WEIRD
WONDERFUL
AMERICA

WEIRD WONDERFUL AMERICA

The Nation's Most Offbeat and Off-the-Beaten-Path Tourist Attractions

Laura A. Bergheim

A Tilden Press Book

COLLIER BOOKS
MACMILLAN PUBLISHING COMPANY
New York
COLLIER MACMILLAN PUBLISHERS
London

A Tilden Press Book
Macmillan Publishing Company
866 Third Avenue, New York, N.Y. 10022
Collier Macmillan Canada, Inc.

Library of Congress Cataloging-in-Publication Data

Bergheim, Laura A., 1962-
Weird, wonderful America : the nation's most offbeat and off-the-beaten-
path tourist attractions.
"A Tilden Press Book."
Includes index.
1. United States—Description and travel—1981-   —Guide-books.
2. Museums—United States—Guide-books.
I. Title.
E158.B46 1988   917.3 04927—dc19   87-31769
ISBN 0-02-030630-X

Macmillan books are available at special discounts for bulk purchases for sales
promotions, premiums, fund-raising, or educational use. For details, contact:

Special Sales Director
Macmillan Publishing Company
866 Third Avenue
New York N.Y. 10022

10 9 8 7 6 5 4 3 2 1

Printed in the United States of America
Typesetting by Chronicle Type & Design

Contents

South

Sponge Museum (Tarpon Springs)
Swimming Hall of Fame (Fort Lauderdale)
Tiki Gardens (Indian Shores)
Tragedy in U.S. History Museum (St. Augustine)
Tupperware Gallery (Orlando)

Double Barreled Canon (Athens)
Georgia Agrirama (Tifton)
Georgia Guidestones (Elberton)
Girl Scout National Center (Savannah)
Granite Museum (Elberton)
Poultry Park (Gainesville)
Tree That Owns Itself (Athens)
Uncle Remus Museum (Eatonton)
World's Largest Peanut (Ashburn)

Brimstone Museum (Sulphur)
Voodoo Museum (New Orleans)

Checkers Hall of Fame (Petal)

Belhaven Museum (Belhaven)
Gourd Museum   (Fuquay-Varina)

Enterprise Square, USA (Oklahoma City)
Gene Autry, OK   (Gene Autry)
Wrestling Hall of Fame (Stillwater)

Criminal Justice Hall of Fame (Columbia)
Dental History Museum (Charleston)
Rice Museum (Georgetown)

Midwest

Circus World Museum (Baraboo)
Crane Foundation (Baraboo)
Dickeyville Grotto (Dickeyville)
Experimental Aircraft Museum (Oshkosh)
Honey of a Museum (Ashippun)
House on the Rock (Spring Green)
Largest Talking Cow (Neillsville)
Medical Progress Museum (Prairie Du Chien)
National Freshwater Fishing Hall of Fame (Hayward)
Water-Powered Museum (Augusta)
World's Largest Loon (Mercer)

West

Hi-Jolly Monument (Quartzsite)
London Bridge (Lake Havasu City)
Meteor Museum (Flagstaff)
Mouse House Museum (Phoenix)
Mystery Castle   (Phoenix)
Petrified Wood Museum (Holbrook)
Titan Missile Museum (Green Valley)
Tom Mix Monument (Florence)
World's Largest Rosebush (Tombstone)

Antone Martin Park (Yucca Valley)
Barbie Doll Hall of Fame (Palo Alto)
Max Factor Museum (Los Angeles)
Museum of Modern Mythology (San Francisco)
On Location (Los Angeles)
Pet Memorial Park (Calabasas)
Ripley's Memorial Museum (Santa Rosa)
Roy Rogers–Dale Evans Museum (Victorville)
Tattoo Art Museum (San Francisco)
Trees of Mystery (Klamath)
Unknown Museum (Mill Valley)
Western Ski Museum (Soda Springs)
Winchester Mystery House (San Jose)

Introduction

America is a land with so many faces, facades, and fascinations that it is nearly impossible to capture its idiosyncratic soul with a single word, thought, or insight. To discover America as it is now, growing up in a thousand gnarled or blossoming offshoots of its original roots, you've got to explore it on its own terms. When you stand in the shadow of the World's Largest Loon in Mercer, Wisconsin, visit the Barbed Wire Museum in La Crosse, Kansas, stroll through the living room of the Paper House in Pigeon Cove, Massachusetts, or wander the grounds of the Coon Dog Memorial Graveyard in Tuscumbia, Alabama, you come face to face with the land and its people as they really are: often weird, usually wonderful, and undendingly inventive.

Major museums such as the Smithsonian Institution do a remarkable job of reflecting American history and talent, but such facilities tell only part of the story. All across the country, there are tiny, less-well-known exhibits and attractions that bring our delightful eclecticism and spirit into a sharper, more personal focus. From coast-to-coast, America is blanketed with offbeat and off-the-beaten-path collections, shrines, and statues—monuments to animals, hobbies, religions, personalities, industries, philosophies, and on and on. There are religious shrines made from gaudy costume jewelry, museums devoted to the history of the Barbie doll, the soup tureen, and violent American tragedies. There are giant statues of cows, guitars, mules, and even a bug. There are whole collections devoted to the history of rubber, tobacco, food containers, and potatoes. There is a coral castle built by a jilted lover, and a city park built to honor poultry.

This book is about these places—how to find them, and what you'll find when you get there. It is a guide to an America that many people have never seen or even heard of, a tribute to attractions that many travel books ignore in favor of more established sites. It is by no means a comprehensive listing—there are many, many attractions not included here. It is an admittedly subjective selection.

It's usually a good idea to phone ahead to places you plan to visit. Many of these attractions are mom-and-pop operations that are likely to close for an afternoon—or a week—without warning, and many proprietors like to know they've got visitors coming so they can roll out the proverbial red carpet. Of course, hours and prices—accurate at publication time—are subject to change.

If you know of other weird and wonderful places, let me know about them. Write to Weird, Wonderful America, Tilden Press, 1001 Connecticut Ave. NW, Washington, DC 20036.

Special thanks are due to many people who helped track down these and many other places, including the good folks at tourism bureaus, chambers of commerce, and city halls throughout the United States; friends who called night and day with ideas and encouragement; and the fascinating people who built and run the places in this book, who gave their time, energy, insights, and postage stamps to reveal the whys and wherefors.

More specifically, thanks to: Joel

Makower, for his velvet-handed whip-cracking and editing/production sweat and savvy; Lindley Boeghoeld and Elisa Petrini, for keeping the publishing ball rolling; Laurie Jackson, for her on-target editing; Sharon Rogers and Jojo Gragasin, for matters of design and production; John Rankin and James S. Turner, for research help; my family, for love, wisdom, detours, and fast pens; and Jim Medwid, for hand holding and mashed potatoes.

WEIRD
WONDERFUL
AMERICA

East

Connecticut

Making Time

American Clock and Watch Museum

100 Maple St.
Bristol, CT 06010
(203) 583-6070

Hours: April-Oct. 11 a.m.-5 p.m.
Admission: Adults, $2.50; children, $1.25
Getting There: Bristol is to the southwest of Hartford. From I-84, take U.S. Hwy. 6 southwest to Hwy. 229 and drive south to Woodland, then turn west on Woodland to where it intersects with Maple. The museum is just to the south, on Maple.

You've got to hand it to them: the folks at the American Clock and Watch Museum have put together a timeless col-

lection. If Alice in Wonderland's white rabbit were living in modern-day Connecticut, he'd be right at home here in the former Miles Lewis House. The rooms overflow with timepieces, many displayed not as dusty, musty exhibits but as integral parts of the household, which is why you may feel as if you've walked into the home of some eccentric grandmother rather than into a museum. While much of the original furniture remains intact, the walls, mantelpieces, tables, and bookshelves spill over with clocks and timepieces of all sizes and varieties. The only really museum-like note is struck with the glass cases that hold pocket-watches, smaller timepieces, and artifacts, ranging from gem-encrusted classics to witty Mickey Mouse originals. Tools of the horologist's trade are also on display, including wonderfully delicate screwdrivers. Sadly, in this modern world of miniature batteries and digital quartz "movements," this profession has nearly run out of time.

Lock Nest

Lock Museum of America

130 Main St. (Rte. 6)
(P.O. Box 104)
Terryville, CT 06786
(203) 589-6359

Hours: May-Nov., 1:30-5 p.m.
Admission: Free
Getting There: Terryville is west of Hartford, near the New York-Connecticut line, and can be reached by taking Connecticut Rte. 6 (Main St. as it runs through town). You can get to Rte. 6 going east from Rte. 8 (Exit 34) or by taking Rte. 84 to Rte. 229 (Exit 31), until it feeds into Rte. 6 heading west.

'erryville takes pride in its legacy as
'the birthplace of the cabinet and trunk
ock industry," as well it should: for
nany years, this was the hometown of
he Eagle Lock Company. In 1972, to
ecure their place forever in the annals
f lock history, Terryvillians opened a
nuseum devoted to locks, keys, and
ther security contraptions. Within the
iallowed walls of the plain little muse-
im building (it looks more like a bank
r a real estate office) where the collec-
ion was moved in 1980, there are some
18,000 locks and other things tracing
he evolution of lock craft.

There certainly are lots of locks here.
There are mail locks and padlocks and
ld locks and new locks and enameled
ocks and iron locks and many, many
Eagle Locks. There are also some unusually ornate keys and a chunky wood-
n padlock sculpture. The older
ocks—notably a 4,000-year-old tum-
le lock from Egypt—are particularly
ascinating for their simple yet func-
ional design.

The collection is displayed on two
loors and divided into theme rooms.
The decor includes carpeting with inter-
ocking patterns and lock-and-tumbler
vallpaper. Although the overall effect of
he museum's ambience harks back to
hat of a 1950s model home (complete
vith wood paneling and dingy overhead
ighting in some rooms), the collection is
ecure in its uniqueness.

Sub Culture

Nautilus Memorial/ Submarine Museum

Naval Submarine Base New London
(Box 571)
Groton, CT 06439
(203) 449-3174

Hours: Mid-April–mid-Oct., Wed.-Mon. 9
a.m.-5 p.m.; mid-Oct.–mid-April, Wed.-Mon.
9 a.m.-3:30 p.m.; closed on Tues., major
holidays, and during the third full weeks of
March, June, and Sept., and the second full
week of Dec.
Admission: Free
Getting There: From I-95, take Hwy. 12
north and follow signs to the New London
Submarine Base, which is just north of
Groton.

Nuclear museums seem to be the vogue,
what with Arizona's Titan Missile Museum, New Mexico's National Atomic Museum, and New Mexico's Los Alamos
Historical Museum. But the West hasn't
cornered the radiation market just yet.

his Connecticut museum is devoted to
he United States submarine forces in
eneral and to the country's first nucle-
r submarine, the *Nautilus*, in particu-
ar. The museum, housed in a building
hat overlooks the permanently berthed
Nautilus, has all the trappings of a sub-
narine fanatic's dream, complete with
vorking periscopes, midget submarines
rom around the world, and an authen-
ic control room. In the museum's entry-
vay is an 11-foot reproduction of Cap-
ain Nemo's *Nautilus* from Jules Verne's
0,000 Leagues Under the Sea. Once
ou've gone through the museum, you
an dive into a self-guided tour of the
ictional sub's namesake—the real *Nau-
ilus*. It's been put out to pasture, so to
peak, allowing visitors a fascinating
xploration of its nuclear-powered won-
lers. There's also a research library in
he complex for those who want to sub-
nerge themselves in the topic.

Nuts to You

Nut Museum

03 Ferry Rd.
Old Lyme, CT 06371
203) 434-7636

Hours: May-Oct., Wed. and weekends 2-5
.m. or by appointment
Admission: Adults, one nut and $2; children,
one nut and $1
Getting There: From I-95, take Exit 70 to
Conn. Hwy. 156 and follow it to Ferry Rd. The
museum is truly "a nut's throw from I-95," as
he owner says, but the sign is small, so watch
arefully.

Elizabeth Tashjian is a nut—but she's a
avvy one. She's turned her obsession
vith nuts into more than just a museum;
he's turned it into a media event. John-

ny (Carson) and Dave (Letterman) are
merely names she tosses off on her long
list of interviewers. Letterman even
called her a "Nut Visionary" on his late-
night talk show, a title Tashjian took to
heart and now uses to describe her unusual relationship with nuts.

The Nut Museum is housed in
Tashjian's rambling, weather-beaten
Victorian mansion in Old Lyme, set off
in a woody area overgrown with specimen trees, including a 99-foot fir and a
tropical balsa tree, as well as a variety of
nut trees (filberts, chestnuts, hazelnuts,
and walnuts). From these you can select
the nutty half of the requested admission donation fee; you'll have to shell
out the other half yourself—money
doesn't grow on trees. As you admire the
foliage, Tashjian hustles you into her
house to see the museum. From this moment on, it's hard to tell which the real
show is—the nuts on display, or the lady
who loves them.

Tashjian is a seventyish woman with
more zest for life than kids 10 times
younger. She is both aggressively eccentric and endearingly self-promoting as
she shows visitors around the house.
The collection is smaller than all the
hoopla over her museum would lead one
to think; the bulk of it is in the living
room area, although bits and pieces of
nuts and nut art are scattered throughout the house. But it's not the size that
counts, it's the substance—and these
are nuts to be reckoned with.

Take, for instance, the 35-pound
double coconut from the Seychelles Is-
lands. This nut, an example of the largest variety in the world, is a sort of organic Rorschach test unto itself.
Depending on the viewer, it can bear an
uncanny resemblance to Siamese twin
footballs or look exactly like a curvy

lower female torso. The nut rests in an appropriate place of honor on an ornately carved chair. Aside from this big nut, which has grabbed almost as many limelights as Tashjian herself, the major portion of the collection sprawls across a mirror-covered, seven-foot-long wooden table that stands on four legs carved to resemble nutcrackers. Reflected against the table-top are a variety of nutcrackers, nut souvenirs (nut dishes are prevalent), nut sculptures (including jewelry made from nuts), and just plain old nuts.

As Tashjian takes visitors on a tour, she stops here and there to spout bits of her personal nut philosophy ("Nuts are more than tasty treats, they're beautiful, modern fossils;" "You'll never find two nuts exactly alike"), or pauses a moment to break into a chorus of the "Nut Anthem" that she has sung on national television to cheering studio audiences ("Nuts can be so bee-oo-tee-

ful . . ."). At one point, she models her collection of nut masks, then swerves into a feminist lecture on male/female roles.

This change of pace comes when Tashjian shows off one of the sculpture from the vast collection of nut art that she has created over the years. This piece, titled "Nuts Grew in the Garden of Eden," consists of an aluminum torse draped with chains on which two suggestively placed nuts dangled conspicuously. She took this to one of her Carson appearances, and boy, what a response

Tashjian is a graduate of the National Academy School of Fine Arts in New York, and her formal training was obviously not wasted—her sculptures and surrealistic nut paintings are the result of a prolific, if one-track, talent. So how did the obsession start? Tashjian says her family always had nuts around the house—in bowls, on plates, in every room—and one day in her nutty youth she realized how immensely beautiful they were. From there, it was a short leap to artistic representation, and then to collecting and exhibiting nutty finds But she wasn't obsessed with what she calls her "mission to remove the demeri mark from nuts" until a couple came to visit the museum, and the husband offered his wife as his "nut" donation. The wife was so angry, Tashjian says, she wouldn't even allow her husband to see the collection. Then and there, Tashjian says, she realized that nuts have had a bad rap for too long, and her little museum became a launching pad for her talk-show career as a philosophical nut discourser. She doesn't mind the label of "Nut Lady" that was given her long ago; in fact, she revels in it. To call Elizabeth Tashjian a nut is, in her eyes, a fine compliment indeed.

Weight Watchers

Streeter Collection of Weights and Measures

Medical Historical Library
Yale University
33 Cedar St.
New Haven, CT 06510
(203) 785-4354

Hours: Mon.-Thurs. 8:30 a.m.-midnight; Fri.-Sat. 8:30 a.m.-1 p.m.; Sun. 11 a.m.-midnight; call for holiday hours

Admission: Free

Getting There: The collection is housed on the first-floor exhibit area of the Yale Medical Library, located on the university campus.

Standardized measurements of distance and weight have played a remarkable, but largely unsung role in our evolution from grungy hunter-gatherers to blow-dried salad-bar grazers. The weights and measures in the Edward Clark Streeter Collection remind us just how important order and system have always been to humankind.

Streeter, a physician, began collecting weights and measures in 1923, in the belief that metrology (the science of weights and measures) is a cornerstone of technological advancement. He later helped found the Yale Medical Historical Library, and donated his collection in 1941.

There are rather weighty weights—at least in terms of historical and archaeological significance—on display here. There are more than 500 weights from the Classical world alone, including ancient Babylonia, Assyria, Rome, Greece, and Egypt. These were mainly carved from stone into decorative or functional shapes and sizes, for use as standard measures to weigh everything from salt to gold.

Among other holdings in the collection are a rare fourteenth-century triangular weight used for the Charles V gold franc, as well as more than 100 coin and apothecary scales and weight boxes dating from as early as the 1600s. There are also plenty of amusing things in the collection, including a charmingly etched advertisement for "Chesterman's Patent Spring, Metallic, Steel, & Other Measuring Tapes; Land Chains,

JAMES CHESTERMAN & CO.,
BOW WORKS, SHEFFIELD,
ENGLAND,

Sole Manufacturers of

CHESTERMAN'S PATENT SPRING,

METALLIC, STEEL, & OTHER

MEASURING
TAPES;

½-Size Chesterman's Patent Steel No. 28 L., 66 Feet.

¼-Size Chesterman's Patent Metallic Tape, No. 34 L., 66 Feet.

LAND CHAINS, STEEL RULES, AND STRAIGHT EDGES, ETC., ETC.

Steel Rules, and Straight Edges, Etc., Etc." On a scale of 1-10, metrologists give this collection a perfect score.

Delaware

Spin One for the Nipper

Johnson Memorial

Bank Lane and New St.
Dover, DE 19903
(302) 736-3262

Hours: Tues.-Sat. 10 a.m.-4:30 p.m.; Sun. 1:30-4:30 p.m.
Admission: Free
Getting There: I-113 and Rte. 8 converge in Dover; the memorial is at the intersection of Bank Lane and New St., a block west of S. Governors Ave.

You could say that phonographs were his master's vice, so obsessed was Eldrige Reeves Johnson with the business of record players. While Johnson's name may not be a household word, the company he founded became the fulcrum of that modern behemoth, RCA. To preserve Johnson's memory, his son,

"HIS MASTER'S VOICE"

Fenimore Johnson, built the museum in Dover. Although it is run under the aegis of the state Bureau of Museums and Historic Sites, don't let the state's stewardship steer you away—this little museum is full of music.

Eldridge Johnson founded his Victor Company in 1901 and sold it to the tune of $29 million 26 years later (finally it ended up in the hands of RCA)—but, oh, those 26 years. Although Thomas Edison actually invented the "talking machine," it was Johnson who perfected the flat-disk mechanism that gave birth to the record playing and production industry.

There are many faces to the Johnson memorial. One is the decidedly fuzzy visage of Nipper the dog, whose fascination with "His Master's Voice" became an indelible image in the history of advertising. Nipper can be found throughout the museum, in the form of jigsaw puzzles, needle tins, salt and pepper shakers, and even an automobile radiator cap. The Nip also shows up in his original form (no, not stuffed): an 1899 oil painting by Francis Barraud. The model was Barraud's brother's fox terrier. Legend has it that Barraud originally created the painting to sell to Thomas Edison; Edison didn't want it, so Barraud painted out Edison's Gramophone and painted in Johnson's Victor Talking Machine.

The gift of mechanical music that Johnson gave to the world is lovingly remembered in the coziest section of the memorial. Designed to resemble a 1920s Victrola store, it offers authentic window displays, listening rooms, vintage Victrolas, and thousands of early recordings. Visitors can settle into a comfortable chair, browse through the music catalog, and request a disk, which

ne of the museum guides will gladly
oin. The choice of machine will depend
n the musical selection, so you might
e treated to hearing Enrico Caruso
roon through an elaborate 1912 Vic-
rola floor model, or to a country ditty
ing from a simple 1902 table model.

Other exhibits include tributes to the
fe of Johnson as a young inventor (an
arly business card reads "Eldridge
eeves Johnson/Machinery and Novel-
es"), as a corporate head (his office
as been reconstructed here), or as a
realthy adventurer (a model of his ar-
haeological expedition ship the *Caro-*
ne is on exhibit). There are also trib-
tes and mementos featuring some of
is company's greatest recording stars,
mong them Maria Jeritza and Maud
owell. There's an entire case devoted
o Caruso memorabilia, with a sculpture
ne great-voiced man created of himself
s a gift for Johnson.

Indeed, the music machine was only
art of Johnson's lyrical legacy. He is
onored as much for the extraordinary
ssemblage of musical artists (mainly
peratic) he garnered for his record la-
el as he is for creating the device on
hich the music was played. Caruso's
xclusive 10-year contract with John-
on's Victor Company resulted in some
f the most remarkable and rare record-
igs in the history of modern music.
ohnson was also the father of "musical
ppreciation" as a course of study. Mil-
ons of groggy-eyed schoolchildren
ave him to thank for having to endure
ong-winded lectures in musicality,
rhich he originally conceived as a way
f ensuring record sales to future
enerations.

For all the other honors and tributes
isplayed here, the objects that best
park the imagination and set the mind

to wandering are the Victrolas. They
abound throughout the museum and
are as beautiful to see as they are (many,
anyway) scratchy to hear. But there is
still more sophistication and glamour in
any of these old crank-and-megaphone
players than in all of today's modern CD
players with ceiling-high speakers. Appropriately enough, the only woofer in
this museum that has withstood the on-
slaught of high-tech hi-fi is Nipper. The
little black-and-white dog still sits with
his head cocked to one side, listening so
very intently to the Victrola. He seems,
even today, to hear His Master's Voice,
which has long ago taken on the musical
resonance of the ages.

District of Columbia

This Spud's for You

Potato Museum
704 North Carolina Ave. S.E.
Washington, DC 20003
(202) 544-1558

Hours: By appointment only
Admission: Free; donations encouraged
Getting There: Located seven blocks from
the U.S. Capitol building. It is easily reached
by going north on North Carolina Ave. from
the Southeast sections of either Pennsylvania
or Independence Aves. The museum is in a
townhouse at the intersection of North
Carolina Ave. and Seventh St. N.E., and is
marked only by its house number.

Forget the Air and Space Museum and
the Museum of Natural History. A
steady diet of spaceships and dinosaurs
can easily dull one's palate. Venture instead off the Mall to the delightful little
Potato Museum, less than a mile from
the Capitol. This museum can add spice

CLARK'S NO. 1 POTATO.

to an otherwise routine menu of touring. It is a side trip well worth the effort.

The museum first sprouted in 1975, in Brussels, Belgium, where Tom Hughes was teaching fifth grade. A newspaper story noting the worldwide lack of a museum honoring the *Solanum tuberosum* (a.k.a. the potato) prompted Tom and his students to study and collect potato-related items, and the museum began to take root. After four years, the Hugheses brought their museum to the nation's capital.

The Potato Museum, located in the townhouse of Hughes and his wife Meredith, is actually a basement-filling sampling of the collection the couple has gathered over the years. Their love and admiration for the potato—Meredith calls it "the perfect food"—has kept their ardent procurement of potato objects blossoming over the years.

The somewhat cramped quarters of the collection add a surprising charm to the museum. Unlike typical exhibit halls, where items are often preserved in sterile environments under alarm-wired glass, the Potato Museum more closely resembles the back room of a country antique store. The basement where much of the collection is displayed over flows with potato paraphernalia. Among the highlights: Mister, Missus, and baby Potato Heads, sharing shelf space with a "Spudsie" game, a set of KP postcards, and a package of "Spud" cigarettes, the first menthol cigarette sold in the U.S., and the first cigarette made from potatoes. There are also antique and modern potato chip tins and bins, a Belgian potato plow, and a Maine potato barrel that spills over with stuffed potato dolls and pillows.

The walls are hung with dozens of framed cartoons (one titled "How She Mashed the Murphys" shows a woman flirting with potatoes), reproductions (including, of course, Van Gogh's "Potato Eaters"), original artwork, and posters. There's more: small planting machines, picking bags, barrels, and other items from around the world; po

to comic books, stamps, and cook-
ooks; a collection of (dead) potato
ugs, the potato's worst enemy; shirts
d coats made from potato sacks; and
 and on. A veritable potato potpourri.

Wherever possible, a small white card
plains each item's origin and impor-
nce. But the information imparted in
e or two typed lines cannot compete
ith the lively commentary Tom
ughes provides as he shows visitors
ound the museum. As he darts from
ject to object, Hughes gives an eco-
mic, political, social, and nutritional
story of the potato. Picking up a
lighted potato encased in clear plastic,
 relates the history of the Irish potato
mine, then moves to a box containing
ried potatoes called "Chuno" and tells
e story of how mountain people dehy-
rate, store, and stew them during the
inter months.

"Potatoes have become a way of life
r us," Hughes explains as he sits on a
ictorian settee in his elegantly eclectic
ving room. "We've now got more than
,000 items, and a reference library
ith at least two-thirds of the material
ver published about potatoes."

As Tom Hughes talks, he gently un-
raps a pre-Columbian pot in the shape
 a potato, on loan from a private art
llector in Arizona. His fingers trace
e potato eyes carved on the pottery
rface as he launches into a brief dis-
rtation of the role potatoes played in
e diets of ancient cultures.

The beauty of potatoes is more than
kin deep. It is a major international
op: the Soviet Union grows 25 per-
ent, China 19 percent, Poland 12 per-
ent, and the United States 5 percent of
e world's annual 300-million-ton po-
ato crop. Potatoes provide more food
alue per acre planted than wheat or

rice, the world's other two leading food
crops.

To spread the potato gospel, Hughes
publishes *Peelings*, a monthly newslet-
ter (circulation: "almost 300"). Says
Meredith: "People from all over send us
potato things in the mail, call to tell us
anecdotes or give us recipes. We
touched a nerve in a lot of potato-loving
people." She says there's a surprising
amount of interest in potatoes. "We get
calls and inquiries from horticulturists,
agriculturists, ancient historians, and
students who want to use our library or
study some of the items in the
museum."

Tom Hughes believes some people are
drawn to the Potato Museum because it
is more intimate and fun than the larger
"warehouse" museums like the Smithsonian. "People have a fixed notion
about museums—that everything is behind glass, and that you can't touch
anything," he says. "But our museum
lets visitors get closer to the display. And
it's got a sense of humor.

"We're still a small-potatoes opera-

tion," he says with a grin. As it is, the Hugheses live in and around their museum, often interrupting daily family activities to show a busload of tourists through the area.

The only question the Hugheses can't answer is why theirs is the first and only museum devoted to potatoes. "There are so many damned museums to war—weapons, battlefields, soldiers," says Tom. "We think it's important to have a museum in tribute to the constructive side of mankind. The potato is historically and socially the most important food known to man. That's worthy of a museum."

His enthusiasm is backed by a vision, and his eyes grow misty as he describes it: "A high-tech Potato Museum, with

laser and light shows, movies, videotapes, and hands-on exhibits. And a l of eating, too."

Maine

Hot Stuff

Bryant Stove Museum
Main St.
Thorndike, ME 05986
(207) 568-3665

Hours: Mon.-Sat. 9 a.m.-5 p.m.
Admission: Free
Getting There: Thorndike is less than an hour's drive from Bangor, Augusta, or Belfas

The museum can be reached by taking Rtes. 137 or 139 and following the orange signs that lead to the Bryant Stove Works.

The wood-burning stoves in this museum put newfangled gas and electric ranges to shame and virtually banish microwaves to postmodern purgatory. These old stoves are some of the funkiest, funniest, and most endearing home furnishings ("appliance" is too cold a term for these hot properties) ever to hold court in Grandma's kitchen.

Many of the stoves in the Bryant Stove Museum are deliciously ornate, with all the flourishes and froufrou design elements so dear to the Victorians. It's hard to imagine anyone baking a plain old apple pie in one of these exotic hot boxes, much less turning out an overdried meatloaf. The stoves are cast-iron wonders, with intricate claw feet, delicately wrought doors and handles, cornices and ornaments, elaborate name plates, and distinctive engravings.

Many of these wood-burning stoves were built to reflect and advertise their manufacturer's particular image (an 1853 Castle Stove, for instance, resembles a fortress), while others are just plain wacky. One looks more like a deep-sea diving helmet from *20,000 Leagues Under the Sea* than anything you'd bake a cake in, while another, a two-column style from 1845, bears a startling likeness to some sort of Indian altar ornament. Even the "simpler" stoves have delightful lines and shapes—a turn-of-the-century "Charm Crawford" model has the plump form and delicate ornamentation of an old bonbon tin. Also on display are some stunning stove tiles and cute toy stoves.

The Bryant Stove Museum is adjacent to the Bryant Stove Works, a little shop

and store where Bea and Joseph Bryant have been restoring and selling old stoves since 1970. The Bryants opened the museum as a way of preserving and presenting some of the rarer wood-burning stoves and associated paraphernalia. In doing so, they have maintained a reminder of that bygone era when the form of a stove could delight the eye as much as its function could please the palate.

Just Desert

Desert of Maine

Desert Rd.
Freeport, ME 04032
(207) 865-6962

Hours: May 15-June 15 and Labor Day-Oct. 15, 10 a.m.-5 p.m.; June 15-Labor Day, 8:30 a.m.-dusk
Admission: Walking tour: adults, $2.75; children, $1.50. Safari coach tour: adults, $3.75; children, $1.75
Getting There: Located just south of Freeport Village on Desert Rd., just 2 miles from U.S. Rte. 1 and I-95 (Exit 19 from both). Follow signs.

It's hot. The sun is baking down. The desert seems to stretch as far as the eye can see. A gust of wind picks up clouds of sand as the dunes shift listlessly in the heat. You're in the Gobi, right? Or maybe the Sahara? No way, this is Maine! Just outside of charming little Freeport, home of that quintessentially Maine-line establishment, L.L. Bean, there is, indeed, a real desert. It stretches for several hundred acres, though how many, exactly, no one's really sure. That darned desert just keeps right on spreading.

Visitors to the Desert of Maine can either run barefoot through the soft, sandy dunes or jostle along in a safari-style coach that has the look and feel of a movie studio tour tram. Either way, you'll get a proper feel for the closest thing to a barren wasteland this side of the Jersey Turnpike. And, once you've had your fill of collecting naturally multicolored sand between your toes and in your pants cuffs, you can check out the desert's two museums: the Farm Museum, housed in the only remaining building of the original Tuttle Farm, whence the desert sprang, and the Sand Museum, which provides many grains of wisdom about the nature and variety of sand.

After visiting the museums, you might want to watch artisans making sand paintings in glass bottles, and perhaps buy a few dozen for friends and relatives in the huge gift shop. And don't forget to check out "The World's Largest Sand Painting."

Yes, it is weird that there's a desert in the heart of New England. And the folks who manage what they modestly label "Maine's Most Famous Natural Phenomenon" are the first to admit that their little plot of sand is pretty unusual. But it wasn't always a vast expanse of sand and sky. Once upon a time, the Desert of Maine was a fertile farm.

When, in 1797, William Tuttle moved his family and home (literally: it took 48 oxen to drag the abode) to their new farm near Freeport, the land was lush and fruitful. The family thrived, growing hay and a variety of vegetables. When Tuttle's son John inherited the property, he tried to turn some of the farm acreage into rolling pasture. Unfortunately, his unmannered livestock just kept eating and eating, pulling up clumps of sod and chewing the remaining grass until it looked like a Marine's scalp. The topsoil began to disappear and an enormous deposit of sand and silt emerged to fill in the bare spots. Soon, the sandy areas had spread, forcing the Tuttle family to give up the battle and let the desert bloom across their once-fertile acreage. All that remains of the Tuttle Farm is the barn, which has been converted into a museum depicting the life and times of the Tuttles.

Scientists have long been fascinated by this place, which bears many of the characteristics of the great Asiatic eserts of the world, including the Gobi nd Sahara. While the Desert of Maine oesn't have the usual flora and fauna ssociated with deserts (no cacti or scorions here, just poor scraggly trees halfuried under tons of sand), the patterns f sand-spread and dune-shifting seem) indicate genuine, certified desert maerial. The current theory is that the esert is the result of deposits from an ncient glacier that once cruised hrough on its way to greener pastures. The texture of the sand (sharp and anular rather than the smooth and polshed sand from ocean floors), as well as he particular variety of minerals in the ilt, seem to support the glacial deposit heory.

Perhaps the strangest thing about the)esert of Maine is its contrast with the urrounding countryside. As you drive hrough the fertile landscape, you'll ave a hard time believing there's a esert within this forestland. But once ou enter the desert, you step quite sudenly into a very different world. It's an oasis in reverse: a little island of barrenness amid a lush sea of green.

Pole Cats

Peary-MacMillan Museum

Hubbard Hall
Bowdoin College
Brunswick, ME 04011
(207) 725-3416

Hours: Sept.-May, Tues.-Fri. 10 a.m.-4 p.m.; Sat. 10 a.m.-5 p.m.; Sun. 2 p.m.-5 p.m; call for summer hours
Admission: Free
Getting There: From I-95 or Rte. 1, take the Brunswick exit and follow signs to Bowdoin College. The museum is on campus in Hubbard Hall.

Icy memorabilia and artifacts abound in this collection devoted to the exploits of two frigid Bowdoin alumnae, Admiral Robert E. Peary (Class of 1877), the first man to reach the North Pole, and

his Chief Assistant, Donald B. MacMillan (Class of 1898). Divided into three sections, the museum traces Peary's career from his early exploits to his famous frozen feat (and feet, from the looks of the snowshoes on display). Among the items collected here are the North Pole expedition's pickaxes, navigational instruments, knives, guns, and a sledge. MacMillan's North Pole log is also exhibited, as is the fur suit he wore, which probably scared as many polar bears as Eskimo women. Stuffed Arctic animals are here, too, along with some cool Eskimo art.

Orgone Conclusion

Wilhelm Reich Museum
Orgonon
Rangeley, ME 04970
(207) 864-3443

Hours: July-Aug., Tues.-Fri. 10 a.m.-5 p.m.; Sat.-Sun. 1-5 p.m.; Sept., Sun. only, 1-5 p.m.
Admission: Free
Getting There: Rangeley, in the northwestern part of the state, can be reached by taking Hwy. 4 N. from U.S. Hwy. 2.

Talk about one-track minds. Almost all of Wilhelm Reich's scientific studies kept leading him back to sex. His most famous (and infamous) theory—that orgasm releases a biological power source, "orgone energy"—eventually landed him in jail, where he perished in 1957. But by that time Reich had a large following of believers in "pelvic freedom," who have maintained Reich's estate and research complex, Orgonon, as a museum-shrine-study center.

The museum building was constructed by Reich in 1948-49 as an observatory and laboratory for his research into the laws of orgone energy. Much of the scientific atmosphere has been preserved, as have Reich's original research library and other areas where he worked and relaxed. There is a frozen-in-time quality about the museum, as though nothing has been disturbed since the day Reich stepped out the door. Wood still stacked in a shelf next to the fireplace in his study, and his desk is still strewn with pens and paperweights.

Many of Reich's inventions are on display in the museum, including an amusingly frightful machine called a "Stormbuster" (the ray guns from the film "Ghostbusters" bear a suspicious resemblance), which Reich believed could control the weather through the principles of orgone energy. Among the other inventions here are the infamous "orgone accumulators" that were outlawed during Reich's later years; Reich's continued research use of the accumulators eventually led to his imprisonment for criminal contempt.

Reich's theoretical linking of orgasm with organic energy is not really surprising, given that he was one of Sigmund Freud's most avid and talented pupils in Vienna. Although his dictum of sexual freedom seared his name in the consciousness of a still-repressed 1950s society, Reich was also a pioneer in cancer studies and research into gravity and antigravity.

He is buried in a woody area on the grounds of Orgonon, in a tomb that bears a bust of his head atop a simple memorial with a stone façade. Reich left behind a legacy of baffling scientific research that has never been confirmed, but his theories sparked a debate more potent than any organic energy he might have discovered.

Maryland

House of Ruth

Babe Ruth Museum
216 Emory St.
Baltimore, MD 21230
(301) 727-1539

Hours: April-Oct. 10 a.m.-5 p.m.; Nov.-March 10 a.m.-4 p.m.
Admission: Adults, $2.50; children (12 and under), $1.25; senior citizens, $2
Getting There: Located in Baltimore, seven blocks from the Inner Harbor and five blocks from the Baltimore Arena. It is a block south of Pratt St. and a block west of Greene St.; signs abound throughout the neighborhood.

On Feb. 6, 1895, in an upstairs room of this simple rowhouse in the heart of Baltimore, George Herman Ruth was born. Despite his obvious youth at the time of his birth, the "Babe" got his moniker 18 years later when he was signed by the Orioles' owner, who had to become Ruth's legal guardian so the tender rookie could play with the big guys.

Although Ruth spent only a short time in this house (his parents later bundled him off to a school for juvenile delinquents), it's the only remaining link to Baltimore's claim on Ruth's childhood. Even the legendary sandlot where the tyke played ball has been replaced by a electric power station. The house has been refurbished to include as much Babe-phernalia as it can hold, as well as the collections of the Maryland Baseball Hall of Fame and the Baltimore Orioles Official Museum.

The "Sultan of Swat" is in evidence throughout the museum, from an animated robot of the Babe that chats up delighted youngsters, to the Babe Ruth family album. His baseball career is exhaustively represented in exhibits that include the necessary statistics for each of his 714 lifetime home runs, his uniforms and gear, and plenty of other bits and pieces of the Babe's life as witnessed through videotapes and slide shows.

The Maryland Baseball Hall of Fame and the Orioles Museum extend the roster of players but narrow the field to the home state and home team. There are "touchable" exhibits of uniforms, gloves, bats, balls, and programs, as well as the stats, pix, and multimedia moments that are *de rigeur* in all sports museums. This is one of the more enjoyable ones, partly because of the history of so many varied players and clubs, and partly because it is blessed with the benevolent ghost of the Babe, the greatest among greats.

Do It Yourself

Duvall Tool Collection

Patuxent River Park
16000 Croom Airport Rd.
Upper Marlboro, MD 20772
(301) 627-6074

Hours: Sun. 1-4 p.m., or by advance reservation
Admission: Free
Getting There: Take the Capital Beltway (I-495) to Exit 11A E. (Pennsylvania Ave.). Continue to Rte. 301 and drive 2 miles to Croom Station Rd. Go left and follow it to the end, then turn left onto Croom Rd. Drive 2 miles further to Croom Airport Rd., turn left, and follow signs to the park.

Nestled in the Jug Bay Natural Area of the Patuxent River Park, this little museum houses the antique tool collection of the late W. Henry Duvall. There are more than a thousand nineteenth-century tools, including farm implements

and kitchen items. There are cooper's tools and cobbler's tools, and over 100 carpenter's planes. If nothing else, gazing at these tools from days gone by will make even the most hardened do-it-yourselfer give thanks for the advent of the power drill, the washing machine, and the rider lawnmower.

Fowl Friends

Poultry Hall of Fame

USDA National Agricultural Library, 2nd Floor
10301 Baltimore-Washington Blvd.
Beltsville, MD 20705
(301) 344-3355

Hours: Mon.-Fri. 8 a.m.-4:30 p.m.
Admission: Free
Getting There: Take Rte. 1 (Baltimore-Washington Blvd.) though Beltsville. From I-95, take Exit 29 and drive east on Hwy. 212 (Powder Mill Rd.) to Rte. 1; or take Exit 25 from I-495 (the Capital Beltway) to Rte. 1.

The big names in the poultry biz are honored in this informative though uninspiring tribute to the men and women who have helped put a chicken in every pot over the past century. Exhibits in the Poultry Industry Hall of Fame are devoted to portraits of these great lead-

s, with special attention paid to the est inductees, of which there are five rm-fresh ones every year. Examples of cent honorees: M. C. Small, editor of *urkey World* and active in the World's ultry Congress; Dr. T. C. Byerly, who orked on the development of the Beltsle turkey and the Chicken of Tomorw Program; and Henry Saglio, honed for his vision in recognizing the dustry's "need for a fast-growing hite-feathered meat bird of superior nformation." Who knows what the ture may hold for the poultry dustry—if chickens had lips, maybe ey could tell us.

Massachusetts

Clear Vision

lindiana Museum

rkins School for the Blind
5 N. Beacon St.
atertown, MA 02172
7) 924-3434

ours: Mon.-Fri. 8:30 a.m.-5 p.m.
dmission: Free
etting There: Watertown is west of Boston
d can be reached via U.S. Rte. 20 (N.
acon St. as it runs through town and passes
e Perkins School). The museum is on the
rkins campus, in the Howe Building.

a certain extent, the Blindiana Musen is a redundancy. The Perkins School r the Blind, which you can tour, is, in d of itself, a living memorial to the story of education for blind and deaf rsons. Nevertheless, the museum proes a fascinating glimpse at the develment of this lesser-known and diffilt realm of teaching.

Among the items displayed in the museum are early photographs of classes, various teaching aids and appliances, games and other recreational/educational paraphernalia. There are also Braille and embossed books, some of which are as beautiful to the eye as they are to the fingertips. As a tribute to Helen Keller, there's a collection of her speeches and books, as well as mementos of her life.

Established in 1829, Perkins was the first school for blind persons in the United States. The school soon developed a reputation for firsts and foremosts —from the education of Helen Keller (and her teacher, Annie Sullivan) to the development of the Perkins Brailler. The Blindiana Museum and Library were founded in 1870 to preserve the historic progresses that were being made in the field of education for the blind and deaf population. In a world where memorials to other forms of valor (mainly military) number in the thousands, this study and preservation of "blindiana" is a rare commodity.

Mail Chauvinism

Cardinal Spellman Philatelic Museum

235 Wellesley St.
Weston, MA 02193
(617) 894-6735

Hours: Tues.-Thurs. 9 a.m.-4 p.m.; Sun. 1-5 p.m.
Admission: Free; donations encouraged
Getting There: Weston is 14 miles west of Boston. Take I-90 (the Mass. Turnpike) or Rte. 128 (at the intersection with I-90) to the Weston/Wellesley Rd. exit and drive north to the museum.

During his life, Francis Cardinal Spellman gathered thousands of stamps from around the world in the belief that planetary understanding and harmony could be had with stamp diplomacy. In 1948, Spellman donated his collection to the Sisters of St. Joseph, in memory of his beloved aunt, Sister Mary Philomena. The museum corporation was set up, a brand new building (the only one ever designed specifically for a philately museum) was finished in 1960, and the gum-backed beauties have been living here ever since.

The museum claims to be the only accredited museum in the United States devoted solely to stamps. Aside from the Spellman collection, the pink brick building houses the entire Eisenhower Collection, General Ridgeway's collection, and the largest Vatican collection (outside the Vatican, that is) on special gold-illuminated pages. The museum also holds nearly complete collections from Poland (even stamps issued from concentration camps), Japan, China, Great Britain, and the United States, as well as large collections from virtually every other country—a total of more than three-and-a-half million pieces.

And in case the excitement of this enormous collection gets to be too much, there's a charming post office in the building where you can get away from it all for a mailman's holiday.

Berry Interesting

Cranberry World Center
Ocean Spray Cranberries, Inc.
225 Water St.
Plymouth, MA 02360
(617) 747-1000

Hours: Apr.-Nov., daily, 9:30 a.m.-5 p.m.; extended weekday evening hours, July and Aug., until 9 p.m.
Admission: Free
Getting There: The center is approximately 40 miles south of Boston and most easily reached by taking Rte. 3 to Rte. 44 (Plymouth Exit). Cross Rte. 3A and turn left at the waterfront traffic circle. Cranberry World is in the fourth building on the right.

New York City may be the Big Apple, but Plymouth is undoubtedly the Bog Apple. Just a few blocks away from the Pilgrim rock of ages, the Cranberry World Visitors Center beckons the curious to enter and learn the mystery and history of the *Vaccinium macrocarpon*. After all, who could resist discovering the answer to that timeless question "What's in a Bog?"

In fact, Cranberry World is crammed full of bogs, and what's in them. Outside, the half-acre "What's in a Bog?" exhibit answers the question once and for all: soil, sand, water, bugs, among other things—and, of course, cranberries. And just so rainy days won't get you bogged down, inside the two-level, 5,000-square-foot pavilion, there's a miniature cranberry bog diorama that'

most like being there (if you're about
n inch-and-a-half tall). But bogs are
ist the beginning; this place is virtually
rimming over with cranberry lore.

The story of cranberry harvesting and
roduction is told with a display of tools
nd machines. In the early days, cran-
erries were hand-harvested with the
id of scoops to break the berries loose
om the vines. Scooping gradually gave
ay to mechanical dry-harvesting,
hich in turn, has given way to the
nodern method of wet-harvesting, a
ystem that uses wheels with rods to
ropel them to shake the submerged
erries loose and send them floating to
ne flooded bog's surface. From scoops
o rod wheels, the tools are all here, as
re production machines—including a
eparator, an amusing sorter that judges
good berry from a bad one by how
igh it can bounce.

Another highlight is a beautiful
"Italio," an etched-glass depiction of
the effects of seasonal changes on the
cranberry plant. And don't miss the giant cranberry model, politely vivisected
to show its many layers. If all this whets
your thirst for knowledge, there are free
samples of cranberry cooking and
Ocean Spray juices for everyone.

The officials at Ocean Spray Cranberries, a farmers' cooperative, say they
created Cranberry World Visitors Center as a way to give something back to
the town of Plymouth, which has harbored it over the years. According to the
company, another primary objective for
building the center was "to enhance the
understanding and awareness of the
cranberry among current and potential
consumers of the cooperative's products." Since the 1977 opening, nearly 3
million current and potential cranberry

consumers have had their understanding and awareness of Ocean Spray products enhanced here.

Cycles of History

Motocycle Museum

33 Hendee St.
(P.O. Box 3, Highland Station)
Springfield, MA 01139
(413) 737-2624

Hours: Mon.-Sun. 10 a.m.-5 p.m.
Admission: Adults, $2; children, $1
Getting There: Take the St. James Ave. exit from I-95 in Springfield and turn right onto Page Blvd. Go about a quarter of a mile until you come to Hendee St. Turn right. You'll see signs to the museum once you've passed the railroad yard and gone into a large parking lot.

Everyone knows Henry Ford revolutionized the world with his automobiles, but not many know the story of the Indian Motocycle Company's contribution to two-wheeled cruising. This museum presents some vrooming good examples of early and later model Indians, as well as a wicked collection (probably the world's largest) of toy motocycles and some fun cycling memorabilia.

The Indian Motocycle Company was the first cycle manufacturer in the United States when it was opened in 1901 by George M. Hendee, a "high-wheel champ," and Oscar C. Hedstrom, a fellow racer who invented the Indian Motocycle. Until the company went out of business in 1953, it manufactured a startling variety of fast and furious motocycles that are still considered among the finest ever made. Part of the glory that was an Indian Motocycle was its simplicity (its engine was about as in-tricate as a lawnmower's) and its economy (it could get an oil baron's nightmare of 75-100 miles per gallon of gas).

The cycles in this museum range from one of the original, early Indians that has an elegantly daring look about it to later versions that could do everything from squeeze into a tube (for transport with World War II paratroopers) to ski down a snowy mountainside. The toy motocycles are also charmers—their tiny wheels and intricate detailing (right down to the paint jobs and decals) are wonders of miniaturization.

Other exhibits include plenty of Indian cycler paraphernalia, and a look at the history of women on wheels. Also displayed are examples of other items the company manufactured, including outboard motors, home-unit air conditioners, and airplane engines. But the motocycles zoom ahead to steal this show.

You Read It Here First

Paper House

Pigeon Hill St.
Pigeon Cove, MA 01976
(617) 546-2629

Hours: July-Aug. 10 a.m.-5 p.m.; also open intermittently in spring and fall, depending on availability of caretaker
Admission: Adults, 50 cents; children, 25 cents
Getting There: Take Rte. 128 north from Boston to Cape Ann, Mass., all the way to the end. Go east on Rte. 127, past downtown Rockport, and follow the signs to the Paper House, located just off the main road. (The signs are hard to see, but look for the first one at an intersection, where the Cape Ann Tool Company is located. The road to the Paper House curves off to the left at this point.)

An hour north of Boston, on the "other
Cape," there's a house where the concept of wallpaper takes on a whole new
meaning. From afar, the Paper House
looks like an airy little bungalow built
for summer parties—but when you step
onto the porch the uniqueness of the
construction becomes apparent. The
outside walls, which at first look like
moss-coated wood, are formed from
tightly packed, yellowed triangles of
newspaper; the "bead" curtains that
hang in the windows reveal themselves
to be intricately twisted magazine
pages. Stroll inside, and you'll find that
everything from the grandfather clock
to the fireplace mantel is built from old
newspapers.

While this place would give even the
bravest of paperboys nightmares, the
Paper House was a dream come true for
its creator, Elis Stenman. Stenman, a
Swedish immigrant who read at least
five newspapers a day, began work on
his monument to the Fourth Estate with
a simple goal in mind: he wanted to find
a utilitarian way to save newsprint. He
hit upon the idea of a house and, in
1922, put his family to work, folding
and pasting, pasting and folding
newspapers.

Twenty years later, the house was finished. It took 215 thicknesses of newspaper to construct the walls, and by the
time the furniture and other interior
items were fashioned, 100,000 newspapers (largely from Boston) had been incorporated into the structure. Despite
the sheer mass of papers that went into
building the house, Stenman never gave
up on the details. His imagination led
him to devote entire pieces of furniture
to heavily reported news events or to
collections of particular newspapers.

The most tantalizing example of
Stenman's thematic building is a sturdy

little writing desk created from accounts of Charles Lindberg's historic flight. The desk, like the rest of the furniture, is fashioned from tightly rolled sticks of newspaper. From across the room it looks like an ordinary bamboo or rattan desk, but, as with everything in the house, a closer inspection reveals yellowing bits of type and fading photographs. A framed portrait of "Lucky Lindy" hangs on the paper-montage wall above the desk.

Another desk in the house is fashioned solely from issues of the *Christian Science Monitor*, and there's a nearby bookshelf made from foreign papers. A cot gives less-than-sweet dreams with World War I newspaper accounts, while a radio cabinet was formed from accounts of the 1928 Hoover campaign.

And the grandfather clock was created with papers from the capital cities of the (then) 48 states. But not everything in the house is made completely from newspapers: a piano is only covered with paper rolls, and the fireplace is made of brick. (Now really, who would build a fireplace from newspaper?) Even so, the mantel is made from the rotogravure section of the *New York Herald Tribune* and the *Boston Sunday Herald*.

The Paper House is pretty tiny—really only one room, and it doesn't take much time to tour. This is one of those classic examples of weird, compulsory building that have to be seen to be believed. When it comes to tourist attractions, this house is a headliner.

Witch Watch

Salem Witch Museum

19½ Washington Square N.
Salem, MA 01970
(617) 744-1692

Hours: Year round 10 a.m.-5 p.m. except July & Aug. open until 7 p.m.; presentations begin every half-hour
Admission: Adults, $2.75; children, $1.50; senior citizens, $2.25
Getting There: The museum is hard to miss when you drive through central Salem. It's across from the common in the heart of the town, housed in an imposingly Gothic ex-church. Salem can be reached by taking Rte. 128 (north from Boston, south from upper New England) to the Salem exit for Rte. 114, which runs through town.

In the 1690s, a bunch of bored adolescents put the hex on the rural community of Salem by staging hysterical fits and

accusing prominent citizens of witchcraft. In all, 19 "witches" were hanged (none was burned), several others died in prison, and one elderly gentleman was pressed to death by stone weights. Years later, the finger-pointing brats confessed their histrionics, and Salem's embarrassment was complete.

There was a time when Salem was deeply scarred by this brutal history. Favorite son Nathaniel Hawthorne even added a "W" to his family name, Hathorn, in self-imposed contrition for having descended from one of the witchcraft trial judges. But this bad spell seems to be over with, as the town now fairly thrives on its horrific past. Tourists pouring in by the cauldronful enjoy such sites as the the Essex Institute, where original trial records can be viewed, the Witch House, where pretrial investigations were held, and the Witch Dungeon Museum, where a "live trial" show is the high point of a tour through a recreated dungeon. But the finest educational experience in town is the Salem Witch Museum, a tableau re-enactment of the whole hysterical tragedy in a truly awesome display of Yankee pathos.

The museum building, a onetime church that would have made Count Dracula feel at home, is enough to scare you without ever having to pay the admission price. But go ahead, fork it over, because once inside you'll find yourself standing with a like-minded group of witch watchers in the center of a giant pentagram. The lights dim, spine-chilling sounds abound, and any little kids in the group are guaranteed to start whimpering. Above you, scenes starring waxy witches are slowly illuminated while the story of the growing hysteria that culminated in mass murder is told in dolorous tones. Look up there! It's Tituba stirring an innocent cauldron of soup. And over there is Giles Corey, being pressed to death.

The fact that the museum's phone number ends with the number 1692 (the year when the witch hunt was at its peak) is a hint to the delightful history-in-the-remaking quality of the Salem Witch Museum. Another nice touch is the requisite detour through the witch-kitsch gift shop on the way out of the museum.

Okay, so it's not really a museum in the truest sense of the word. The curators would rather we thought of it as a

"powerful half-hour multisensory presentation." After all, seeing wax figures bathed in scary lighting while you hear eerie music and a spooky narration involves both your eyes and ears. But it's not the kind of episode in American history you'd want to smell or taste, let alone touch with a 10-foot broomstick.

New Hampshire

One-Track Minds

Crossroads of America
Rte. 302 and Trudeau Rd.
Bethlehem, NH 03574
(603) 869-3919

Hours: Tues.-Sun. 9 a.m.-9 p.m.
Admission: Adults, $2.50; children, $1.75
Getting There: Located on the edge of Bethlehem, at the intersection of Rte. 302 and Trudeau Rd.

The entire third floor of an old boarding house is filled with the main exhibit of Crossroads of America—a fact that sort of contradicts the idea of model trains

king up less space than real ones. The
eer size, scope, and intricacy of this
ormous train setup is a joy and a won-
r to rail people.

Much more than just a nicely dis-
ayed Lionel Train or two, Crossroads
America exhibits an entire little
orld, complete with hills and dales and
ucks and trailers and cows and mead-
vs and . . . well, you get the picture.
'e're talking mini-America the Beauti-
l here.

Roger Hinds, the mastermind and
eator of this mammoth minitrain
ene, is a model citizen and electronics
xpert who put his energy and knowl-
lge to creative use when he built Cross-
ads of America. Through a complex
vitching system, Hinds can simulate a
4-hour, day-into-night minidrama de-
icting a typical railroad schedule.
here are enough animated moments in
is little day that you'll have a hard
me keeping track of them all. At one
oint, a tiny cow staggers into the path
f an oncoming train, only to hop back
ut of danger a moment later; at anoth-
r junction, a miniature mail pouch
ounces off of the mail car at its ap-
ointed stop. And so forth, through val-
ys and mountains, over babbling
rooks and rolling rivers, and through
leepy little towns like Bethlehem, the
rain goes ever onward.

According to Hinds, this giant setup is
he world's largest $^3/_{16}$-scale model train
n public display. Model enthusiasts
rom around the world have made
racks to New Hampshire to see it. And,
or those who prefer other forms of
ransport, there are scores of model cars
nd trucks and ships and planes on dis-
lay as well. In fact, the only things that
re life-sized around here (other than
linds and his crew) are the doughnuts

and coffee available in the adjacent
"Mary's Dining Car."

Baby Doll

Doll-Fan Attic Museum
Rte. 175
Ashland, NH 03217
(603) 536-4416

Hours: Daily 10 a.m. - 5 p.m.
Admission: Adults, $2; children, $1
Getting There: From I-93 take exit 25 and
head east on Rte. 175 to the museum.

The Doll-Fan Attic museum is just
that—an attic filled with dolls that
draws fans from miles around. The bottom floor of this little building is occupied by The Roots Seller, a funky store
specializing in paper memorabilia (especially *Life* magazines), so you'll probably browse a bit before climbing upstairs. The museum itself is crammed to
the rafters with shelves of dolls.

The overcrowding, as well as the variety of the dolls in this attic collection, is
a refreshing change from the porcelain
and lace and "don't touch" glass favored by most doll museums. Sure,
you'll still get your fill of cherry-lipped
china numbers, but here there are also
dolls fashioned from loofa sponges,
prunes, and cow bones. There's even a
punked-out Barbie.

The owner of the collection, Monica
Owens, started gathering her little people to use as tools in teaching elemen-
tary school. She quickly discovered that
her students were fascinated by the an-
thropological and cultural significance
of the toys—a fact that explains the
enormous collection of foreign dolls.

Fair Game

Game Preserve

110 Spring Rd.
Peterborough, NH 03458
(603) 924-6710

Hours: Mon., Wed., and Fri. noon-5 p.m.;
weekends by appointment
Admission: Adults, $2.50; children, $1.50
Getting There: From Rte. 101 as it passes
Peterborough, take Grove St. north and turn
left onto Union St. Take Union to Windy Row,
and drive north to Spring Rd. Turn left on
Spring Rd; the Game Preserve is on the left.

So, you thought you'd find some wildlife
here? Not a chance, unless old checker-
boards and card games make you want
to party. The Game Preserve is a witty
name for an equally witty gathering of
antique board and card games, gathered in this quiet bed-and-breakfast/
museum by a friendly couple named
Lee and Rally Dennis.

The Dennises are experts on the lore
and history of games, and they have put
more than 1,000 examples (some dating
back to as early as 1812) on display in
their little corner of New Hampshire.

While many of the amusements preserved here have faded into the same
history that swallowed up pantaloons
and pinafores, there are also some fascinating and funny precursors to games
that have stood the test of time. You can
try your hand at a round of tenpins, hop
onto a carpet made for hopscotch, and
risk a glance at some early casino
games. There are also some dainty old
table-tennis paddles and a few elaborate bagatelles (a game that's descended
to us in the rudely clanging form of
pinball). The Dennises just happen to
operate an antique store nearby where,
if you're game, you can buy some of
these playful pastimes to take home.

Making a Killing

Morse Museum

Rte. 25C
Warren, NH 03279
(603) 764-9407

Hours: Daily 10 a.m.-5 p.m.
Admission: Free
Getting There: The museum is on Rte. 25C,
which can be reached from Rte. I-93 by taking
Rte. 25 south.

This safari museum looks more like it
was put together by Tarzan than by a
great white hunter. Sure, there are the
requisite trophy animals, stuffed and
mounted in "natural" poses, but there's
also such an overflow of curios that the
collector's love of the culture of foreign
lands shines through as much as his love
of hunting foreign game. The collector
in this case was Ira Morse, a farm-bred
New Hampshire man who squeezed six
safaris and countless trips abroad into
his lifetime even as he was making a
killing in the retail shoe business.

During his boyhood, Morse was fascinated by tales of African jungle adventure, and dreamed of stalking lions and
elephants through the bush. His grandfather's best milking cow and innocent
neighborhood squirrels were early vic-
tims of Morse's big game fantasies,
which he played out with the .22-caliber
rifle he was given as a gift. But Morse
would have a long wait before he fulfilled his dreams—he was over 50 before he went on his first safari. Accompanied by his son, Philip, just graduated
from Dartmouth, Morse embarked on a
seven-month-long hunting expedition
that yielded numerous trophies and fulfilled a lifelong love of travel.

The Morse Museum, built to house his
collection, was dedicated in 1928, in the

heart of the farming community where Morse had stalked his first cow. Aside from an enormous collection of stuffed animals killed by the Morses during their safaris, there are animal skins—leopard, tiger, beaver, monkey—and various other bodily parts mounted on the walls and preserved under glass. An elephant foot hanging at one end of the museum measures 23 inches in diameter, and the ears (6 feet long) and tusks (9 feet long) are nearby. Put them all together and you'd have a beast to reckon with.

The little stone museum building is also home to numerous talismans, weapons, adornments, and eccentric souvenirs collected by the Morses during their travels. Glass cases are crammed with musical instruments, beads, incense burners, carved ivory toys, and other curios from such diverse locales as Ceylon, China, India, and Africa. Throughout, the animals share floor and wall space with teak statuary, tattered flags, maps and prints, butterfly collections, native drums, and woven cloths.

There is an essence of Victorian romanticism evoked by this gathering of esoterica in such a small, quaint location. You can almost smell the cigar smoke of some mythical men's club, where members sat about in red leather chairs daring each other to take 80-day trips around the world. This collection has a charm and cultural resonance that other big-game museums lack, for Morse was a hunter, not merely of creatures, but also of places.

housed in a chalet-like building in the heart of the winter sports country. Aside from a few elaborate slide shows, videotapes, and pushbutton audiovisual exhibits about the business and sport of New England skiing, there are exhibits on the history of skis, ski clothing, and ski art. The collections include unusual bindings and other paraphernalia, some truly embarrassing fads in ski wear, and assorted paintings, posters, sculptures, and stamps about the sport. Exhibits change seasonally, and if what you see gets you in the mood to ski, the tram for popular Cannon Mountain is right next door.

Snow Fun

New England Ski Museum

Franconia Notch
(P.O. Box 267)
Franconia, NH 03580
(603) 823-7177

Hours: May 27-Oct. 16 and Dec. 15-March 31, daily 10 a.m.-4 p.m.
Admission: Adults, $2; children, $1
Getting There: Located on I-93 in Franconia Notch State Park, adjacent to the Cannon Mountain Aerial Passenger Tramway Base Station.

It seems that just about every ski region has its museum, and you've got to wonder why. Maybe it's because the development of skiing in any particular area is directly linked with local tales of snowbound adventure and breathtaking Olympic prowess. Here's another museum, this time devoted to the history of skiing in general and New England skiing in particular.

Like many a ski museum, this one is

Scouts' Honors

Scouting Museum

Camp Carpenter
R.F.D. # 6-Bodwell Rd.
(P.O. Box 1121)
Manchester, NH 03105-1121
(603) 669-8919

Hours: July-Aug., daily 10 a.m.-4 p.m.; Sept.-June, Sat. only, same hours
Admission: Free
Getting There: About an hour north of Boston, Camp Carpenter can be reached by taking I-93 N to Exit 5 and following the signs to the museum (approximately 4 miles).

Helping little old ladies across the street, building matchless fires, and being brave, clean, and reverent, are among the virtues that the Boy Scouts of America has woven into the moral fiber of many a young man's character. Boy Scouts past and present will salute the colorful array of memorabilia on display in the Lawrence L. Lee Scouting Museum.

Lawrence L. Lee was the executive

director of the Daniel Webster Committee, BSA, who helped plan this museum before his death. The knobby, rustic building, dedicated to Lee's honor in 1969, is an ideal setting for this collection of memorabilia and memories, which includes everything from Jamboree buckles to original *Boy's Life* covers.

The history of the Boy Scouts, Cub Scouts, and Explorers is traced through lively displays of badges, buttons, kerchiefs, and caps. Donations to the collection from scouts who made it big include a flag that went to the moon with Alan Shepard. There are also plenty of international scout materials in the collection, reminding visitors of the miracles of youth diplomacy quietly carried out over the years through worldwide

scouting organizations. And for those who want to read up as well as catch up with the story of the Boy Scouts, the neighboring Max I. Silber Scouting Library contains thousands of reference materials, including yearbooks, handbooks, and periodicals.

Through an organized rite of passage (from childhood to adolescence, Cub Scout to Explorer), the Boy Scouts have beaten a path to manhood that's ingrained itself, like Ovaltine and stickball, into the very definition of American male adolesence. But even folks who've never sung endless rounds at a Jamboree or burned hotdogs over a smoky fire will enjoy the pomp and pageantry on display in the Lawrence L. Lee Scouting Museum.

New Jersey

Souperb

Campbell Museum

Campbell Place
Camden, NJ 08101
(609) 342-6440

Hours: Mon.-Fri. 9 a.m.-4:30 p.m.
Admission: Free
Getting There: Take Exit 4 from the New Jersey Turnpike to Rte. 73 to the Cherry Hill exit, and take Rte. 38 West to Rte. 30 West (keep to the far right on Rte. 30). Go 1 mile and look for signs to Campbell Place; when you come to the overpass sign for Campbell Place marked with an arrow, take the next right marked "exit" (stay in the left lane of the exit ramp). Follow signs for Campbell Place into the complex, and drive past the red brick Campbell Soup Company building. The museum is directly ahead.

If you're looking for rooms filled with souped-up Andy Warhol paintings, you've come to the wrong place. The Campbell Museum is mainly dedicated to preserving the history of soup and the extraordinary artistry that accompanied its serving. There are no petrified noodles or dumpling fossils in the collection—but there are plenty of rare and beautiful containers and utensils on display to nourish your understanding of soup's societal significance.

As an appetizer to the museum, visitors who make arrangements in advance can see "Artistry in Tureens," a 20-minute film showcasing and idolizing decorative soup servers. Then it's on to the cream of the crop of soup paraphernalia, including some serving utensils that date back to 500 B.C. The bulk of the collection, however, was cooked up in Europe during the eighteenth century. Artisans of all kinds, from potters to painters, were showered with attention and money from wealthy patrons and royalty during this glorious era of craftmanship, and the extravagance of many of the tureens in the Campbell Museum attests to this artistic pampering.

The elegant and elaborate tureens from this golden soup period are much in evidence in the collection, which includes a rare porcelain Meissen swan-shaped tureen from Saxony (circa 1745). In fact, soup seems to be served most often here by animals: throughout the museum, leaf-encrusted rabbits, fat red hens, mean-looking boars, and wide-eyed cattle embody the artistry and humor of the greatest craftsmen.

Other popular motifs run the gamut from fruits and vegetables to gardenias and galleons. And, while porcelain (in both its hard- and soft-paste forms) is

e favored material, various decorative
d functional touches feature leather,
nd-wrought metal, and cloisonné.
So, you've had your lesson for the
y. You probably feel educated right
wn to your knee socks. Now comes
e fun part: once you've done the tu-
ens, you can visit the lobby adjacent to
e museum to check out a small exhibit
memorabilia from Campbell Soup.
's a tiny but lively collection starring
ose roly-poly Campbell Soup Kids,
ong with early advertisements, origi-
l cans, and other souper stuff that will
ake you miss your mother, even if you
ought her along. All in all, the Camp-
ll Museum is good food—for thought,
d for memories.

Microtropolis

Miniature Kingdom
350 Rte. 31 S.
Washington, NJ 07882
(201) 689-6866

Hours: Tues.-Sun. 10 a.m.-5 p.m. (Closed
Jan. 10-Feb. 14)
Admission: Adults, $4.50; children, $3.50;
senior citizens, $4
Getting There: Located about an hour and a
half drive from New York or Philadelphia, it is
in northwest New Jersey on Rte. 31, a mile
south of the town of Washington. I-95 from
Philadelphia intersects Rte. 31, as do Rte. 57
and Rte. 80.

There's something about the human
spirit that inspires folks to spend their

lives building miniature cities from plaster of Paris, religious shrines from bits of broken soda bottles, and giant dinosaurs from chicken wire. The Miniature Kingdom, built by master minibuilder Arthur Thuijs, is a splendid case in point.

Thuijs was a world-acclaimed miniaturist who created famous little kingdoms throughout Europe, including Holland's "Madurodam." And he was much more than a miniaturist—Thuijs was also, at various times in his life, a pianist, painter, clothing designer (creator of the pedal-pusher, no less), and architect. Yet, despite his many career changes, Thuij's greatest mission in life was to build tiny cities. The Miniature Kingdom became his pièce de résistance.

Thuijs created his itty-bitty masterpiece when living with his family in Holland. Over a 10-year period, he is said to have spent tens of thousands of hours constructing the exhibit, which consists of 50 structures ranging from castles and cathedrals to villas and villages. The buildings were created from Swedish masonite with lead or copper roofs and real glass windows. More than 300 tiny working street lamps line the authentically recreated boulevards, and an international railroad system with six-inch-high cars winds its way through the principalities. There are also 1,000 trees, 10,000 hyacinths, 2,000 people, 400 animals, 150 cars, 40 canal boats and 5 half-foot-high sail and clipper ships, each handcrafted in miniature by Thuijs.

An offer from the Great Adventure amusement park in Jackson, N.J., was too good to pass up, so in 1974, Thuijs emigrated to the United States. Five years later, he built a permanent home

for his collection of models in a 13,000 square-foot castle just outside the tow of Washington, N.J. Although the mas ter builder died in 1984, his wife, Trudy—one can't help wondering if h ever called her "the little woman"— continues to run the Miniature Kingdom.

Strange Stuff

Seashell Museum

2721 Asbury Ave.
Ocean City, NJ 08226
(609) 398-2316

Hours: Memorial Day-Sept., Mon.-Sat. 9 a.m.-6 p.m.
Admission: Free
Getting There: Take U.S. Hwy. 9 to Hwy. 5 N. (Exit 30N) into Ocean City. The museum at the Shell Yard in the heart of Ocean City, or Asbury Ave.

This place has a really strange collectio of mutant mollusks. In fact, what the museum claims to be the only known Si

nese-twin helmet shell is on display
ere, along with a funny and beautiful
ollection of freak shells. While you're
ere, you may also learn a thing or two
om the seashell family-tree display or
ne of the other educational exhibits
oused in the Discovery Seashell Muse-
m. The Strange family, all certified
ivers, built this collection over the
ears. Their outdoor seashell shop, The
eashell Yard, has 10,000 shell varieties
anging from the common clam to the
xotic Glory of India Cone shell, all of
hich are for sale; but if you just want
o look, you can visit both the museum
nd the yard without shelling out a cent.

Place Setting

Spoon Collection
ambert Castle
alley Rd.
aterson, NJ 07503
201) 881-2761

Hours: Wed.-Sun. 1-4 p.m.
Admission: Adults, $1; senior citizens, 50
ents; children under 15, free
Getting There: From I-80 eastbound, take
xit 57 to Rte. 20 to Clifton, bear right, and exit
t Valley Rd. Follow signs to the museum,
vhich is on the right. From I-80 westbound,
nake a U-turn at exit 56 (Squirrewood Rd.)
nd get back on I-80 eastbound to get off at
Exit 57; then follow the directions above.

Utilitarianism is the name of the display
game in many a museum—but
utensilitarianism is rare indeed. The
Bertha Schaefer Koempel Spoon Collec-
ion, showcased in the ornate Lambert
Castle, will inspire even hardened knife-
and-forkers to swoon over spoons.
Koempel began collecting spoons dur-
ng her turn-of-the century girlhood,
and grew up to marry a well-to-do doc-

tor whose friends continued to ladle rare
and unusual spoons on Koempel
throughout her life. The resulting collection contains more than 5,400
spoons, including gem-encrusted implements from Imperial Europe, cloisonné
spoons from Czarist Russia, and thousands of souvenir spoons from world
fairs, presidential inaugurations, and
other memorable events.

There are spoons from every state in
the United States and nearly every
country in the world, as well as what
could only be called sentimental spoons,
given to Koempel by family and friends
to commemorate anniversaries and
birthdays. Some spoons are decorated
with paintings or appliqued photographs on the bowls, while others are
crafted from exotic materials, including
mother-of-pearl from China and filigreed metals from the Near East.

The Lambert Castle Museum, where
the spoons are displayed, is an art-filled
mansion with plenty of winding stair-
cases and turrets. Once the home and
collector's showcase of the millionaire
Cathola Lambert, the castle still exudes
its creator's affection for grandeur and
intricate decoration.

New York

Under Cover

Alling Coverlet Museum
122 William St.
Palmyra, NY 14522
(315) 597-6737

Hours: June-3rd Sun. in Sept., daily 1-4 p.m.
Admission: Free
Getting There: From I-90 (N.Y. Thruway), take Exit 43 to Rte. 21 north and drive 7 miles to Palmyra. Turn right at Main St. (Rte. 31), then left onto William St., where the museum is on the right.

The Alling Coverlet Museum holds the largest collection of hand-woven coverlets—bed covers—in the United States, thanks to Mrs. Harold Alling's 30-year career as a peerless coverlet hoarder. Now all the world can enjoy her collection, which includes dozens of beautiful geometric weaves as well as some intricate designs devised with Jacquard punch-card loom attachments. The coverlets are lovingly displayed in a two-story brick building in historic Palmyra, known far and wide for the great loom artisans who made the town a virtual coverlet mecca in the nineteenth century.

Memorial Memorial

Memorial Day Museum
35 E. Main St.
Waterloo, NY 13165
(315) 539-2474

Hours: Memorial Day-Labor Day, Tues.-Fri. 1:30-4 p.m.
Admission: Free
Getting There: Rtes. 96, 5, and 20 all run right through the small upstate town of Waterloo, with Rtes. 5 and 20 becoming Main St. as they cut through town. The museum, prominently signed, stands in the heart of the town. It is hard to miss.

It is strangely fitting that the place where so many of Napoleon's army fell in battle should share a name with the New York town that started the tradition of Memorial Day. The observance started in 1866, when Henry Welles and General John Murray came up with the idea that Waterloo should have a holiday to honor its war dead. The concept of Memorial Day spread rather slowly, first being celebrated in Waterloo, then in the surrounding towns, and finally working its way into the hearts, minds, and leisure plans of the rest of the nation. In 1966, President Johnson proclaimed Waterloo the birthplace of Memorial Day, and the town opened the Memorial Day Museum to memorialize its own place in holiday history.

History is alive in this museum, housed in a lovely 20-room mansion that looks out over the town's quiet Main St. Like many museums and historical-society collections that depict slow-to-change communities, there is an immediacy to the preservation of a past that could almost—but not quite—be the present. You can almost taste the sour lemonade, smell the sweet honeysuckle, and see the crowd of wom-

n with parasols and men in straw hats trolling down the street during that first Memorial Day's festivities, as they do in the photographs and accounts displayed here. It is the little bits and pieces of that era exhibited here—the dress ribbons, newspapers, and nickknacks—that bring time to a warm summer standstill.

Along with artifacts from early Memorial Day celebrations, the museum makes an effort to retain the roots of the reasoning that spawned the town's claim to fame. Post-Civil War conflicts are remembered here in exhibits about those who fought, and why.

America is older, more battle-scarred, and more bitter than it was when the people of Waterloo decided to honor their dead war heroes. Memorial Day has taken on a less patriotic meaning than it had in 1866. But thanks to the Memorial Day Museum, honor seems

more honorable when held up to this mirror of the past.

Now You See It

Museum of Holography

11 Mercer St.
New York, NY 10013
(212) 925-0581

Hours: Tues.-Sun. noon-6 p.m.
Admission: Adults, $3; children and senior citizens, $1.50
Getting There: The museum is housed in a landmark cast-iron building in the heart of lower Manhattan's SoHo section. Subways and taxis are the best way to get around; while the Holland Tunnel is only a few blocks away, drive and park at your own risk.

Anyone who's got a wallet full of plastic already carries around a personal, hip-pocket hologram collection: those shimmering three-dimensional images of flying birds and spinning globes that adorn most major credit cards are one common manifestation of the strange and fascinating technology of holography. But there's more to holograms than meets (or fools) the eye. Aside from theft-proofing credit cards, these flickering images are turning up with increasing frequency in the worlds of art, entertainment, and business. The Museum of Holography provides a small but worthwhile showcase for this high-tech world of ghostly elegance.

The museum was founded in 1976, only five years after Dennis Gabor received a Nobel Prize for inventing the technique of holography. Since then, the growing number of artists and technicians using holography has provided exhibition material for the museum's three-room display area.

Here, awe-struck kids and their equally wide-eyed parents stand mesmerized by images of flickering candles, fierce gunfighters, and glittering cityscapes. These are no ordinary canvases or photographs: each scene takes on an otherworldly life of its own, jumping back and forth, fading to black and then reappearing, and fuzzing in and out of focus—all on flat surfaces that appear totally blank until infused with light.

The art (and, some would say, torturous technology) of holography involves using laser light to imprint an image onto an emulsion-coated piece of film or glass. The image is totally invisible until light is shone onto the surface. Then the imprint reappears and seems to float magically in the air, a three-dimensional resurrection of an object or person. But try to reach out and touch it, and it's gone.

You've got to stand at just the right angle and height to see a hologram, which is why the works in the museum have been placed at the average eye level of adults. Metal crates are provided for kids and shorter people to stand on, but basketball players will just have to stoop a little.

Glass Act

National Bottle Museum

20 Church Ave.
(P.O. Box 621)
Ballston Spa, NY 12020
(518) 885-7589

Hours: Year 'round, Mon.-Fri. 10 a.m.-4 p.m.; June-Sept., same hours, including weekends
Admission: $1
Getting There: Take I-90 (N.Y. Thruway) to Exit 27 (Amsterdam) and follow the Rte. 67 signs into Ballston Spa. Take Rte. 67 to where it joins Rte. 50 at the first traffic light in town and turn right at the light. Verbeck House, where the museum is located, is the third building on the right.

Established in 1979 for the preservation, study, and promotion of the history of bottle- and glass-making in the United States, the National Bottle Museum lives up to its task. While many of

e bottles have a self-contained ele-
ance, some of the most interesting
ems are those depicting other facets of
e glass-making industry. Take, for in-
ance, the display of chains and canes
ade from glass—a strange and fragile
aterial for such utilitarian items. And
e nineteenth-century ink bottle collec-
on is well worth a glance.

Other exhibits include a bottle-dating
isplay that shows visitors how to tell
e age of their own favorite flagons,
nd a history of glass blowing that
howcases various tools of the trade, as
ell as some rare blown-glass pieces.
isitors to National Bottle Museum will
ome away with at least a few shards of
nteresting information.

an You Dig It?

etrified Creatures
Museum
.S. Rte. 20, RD #2
chfield Springs, NY 13439
15) 858-2868

ours: Daily, except where noted. May 15-
une 23, 10 a.m.-5 p.m.; June 24-Sept. 10,
a.m.-dark; Sept. 11-Oct. 15, 10 a.m.-5 p.m.
losed Tues. and Wed. in May and Oct.; open
eekends until snow falls after Oct. 15
dmission: Adults, $3; children, $2
etting There: Located on U.S. Rte. 20, 11
iiles north of Cooperstown, and 4 miles east
f Richfield Springs. From U.S. Hwy. 90 (the
.Y. Thruway) take Exit 29 (Canajaharie) onto
wy. 80 and drive south 25 miles to Hwy. 20.
hen drive west on Hwy. 20 to the museum,
hich is on the south side of the road.

he Petrified Creatures Museum turns
uch dry subjects as geology and pale-
ntology into nearly lively arts. Al-
hough the museum's displays, in and of
hemselves, are standard natural history

fare (fossils, taped narrations of the
meaning of it all, and so on), the museum grounds turn fossils into fun. Life-
sized dinosaur "restorations" (as the
museum calls them) dot the landscape,
their chunky, pastel-painted papier mâché and chicken-wire bodies adding an
amusing, lumbering elegance to the
woods, which were once a prehistoric
seabed. Today, the land is rich in fossils,
and visitors are invited to dig, dig,
dig—and keep what they find for free.
"Uncover the life that swarmed over
this area 300 million years ago!" reads a
brochure, which goes on to explain that
"Finding free fossils is an encounter
with the first kinds." And what first
kinds might one encounter? Sharks, in
the forms of their teeth, petrified wood,
coral, starfish, sand dollars, and more.
Among the rocks and minerals given up
by the earth in this region are turquoise,
lapis lazuli, garnet, amber, jade, and
pyrite. The Petrified Creatures Museum
is probably the only place around where
you can dig for the treasures of nature
and time in the shadow of a lilac-colored
Brontosauras.

What's Shakin'?

Salt Museum
Onandaga Lake Park
Onandaga County Dept. of Parks and
Recreation
Box 146
Liverpool, NY 13088
(315) 457-2990

Hours: Weekdays 10 a.m.-5 p.m.; weekends
10 a.m.-6 p.m.
Admission: Free
Getting There: From I-90 (N.Y. Thruway),
take Exit 38 to Hwy. 370 north (Onandaga
Lake Parkway). Follow signs to Onandaga
Lake Park, where the museum is located.

Lake Onandaga's saline marshlands provided a briny livelihood for this tiny upstate town and its larger neighbor, Syracuse, during the 1900s. By the 1860s, Syracuse area salt-makers were turning out 9 million bushels of salt a year, more than half the total national production. But by the 1920s, what with modern import and production methods, the New York salt business had petered out completely. Nevertheless, Liverpool didn't forget its its sodium story.

Built during the Great Depression as a work-relief project, the Salt Museum resides in a replica of an early "salt block" (the name given to salt production complexes because of the blocks where giant salt-boiling vats were placed). The museum focuses on the salt industry as it existed in the region during the height of the Industrial Revolution. Exhibits include displays of tools, photographs, and documents, as well as demonstrations of the long-lost art of salt production. Even well-seasoned tourists will be pleasantly surprised by this little-known part of New York's industrial heritage.

Soar Subject

Soaring Museum
R.D. #3, Harris Hill
Elmira, NY 14903
(607) 734-3128

Hours: Daily 10 a.m.-5 p.m.
Admission: Adults, $2; students and senior citizens, $1.50; children under 12 free when accompanied by adult
Getting There: Take Hwy. 17 to Exit 51 and follow the signs to the museum on Harris Hill.

here is a beauty, a daring, a gravity-defying freedom about glider flying that engine-powered machines just can't match. The National Soaring Museum brings that exhilaration to life in a series of changing exhibits that often have as much energy and liveliness as the sport that inspired them.

Although the original museum building burned down in 1977, a larger, more effective exhibit space was opened in 1978. Here, you can settle into a cockpit simulator for a flight of the mind, meander through exhibits on meteorology, aerodynamics, and soaring history, or watch real sailplanes doing their thing from the adjacent glider field. The strong of stomach and brave of soul can soar along with them, thanks to a company that specializes in passenger joy-rides for a fee. While gliding can be a short-lived high compared to jumbo-jet jaunts, the planes and paraphernalia on display in the National Soaring Museum seem to lift off in spirit where engine planes drag behind.

Eclectic Circus

Southeast Museum
Main St.
Brewster, NY 10509
(914) 279-7500

Hours: Tues., Wed., and Thurs. noon-4 p.m.; Sat. and Sun. 2-4 p.m.
Admission: Free
Getting There: Take I-84 to the Brewster exit and follow signs to town. The museum, housed in the first floor of the Old Town Hall, is located on Main St.

If you're into circuses, condensed milk, train wrecks, or salt-and-pepper shakers, this small museum is for you. The Southeast Museum is one of those eclectic collections that has a little bit of everything from its region's history. In this case, the history revolves around the winter quarters of early circuses, the Borden Condensed Milk factory, and the Harlem-Hudson Train Line.

The circus memorabilia collection includes posters, wagons, and other festive items from the time when the earth had more than one "Greatest Show" to offer and small traveling circuses called Brewster their home during the winter months. While the circus was coming (and staying), Gail Borden was creating his condensed milk dynasty in Brewster. On display in the Borden Exhibit are such pertinent items as Borden's desk, and some wonderful old milk labels, bottles, and toys. As for the Harlem-Hudson Line memorabilia, along with the usual timetables and signal flags there are some morbidly fascinating photos and accounts of train wrecks. But the hands-down winner in this museum is the collection of more than 250 salt-and-pepper shakers. Why are they here? Who knows? All that matters is that they *are* here, and that they come in many delightful forms, from playful puppies to crying babies.

Strong Sense of History

Strong Museum

1 Manhattan Rd.
Rochester, NY 14607
(716) 454-7639

Hours: Mon.-Sat. 10 a.m.-5 p.m.; Sun. 1-5 p.m.
Admission: Adults, $2; children (4-16), 75 cents; students, $1.50; senior citizens, $1.50
Getting There: Located in the heart of downtown Rochester in upstate New York. Take the inner loop from I-490 to the Monroe Ave. exit and go north; the museum is at the next intersection.

Margaret Woodbury Strong collected lots of stuff during her 72-year life—tons of stuff, in fact. Little stuff, big stuff, cheap stuff, expensive stuff, silly stuff, weird stuff, ugly stuff, tacky stuff. Because she also had lots of green stuff, she left $60 million of it for the creation of a museum to house and interpret her collection. And, while it was a difficult task to eke out recurring historical and societal themes from the more than 300,000 objects Strong had left behind, the collection was eventually tamed, and the museum was opened to the public in 1982.

As delightful as it is kitschy, the Margaret Woodbury Strong collection provides an amusing and slightly embarrassing look at American taste and culture from 1820 to 1940. No Van Goghs grace the inner sanctums of this friendly museum; nor do ancient Egyptian burial cloths or rare pre-Columbian pots while away the centuries in temperature-controlled glass vaults. Instead, the treasures here are mechanical banks, kewpie dolls, picture books, car

games, snuff bottles, advertising posters, "potty" figurines, bicycles, ink
wells, gilded and wicker furniture,
washboards, "Brownie" stories, Flow
Blue china, lighting devices, and a
countless array of other mass-produced
fancies.

Strong's passionate collecting was
sparked by a lonely, precocious childhood during which she traveled the
world with her wealthy, middle-aged
parents. During these trips, her parents
would routinely hand the child an empty shopping bag, encouraging her to fill
it with whatever caught her eye.
When the bag was full, her
spending spree was over,
only to be renewed with
another empty bag the
next day.

Strong's father,
an avid coin collec-
tor, made his fortune
as a buggy whip manu-
facturer and investor; her
mother is said to have been
a forceful woman whose favorite hobbies included controlling her daughter's
life and buying miniature carved Japa-

nese utensils. The coins and miniatures
of Strong's parents are included in the
museum along with the massive roster
of items accumulated by their daughter,
whose compulsive collecting habit they
undoubtedly shaped.

During a life that was increasingly
characterized by isolation (her husband
and only companion was 20 years her
senior and became senile when she was
still a vigorous woman) and tragedy
(her only child, a rebellious daughter,
died at age 25), Strong turned much of
her attention to her growing assortment
of knickknacks. In the last decade of her
life, she became an eccentric loner,
dressing, some said, as if she were a
charwoman and spending most of her
time scouring flea markets, second-
hand stores, and street vendors in
search of collectibles. She eventually
built additions to her mansion to catch
the overflow of her collection, which,
she hoped, would one day become the
basis for a "museum of fascinations."

Strong's dream came true. This truly
is a museum of fascinations, housed in
an airy, modern building with thematic
exhibits on the ground floor and a virtu-

Cabbage Patch dolls are in this generation.

The Margaret Woodbury Strong Museum is a mecca for anyone who grew up reading the backs of cereal boxes, who delights in the fare of roadside gift shops and carnival game prizes, and who still remembers the tinsel-fringed joy of childhood treasures. Bring an empty bag and fill it with wonder.

Hot to Trot

Trotting Horse Museum

240 Main St.
Goshen, NY 10924
(914) 294-6330

Hours: Mon.-Sat. 10 a.m.- 5 p.m.; Sun. noon-5 p.m.
Admission: $1
Getting There: Goshen is located on Hwy 17, just south of I-84 (Exit 121); the museum is on Main St.

al attic of pleasures in the upper level. The organized exhibits focus attention on the Industrial Revolution's impact on societal values, entertainments, and work habits. "The Great Transformation," for instance, highlights the metamorphosis of the middle class into a leisure class with the advent of mass-produced household appliances and conveniences, while "A Century of Childhood: 1820-1920" displays enough gimcrack toys and games to give Santa Claus a complex.

The upstairs "open storage" area gives a less organized but even more charming review of the collection, for it is here that the sheer breadth, range, and scattered sensibilities of Strong's passionate, endless search for fascination become evident. Ironically, the one thread that strings together this charm bracelet of a museum is that of relative ordinariness. While most of these items are rare today, in Strong's time (particularly her childhood) they were as commonplace as pocket calculators and

From the looks of it, Hambletonian must have died with a smile on his face. The frisky stallion, considered the "father of trotting," took his title very seriously; if the stud service records on display at the Trotting Horse Museum are accurate, he sired at least 1,331 foals before he died.

But Hambletonian did more than just roll in the hay; he was the start of a tradition of trotting-horse racing and breeding that has lived on in this sleepy upstate New York town for more than 100 years. The Trotting Horse Museum is dedicated to bringing this horsey history to the public, and it does so with an almost unbridled passion.

The museum is housed in the onetime "Good Time Stable" where stalls and entryway have been cleverly converted to exhibit spaces. Each stall holds a ollection or display relating to some aspect of the history of trotting. ambletonian's exhibit stall, with his Records of Services Rendered," is just he beginning. Other stalls have memobilia of great trotters, pacers, riders, nd races. Also featured is the fashionble "What the Well-Dressed Pacer Will 'ear" display. But the most charming xhibit of all is the "Living Hall of Fame nd Immortals Room," with its 14-ch-high statues of great riders. Each atue, encased in an acrylic box, is accompanied by a replica of a favorite og, saddle, and so forth, created from its of wood, paper, plastic, and leather.

An upstairs loft is devoted to the evotion of the sulky (the buggy in which he driver stands), from the early, tall our-wheeled models to the "bike" lkies driven today. Other upstairs exibits include a display of wooden toys nd whirligigs starring trotting horses, nd a replica of one of the stable's original stalls.

The saucy history of sulky racing is epicted throughout the museum, with arly race reports and paraphernalia. uring most of the nineteenth century, lky racing was illegal, but the matches ould break out anyway—and anyhere. Rakish gentlemen out with their

horses would meet unexpectedly at a crossroads or on an open stretch of road, size up each other's team, and a race would begin. Local constables found this quite discomfiting, as did religious zealots who proclaimed that only fast people owned fast horses. But despite this opposition, the sport eventually gained respectability, and formal trotting came to be.

Pennsylvania

Bon-Bon Voyage

Candy Museum

46 N. Broad St. (Rte. 501)
Lititz, PA 17543
(717) 626-1131

Hours: Mon.-Sat. 10 a.m.-5 p.m.
Admission: Free
Getting There: Lititz, in Pennsylvania's Lancaster County, lies along Rte. 501, which cuts across the state in a north-south line. The town is south of the Pennsylvania Turnpike, and the museum, located in the Wilbur Chocolate Factory, is on Rte. 501 (Broad St. as it runs through town).

The first thing you notice is the smell. Even before you enter, it wafts thickly through the air on the street outside the ancient brick facade of the building: Chocolate. Chocolate. And more chocolate. Passing through the factory outlet store to get to the museum is perhaps the finest test of willpower known to modern chocoholics. But once you're beyond the grasp of the of six-foot chocolate bunnies, a tasty treat awaits.

The three rooms of the museum overflow with the tools and triumphs of the candy trade. There are colorful old boxes and wrappers, countless stirrers, pourers, and molds, and a strange and amusing array of candy memorabilia.

On one wall, a photomontage proudly depicts Muhammed Ali's visit to the factory and museum. With the kind of appetite for chocolate it seems "The Greatest" indulged, it's a small miracle he was able to float like a butterfly.

In the same room, on another wall, a dog-earred wheel divulges "Your Candy Horoscope." Among its many insightful commentaries on human nature is the description of Cancer as a "hard worker" who will, by the way, appreciate "a gift of packaged confections in a large quantity for a low price." (The determined Capricorn, however, prefers the longevity of an "all-day sucker.") Around the corner, on the lower shelves of a display case, is a collection of unusually shaped candy molds, some of which are real appetite suppressants—most notably the molds depicting an agonized Christ on the cross.

In another area, a glass-encased wall is lined with dozens of lovely porcelain chocolate pourers that date from 1700 to 1900. Among these are several artful pieces of Limoges, Nippon, and Haviland. Also fascinating is the display of tools used to harvest and prepare cacao, including a wicked-looking South

American machete for clearing the vegetation surrounding cacao trees.

The documentation leaves something to be desired. There are descriptive cards here and there, but many objects, if identified at all, are merely noted on stick-on labels pasted on the display.

While most of the objects are undated, one tool is described as "A Very Old Wooden Candy Mold." As with a box of candy, it's the thought that counts.

Despite its small size and lack of documentation, the Candy Americana Museum's abundance of funny and intriguing candy relics places it in the ranks with some of the better blink-and-you-miss-something mom-and-pop museums. This is the kind of museum to savor as you would a piece of designer chocolate—for a minimal investment (in this case, nothing), it will leave a pleasant taste for the rest of the afternoon.

Death and Taxidermy

Fin, Fur, and Feather Wildlife Museum

Star Rte. (Box 59)
Lock Haven, PA 17745
(717) 769-6620

Hours: April 15-Dec. 14, daily 9 a.m.-5 p.m. Dec. 26-April 14, Fri.-Sun. 9 a.m.-5 p.m.
Admission: Adults, $4; children, $2
Getting There: Although the mailing address reads Lock Haven, the museum is almost 20 miles to the north, in Haneyville. You can get there by taking Rte. 220 to Lock Haven and picking up Rte. 664 N. Take it to the end, where it hitches up with Rte. 44, and head north. The museum is up the road on the right.

Sure, you can go to the zoo to see real animals, but the darned things keep moving. This is one place where they stand still, so you can get a good long look at those sweet brown eyes, those nasty white fangs, and that soft, thick mane. Suffice to say that Dr. Doolittle

uld faint as soon as he walked in the
or. What we have here is a sports-
n's paradise.

As the name implies, no variety of the
d kingdom's inhabitants, from fish to
vl to furry friend, has been left out.
e results are both chilling and awe-
piring. There are more than 500 ani-
ls on exhibit here, all bagged by Paul
d Carole Asper, who also run the mu-
m and adjacent gun and gift shop.
iong the spoils of the Aspers' world-
le hunting trips are creatures from
ngolia, Russia, Australia, India, Ne-
, Mexico, Alaska, Iran, Canada, and
ica.

The Aspers certainly know how to

hunt—Paul has made it into the Safari
Club's "Record Book of Trophy Animals" more than 100 times—and the
mounted kills on display in their museum are a tribute to their prowess. All
"top five" big game biggies are represented: leopard, lion, elephant, rhinoc-
eros, and cape buffalo. You can also find
some rare trophy animals, including a
Marco Polo sheep, a Persian brown
bear, and a dwarf buffalo.

All these trophies have been nicely
stuffed and mounted, surrounded with
painted scenes of their habitats and, in
some cases, photographs of the actual
kill. Other trophies are mounted à la
carte on the walls—long rows of horned

and furred heads stretching the length of the room.

Aside from animals, there's plenty of other hunting memorabilia, including weapons and firsthand accounts of the kills. Until recently, the National Taxidermists Association Hall of Fame was also housed here, but it's been replaced by a collection of sporting art that celebrates hunting and fishing. For those who prefer the wild kingdom a little less wild, this is an overall fine assemblage of creatures from around the globe.

The Kids of Summer

Little League Museum
Rte. 15 S.
Williamsport, PA 17701
(717) 326-3607

Hours: Memorial Day-Labor Day, 10 a.m.-8 p.m.; Labor Day-Memorial Day, 10 a.m.-5 p.m.
Admission: Adults, $3; children, $1; senior citizens, $1.50
Getting There: Take I-80 to Rte. 15 S. and drive 18 miles to the museum, located on Rte. 15.

Ever wanted to put those little sluggers into a cage? You can do it here. The Little League Baseball Museum is everything its big brother in Cooperstown, Ohio, is, only smaller—and, in some ways, a lot more fun. When a museum takes the viewpoint of a child, it naturally takes on a childlike curiosity and wonderment—touch this, play with that, look in here. That's what makes this place so darned neat.

For real sluggers, there are bat-and-pitch safety cages where kids can have a ball or two and catch their own action on video-replay monitors. Other inter-

active exhibits include "see and touch" displays of Little League equipment various stages of production, from raw wood to smooth bat, and an arcade where buttons and buzzers help test Little Leaguers on the difference between the rules of their game and those of the major leagues. For those who'd rather be spectators than players, films and videos are continuously shown in the Diamond Room and the World Series Room. There's also a colorfully displayed collection of Little League memorabilia tracing the game's history from 1939 to the present, exhibits on safety equipment, and a fiber-optics map that shows the worldwide dissemination of the game.

Don't be put off by the plain colonial style brick building, which doesn't really do justice to the creative collection inside. The Little League Baseball Museum is still a hit.

Unforgettable

Mr. Ed's Elephant Museum
U.S. Rte. 30
6019 Chambersburg Rd.
Ortanna, PA 17353
(717) 352-3792

Hours: March-Dec., daily 10 a.m.-5 p.m.; June 1-Oct. 15, weekend hours extended from 10 a.m.-9 p.m.
Admission: Adults, $1; children, 50 cents
Getting There: Located on U.S. Rte. 30, 1 miles west of Gettysburg and 2 miles east Caledonia State Park.

hen an elephant sits around the
use, it sits *around* the house; when
ndreds of elephants sit around the
use, it's time to get a new house. Ed
Mr. Ed") Gotwalt's wife, Patricia, got
tired of her husband's massive collec-
n of elephant things sitting around
eir house that she told him to open a
useum instead. He did just that, and
e resulting Mr. Ed's Elephant Muse-
n is a delight.

"We feel that we are the only elephant
t shop and museum combination in
e world," says Gotwalt with heartfelt
thusiasm. He is probably right. Mr.
l's beloved "Miss Ellie Phunt," a 500-
und, 9 ½-foot-tall fiberglass ele-
ant extraordinaire, stands at the en-
nce to his museum, chatting up
urists with tape-recorded but pleasant
chyderm patter. Ellie once lived at
io's King's Island Amusement Park
fore packing her trunk and heading
st in a U-Haul pulled by Gotwalt.

But Ellie is just the opening act here,
because inside the museum there are
more than 4,000 elephant-related items
to examine. Gotwalt's collection, an obsession dating back more than 20 years,
comes from all over the world. Anything
that could possibly be made in the shape
of an elephant is on display, from a hair
dryer to a potty chair. There are elephant ashtrays, salt-and-pepper shakers, lamps, playing cards, posters,
pillows—the list is longer than an elephant's memory. People come from all
over to donate their own personal elephants to the museum, and Gotwalt
continues to gather things during his
travels, so the collection is constantly
growing. The adjacent gift shop sells elephants of every variety, along with
candy, dried fruits, and nuts—peanuts,
of course.

The test of a truly great roadside stop
is the bumper stickers it sells. Mr Ed's
pass with flying colors: the yellow sticker with a sketch of an elephant standing
majestically in a patch of grass reads
"You'll Never Forget Mister Ed's Elephant Museum." And you know what?
You never will.

Spore Relations

Mushroom Museum

Phillips Mushroom Place
U.S. Rte. 1
Kennett Square, PA 19348
(215) 388-6082

Hours: Daily 10 a.m.-6 p.m.
Admission: Adults, $1.25; children, 50 cents;
senior citizens, 75 cents
Getting There: Phillips Mushroom Place is
right on U.S. Rte. 1 as it passes through
Kennett Square. The museum is the
centerpiece of the complex.

How much do you really want to know about *Agaricus bisporus*, more commonly called mushrooms? Well, if you answer "Plenty!" this is the place for you. The one-room museum has mushrooms in all shapes, sizes, and media—from a 'shroom slideshow to a real live growing area. Charts, models, and illustrations detail the growth and history of the mushroom industry that fungi fanatics will find exhaustive. The museum even caters to trends in mushroom chic with a recently installed diorama ('shroom with a view?) of a *shitake* mushroom.

Mushrooms have been both revered and feared throughout history—Egyptians believed they were the food of immortality, and the Greeks and Romans made them the dish of royalty—but poisonous and hallucinogenic mushrooms have been the scourge of many a superstitious civilization as well. The Mushroom Museum explores this lore and legend while at the same

time promoting the safe and healthy record of the modern mushroom industry.

The Mushroom Museum is right at home in Kennett Square, which claims the exhilarating title of "World's Mushroom Capital." It's a hard-won honor, to be sure: mushrooms are even more difficult to grow than orchids. This area produces 280 million pounds of mushrooms a year, a figure that makes it Pennsylvania's top crop. California, second largest, produces a mere 108 million pounds a year.

Phillips Mushroom Place began as a growing and packaging factory, but quickly mushroomed into a tourist attraction when the museum opened in 1974. There are a number of other areas in the complex, including the Market Place restaurant, where you can stuff yourself with mushrooms, and the Cap and Stem gift shop, where you can buy fresh mushrooms and bizarre souvenirs "from statuary to staghorns."

Twisted

Pretzel House

219 E. Main St.
Lititz, PA 17543
(717) 626-4354

Hours: Mon.-Sat. 9 a.m.- 5 p.m.
Admission: Adults, 75 cents; children, 50 cents
Getting There: From Rte. 501 (Broad St. as runs through town), drive east on Main St; the Pretzel House will be on your left.

You'll know you've found the Julius Sturgis Pretzel House by the giant pretzel on the porch. Legend has it that the recipe was the gift of a hobo, grateful for a meal provided by Julius Sturgis. After testing it out on his family and friends Sturgis turned his bread bakery into a pretzel bakery, and the rest is—well, twistory.

Visitors take a brief tour of the bakery that includes a chance to earn an "Offi

l Pretzel Twister's Certificate" by
rning to twist a pretzel. Don't miss
e collection of sew-on pretzel patches
d other pretzel-related memorabilia
the display case as you enter the first
om. And while you're in the neighbor-
od, keep your eyes open for the per-
nally inscribed photo of none other
an Mr. (Fred) Rogers.

otloose

hoe Museum

nnsylvania College of Podiatric Medicine
ghth and Race Sts.
iladelphia, PA 19107
5) 629-0300, ext. 219

urs: By appointment only, weekdays 9
m.-4 p.m.

dmission: Free

tting There: Eighth and Race Sts. are
ajor arteries in the heart of Philadelphia; any
y map (or resident) can point you to the
ersection, which is about 12 blocks from
y Hall, and also boasts the Police
lministration Building, the Metropolitan
spital, and, around the corner, Franklin
rk. The museum is on the sixth floor of the
llege. Call a day or two in advance to
ange a viewing; you'll have to sign in at the
eption area.

oes, shoes, everywhere, and not a pair
wear. Starting in the lobby of the
nnsylvania College of Podiatric Medi-

cine, you can gaze at the footwear of the
stars—including the likes of Billy Jean
King and Joe Frazier—all encased in
Plexiglas domes. Once you've made it
past the front desk, taken a short elevator ride, and been greeted by your shoe
guide, you get to study the story of shoes
as it is depicted in the sixth-floor
gallery.

To be honest, "gallery" is a generous
term for the fashion in which the collection is displayed; "hallway" is more appropriate. In fact, it's a long, narrow
hallway (which, it seems, half the students and faculty like to traverse, especially while you're trying to see the museum) that holds a row of glass cases
filled with treasures. There are embroidered tapestry shoes, dyed-leather
shoes, and carved wooden shoes, all of
which have silent stories to tell about the
passing of centuries and places and people and feet. The shoes here might be
called educational, in that many have
historical significance. Take, for instance, the nicely preserved pair of
Egyptian burial shoes, labeled "Mysterious Sandals." Presumably, they were
created for those fashion-conscious
corpses who wished to be properly shod
should they be called upon to walk the
earth again.

Also displayed is a photograph of a
papier mâché cast of a "bound" foot.
The practice of binding feet was once
common in China and other Asian
countries, and involved wrapping a pro-
gressively tighter strip of cloth around
the arch of a woman's foot. There was,
according to Lisbeth Holloway, the museum's director, a "strong sexual conno-
tation" that went hand-in-hand with
the bound foot, which is why such dis-
figured women were highly desirable as
wives and concubines.

As you tour the museum, interesting facts seem to spring forth from out of a vast world of shoe knowledge. Did you know, for instance, that the word "sabotage" is thought to come from the name of "sabo" shoes—common Dutch wooden shoes—that an angry employee would don if he wanted to take agricultural revenge on his tulip-growing boss? Stomping on the budding bulbs with those big shoes did a lot of damage, and while it probably didn't get the saboteur the raise he was hoping for, it sure helped vent his frustrations.

Such erudition is tempered by some delicious kitsch. One case near the back contains a pair of recent-vintage men's canvas leisure loafers emblazoned from ankle to toe with the Budweiser logo. The shoes were worn by a tourist who came to Philadelphia for the bicentennial celebration.

Actually, it was during that time that the Shoe Museum was founded. In 1976, the city of Philadelphia asked local institutions to set up exhibits that might help take the tourism pressure off major attractions during the Bicentennial rush. The Mutter Museum, a Philadelphia medical museum, offered to provide the school with the footwear collection. The expected crush of visitors to the city never quite materialized but in the meantime, the Shoe Museum had its foot in the door of Philadelphia's museum roster.

Once you've learned a lesson or two in the hallway of shoe history, you've earned the chance to peruse the display near the elevator bank, where a more light-hearted look at the world of shoe awaits. There is a case filled with wedding slippers, and another holding the tiny button-up shoes once worn by children. Still another display holds several shelves of dance-related memorabilia, including a pair of plaster casts of the feet of Judith Jamison, the prima-dancer for Alvin Ailey.

A famous-shoes case houses such historical treasures as Mamie Eisenhower's sensible but elegant "wife-of" shoes, and Nancy Reagan's more daring rhinestone-encrusted evening shoes. There's also a pair of what Holloway calls "legendary" ocelot-fur shoes created for a famed 1920s film star who died before she could wear them. Ah, fated feet.

But the best display of them all is "[F]oolish Feet," exhibiting some of the [s]iest shoes ever conceived. There are [s]me wonderful wedgies of gold lamé [th]at are a foot high if they're an inch, [an]d look like they just stepped off some [re]ally groovy other planet. There are [al]so pairs of high heels so lofty they [ca]n't even stand up in the display case, [an]d photographs of some "real people" [ro]ller skates: for the gentleman, a pair [of] wingtips on wheels, and for the lady [of] the house, a rolling rendition of fluffy [be]droom slippers.

[W]ar Is Hell

[S]hrine of St. Kolbe
[St.] Thomas Church
[R.]D. 1, Box 187)
[Ne]w Salem, PA 15468
[(41]2) 245-6279

[H]ours: Always visible
[A]dmission: Free
[G]etting There: From 1-70, take Hwy. 51 [so]uth to Hwy. 119. Go south to Hwy. 21 west, [an]d follow it about 3 miles and turn north [in]to R.D. 1. Drive north (toward New Salem) [to] the St. Thomas Roman Catholic Church.

[H]ere, on the grounds of a Roman Catho[li]c church, is probably the most disturb[in]g shrine in the country. It is dedicated [to] St. Maximilian Kolbe, a Franciscan [pr]iest who died while imprisoned at the [A]uschwitz concentration camp, when [h]e willingly traded his own life for that [of] a family man who had been sentenced [to] death by the Nazis.

[K]olbe's supreme sacrifice is remem[b]ered in a moving, shocking shrine. De[si]gned to recall the bleakness of a con[ce]ntration camp, the humble, block-[sh]aped stone construction is crowned with barbed wire strung in symbolic fencing. Within the shrine, stained-glass windows in the colors of the rising and setting sun offer a quote, both in Kolbe's native Polish and in English, taken from his own preaching,: "Without Sacrifice There Is No Love."

The shrine was created under the guidance of the church pastor, the late Rev. Sebastian Pajdzik. Like St. Kolbe, Pajdzik was a Pole who saw the horrors of the Nazi regime firsthand. He swore never to forget what he had witnessed. Here, many decades later and a continent away, in a quiet corner of Pennsylvania, the Shrine of St. Maximilian Kolbe stands, not only as a memorial, but also as an outcry.

Toot Sweet

Trumpet Museum
Fairway Farm
Vaughan Rd.
Pottstown, PA 19464
(215) 327-1351

Hours: By appointment only
Admission: $2.50 suggested donation
Getting There: The museum can be reached by taking Rte. 100 N. (Exit 23) from the Pennsylvania Turnpike, to Rte. 724 (Kenilworth). Take a right onto Vaughan Rd. from 724. The farm is on the left.

Franz Streitweiser doesn't mind blowing his own horns—considering he's got hundreds to choose from. Aside from running a charming bed-and-breakfast on his Fairway Farm, Streitweiser is the owner and manager of the 500-of-a-kind Trumpet Museum he opened in 1980.

What started decades earlier as a music-school hobby in Austria eventually blew out of proportion, so Streitweiser bought the farm, renovated a barn, and hung up the trumpets. Visitors, who are shown around by the collector himself, get a chance to ogle bugles of every variety, age, and sound. Among the treasures are a rare Tibetan temple horn, a coiled, seven-foot "serpent" horn and a nineteenth-century reproduction of a Viking horn called a lur. There's even a horn that Streitweiser himself was instrumental in creating—it's called a "clarinhorn," and it interprets high-rococo music that was formerly thought unplayable. There are horns for every occasion here, from jazz jams to classical concerts, as well as enough sheet music, mouthpieces, and music stands to outfit 76 trombones. Related items include a collection of glass drinking steins painted with trumpet images and some lively posters of famous musicians.

While the walls and ceilings of the museum barn fairly glow with the polished shine of well-loved brass, the liveliest part of the tour is Streitweiser himself. He demonstrates the trumpet sounds, tells their stories, and generally gives a blow-'em-dead performance for even the most casual of tourists. More formal concerts are often staged in the museum or on the farm grounds, so check to find out whether there are any scheduled perfomances when you plan to visit.

What's In Store?

Wanamaker Museum

8th Floor, John Wanamaker Department Store
Thirteenth and Market Sts.
(P.O. Box 7497)
Philadelphia, PA 19101
(215) 422-2737

Hours: Daily noon-3 p.m.
Admission: Free
Getting There: If you can find your way to City Hall—which is quite lofty, and in the center of Philadelphia—you've found Wanamaker's. Right next to City Hall, the nine-story department store building occupies an entire city block, with entrance from Thirteenth, Market, and Chestnut Sts.

A department store is a mighty weird place to find a museum; the hawking of perfumes, exercise gear, stationery, and underwear just doesn't seem to mesh with the more refined ideals of biographical and historical preservation and exhibition—or does it? When the man whose life is being celebrated was the founder of a great department store, what better place to honor him than in the heart of his own retail empire?

When you step off the elevator at the eighth floor, you enter a cavernous world that is devoid of the noise and push of the store's other floors. Although this floor is sometimes the site of special exhibits (in 1986, there was a Leggo show) or events (the movie "Mannequin" was filmed here), most of the time there is not much happening; spackled ceilings and disembodied sections of drywall are all that remain until the next extravaganza sets up shop. But just around the corner from this emptiness, the one-room John Wanamaker Memorial Museum awaits those few intrepid shoppers and tourists who have

sely studied the store's directory or
e city's travel brochures.

The focal point of the tiny museum is
anamaker's glass-enclosed office. Un-
uched since his death in 1922, the of-
e has been turned into a shrine to a
an and his methods: the grand wood-
desk is still neatly stacked with pa-
rs and memos, his beloved cat sculp-
res still perch on every available table
rner and bookcase shelf, and the ex-
aordinary view of Philadelphia still
ers in from the picture window across
e room. This cozy office, with its scat-
ring of rugs and smattering of nostal-
c knickknacks, bears little resem-
ance to the chrome-and-black-leather
sterity of most modern CEOs' lairs.

If the glowing and funny handwritten
tes and personally drafted newspaper
editorials" displayed on the museum's
alls are any indication, Wanamaker
as a people's person as much as he was
businessman. The memos to staff
embers about customer relations read
e textbook discourses on public rela-
ns. Many of the courtesies and conve-
ences we take for granted in modern
ores—including refund and return
licies, standardized price labeling,
en the very concept of behemoth de-
artment stores—were innovations that
anamaker introduced during his reign
the merchant king of Philadelphia.

The list of Wanamaker "firsts" alone
enough to fill a book. Samples in-
ude: first general restaurant in any
ore opened to the public (1876); first
ectrically lighted store (1878); and
irst Marconi wireless station in Ameri-
a to receive news of the sinking of the
itanic (1912). Many of these events
nd accomplishments are documented
the announcements and souvenirs on
isplay throughout the museum.

But the best stuff here has a less defi-
nite place in the record books. There are
thingamajigs, such as the head-measur-
ing machine used for the correct fitting
of hats, and doodads, such as the souvenir fans from the grand dedication of the
revamped store in 1914 (over which
President Taft presided), and even great
big whatchamacallits, such as the fierce
cigar-store Indian, former guardian of
Wanamaker's now-defunct tobacco
shop.

There's also the chair William How-
ard Taft sat on during the store's dedication ceremony. Ignominiously, but
appropriately for the fattest President
ever, the caning on the seat is broken.

Perhaps the most memorable bit of memorabilia is a placard found among Wanamaker's personal effects after he died, which now rests in a glass case along with some turn-of-the-century gewgaws. On one side of the card, there is the following persuasive statement: "Mothers! Read This! If your child is restless at night; picks its nose; has swelling of the abdomen; unnatural appetite; excessive thirst; is wasting away; has bad breath or great nervousness— Use Frey's Vermifuge for Worms." On the other side, a portrait of a fat, angelically ugly Victorian child is framed by the words "After Using Frey's Vermifuge for Worms."

Even if you have no interest in John Wanamaker as an entrepreneur, you can't help liking a fellow who carried around something as weird as this, even while he was running a serious retail empire.

Hard Bodies and Softballs

Weightlifting and Softball Halls of Fame

York Barbell Headquarters
Rte. 83, Exit 11
(P.O. Box 1707)
York, PA 17405
(717) 767-6481

Hours: Mon.-Sat. 10 a.m.-4 p.m.
Admission: Free
Getting There: Rte. 83 runs along the edge of York as it makes its way from the Maryland border to central Pennsylvania. The Halls of Fame building is on your left as you enter the company complex from Rte. 83, Exit 11.

Anyone who has driven along Rte. 83 heading north into York will remember the strongman. Perched atop the York Barbell factory in an eternally bicep-bunching stance with his barbells over his head, the giant figure, who looks as though he has just stepped off a carnival midway, is a fitting guardian for the factory and halls of fame he overlooks.

In the strongman's shadow stands the Y(for York)-shaped building, which houses a hefty assortment of exhibits about the history of all forms of weight training, as well as a softball hall of fame. It is a gallery of strength, grace, and glory—with a pinch of good-natured hucksterism. Bob Hoffman, the Olympian and barbell tycoon who died in 1985, was also known as the "Father of World Weightlifting" and "Mr. Softball of York, Pa." He gave the town of York many things, including its reputation as "Muscletown" and the Richard M. Nixon County Park, but his greatest gift may have been these lively tributes to strongmen and softballs.

The Weightlifting Hall of Fame, which is the United States Weightlifting Federation's official hall of fame, fills several rooms with exhibits on powerlifting, weightlifting, and bodybuilding. These are interesting enough, but their standard collections of photographs, trophies, and historic time-lines will be of interest mostly to avid fans. More intriguing and fun are the collections devoted to Hoffman himself (in the "Father of World Weightlifting" room) and to the history of strongmanism.

The Hoffman collection includes some of his personal weightlifting outfits and trophies, as well as a lovely display of the various ornate porcelain statues and filigreed cups given as gifts to Hoffman by dozens of countries. One glass case holds a sampling of Hoffman's bear collection, which contains

er 600 bears of "all kinds, shapes, d breeds." Included here are ceramic lar cubs and a little hand-carved ooden grizzly bear.

The collection devoted to the "Mighty en of Old" would make any 98-pound eakling shake in his elevator shoes. ere are the balloon-shaped barbells d giant dumbbells that were the ademarks of circus strongmen. Acmpanying descriptions explain that any of these weights were actually uite light, or even hollow, but were iggered to fill with a heavy substance sually sand or water) in case a heckler t too curious. Circus posters and other ts of strongman paraphernalia are on isplay as well, delightful reminders of a me when weightlifting was an enterinment for the masses rather than the eadly serious sport it is today.

The Softball Hall of Fame is a bit ore sedate, but it has its moments. As ou enter, an almost exhilarating sculpure (made from 20 softball bats and ur balls) depicts the arc of a bat swing nd the curve of the ball it hits. Also orth a glance is the exhibit on the hisry of the game, which, according to

the text, began its "meteoric rise . . . as a popular participation sport" after the 1933 Chicago World's Fair Softball Tournament.

On your way out of the building, stop by the flag-filled grand entrance hall to gaze at the large color photo of Hoffman dressed in formal wear. With the lapel of his patterned silk smoking jacket adorned with a white carnation, he looks more like a self-satisfied Daddy Warbucks than a world-famous Olympian. But look a bit closer—the round, bald head and tough jawline bear a marked resemblance to that big hunk of a strongman who guards over this muscle-bound empire.

Rhode Island

Bush League

Green Animals

Cory's Lane
Portsmouth, RI
Preservation Society of Newport County
118 Mill St.
Newport, RI 02840
(401) 847-1000

Hours: May-Sept., daily 10 a.m.-5 p.m.; Oct.,
weekends only 10 a.m.-5 p.m.
Admission: Adults, $4; children, $2
Getting There: The estate, which overlooks
Narragansett Bay in Portsmouth, is on Cory's
Lane, just off Rte. 114 as it passes through
town. The Portsmouth Abbey and School are
across the street, and St. Philomena's School is
next door.

These topiary gardens are filled with
such wickedly wacky renditions of animals, people, and things that visitors
just might be inspired to head home and
go at their own shrubbery with a carving
knife or two. Elephants, peacocks, don-
keys, lions, wild boars, mountain goats,
camels, and giraffes stand about, frozen
in leafy glory. Though these renditions
are somewhat less than graceful (the
stubby nature of shrubbery defies all attempts at lean and leggy sculpture), the
round, squat nature of the beasts has its
own endearing quality. Who cares if the
giraffe looks more like a low-bellied
dinosaur?

While animals head the list of 80
sculptured trees and bushes, there are
other various subjects, including a po-
liceman and a sailboat. There are also
numerous abstract works—trees spiral
upward like giant green drill bits, round
archways are cut neatly through bushes,
and everywhere you turn, bordered
flower beds twist and curve like sym-

metrical snakes around the ankles of the
statuary.

The aptly named Green Animals estate dates back to the mid-1800s and
became the property of the Preservation
Society of Newport County in 1972.
Other attractions on the grounds include a tiny toy museum in the main
residence and a pet cemetery, which is
surrounded by four urns sculptured
from California privets. Once you've
been privy to the rest of the offerings
here, wander back to the gardens and
lose yourself for a while in this top-
notch topiary, where the lions grow instead of growl.

Lob, American Style

Tennis Hall of Fame

Newport Casino
194 Bellevue Ave.
Newport, RI 02840
(401) 849-3990

Hours: May-Oct., 10 a.m.-5 p.m.; Nov.-Apr.
11 a.m.-4 p.m.
Admission: Adults, $4; children, $2; families
$10
Getting There: Rtes. 114 or 138 will take you
into Newport; just past Newport Harbor,
signs for the Newport Casino begin to
appear. Take Memorial Blvd. as it veers left, up
to Bellevue Ave.

Housed in the stately quarters of the
Newport Casino, the International Tennis Hall of Fame does a fine job of relating the history of the most elegant and
legal form of racketeering known to
man. Once you are beyond its rather
plain façade, you'll find that the
grounds, casino building, and museum
exude a well-manicured sophistication.

Tennis is the name of the game here, and it's absolutely everywhere—from the extensive collections of rackets, fashions, trophies, paraphernalia, and art to exhibits on the history of the courtly sport and some of its better-known practitioners. If you ever wanted a closer look at one of Billy Jean King's tennis getups or one of Jimmy Connors' well-worn rackets, this is the place.

Although gambling was never allowed here, the Newport Casino was *the* club for the likes of the families Astor and Vanderbilt. No doubt a gentleman's bet or two slipped through the house rules during big competitions. The Casino hosted the United States National Tennis Championship (now called the U.S. Open) from 1881 to 1915, and it still sponsors invitational tournaments now and then. In fact, to this day, the playing public can rent court time to knock a few about on the perfectly tended (and increasingly rare) grass courts. While its grandest days are behind it,

there's still a glimmer of Edwardian glamour here—whether you're strolling on the pristine lawns or marching through the Enshrinees Hall, this is a fine place to rub tennis elbows.

Vermont

No Strings Attached

Bread and Puppet Museum

Rte. 122
Glover, VT 05839
(802) 525-6972

Hours: May-Oct. 10 a.m.-6 p.m. or by appt.
Admission: Free
Getting There: From I-91, take Exit 24
(Wheelock) onto Rte. 122 West, just before
Glover. The museum is on the farm owned by
the Bread and Puppet Theater on Rte. 122.

The Bread and Puppet Theater is
known as much for its wild costumes,
masks, puppets, and sets as it is for its
flamboyant mix of politics and drama.
Fans of peace marches and human

rights protests have often seen the giant
puppets of skeletons and world leaders
swaying in the air above the crowd,
while the masks have an equally strong
reputation in guerilla-theater circles.
Rather than storing the famous facsimi-
les in a dark warehouse somewhere, the
company opened a museum in 1974 to
exhibit its dramatic past. Housed in a
125-year-old barn on the former dairy
farm the Bread and Puppet Theater
calls home, the two-story museum is
filled to the rafters with giant figures
and mammoth masks.

The collection is organized in
groupings of size, color, and theme that
are often designed to re-enact scenes
from past productions. Famous for their
sheer size, exaggerated features, and
colorful accessories, these giant props
are the handiwork of street-smart artisans who work from clay designs and

e an array of offbeat materials, in-
ding such "found" objects as rum-
age sale clothes and cardboard boxes.
is exuberant artistry shines through
the spontaneous humor and pathos
e puppets and masks evoke.

Although there are no sweet little
lden-haired marionettes to be found
re, those who like their sugar with a
ain of salt will enjoy the rude, crude,
agic, and tantalizing creations on dis-
ay in the Bread and Puppet Museum.

ock Solid

ermont Marble Exhibit

e. 3
octor, VT 05765
02) 459-3311

ours: Late May to late Oct., daily 9 a.m.-5:30
m.

dmission: Adults, $2.50; teens, $1.50;
iildren 6-12, $1

Getting There: Proctor is in western
Vermont, just northwest of Rutland. Take U.S.
Hwy. 7 to Rte. 3 and follow signs to the
Vermont Marble Company and Marble
Exhibit.

This is the place to put to rest any questions, comments, or ruminations you
may have had about that glossy, multi-
purpose stone: marble. Marble is
formed from the recrystallization of
limestone deposits into grains of the
minerals calcite and/or dolomite. In effect, much of that glorious, glowing rock
that forms the steps of post offices and
colleges comes from calcium carbo-
nate—crushed, compressed shells of
prehistoric sea creatures and other calcium sources. Vermont, which millions
of years ago lay submerged beneath a
vast ocean that engulfed most of the
East Coast, is home to one of the largest
marble deposits on earth.

The Vermont Marble Exhibit, run by
the Vermont Marble Company (the
largest marble production center any-

where), takes you on an hour-long, self-guided tour of the wonderful world of marble. The Hall of Presidents, with bas-reliefs of 38 United States presidents carved in white marble, and the real-live-artist-at-work-on-a-real-live-marble-sculpture are highlights of the tour. The film "Men, Marble, and Machines" is shown in an adjoining theater. And don't forget to pick up some discount marble at the "marble market" on your way out.

West Virginia

A Little Religion

Our Lady of the Pines Church

U.S. 219 near Thomas
Horse Shoe Run, WV 26769
(304) 735-5236

Hours: Weather permitting, 8 a.m.-dusk
Admission: Free
Getting There: The church is on U.S. Hwy. 219, outside of Thomas, just south of the Maryland border.

This itsy-bitsy church claims to be the smallest in the 48 states, although there are others clamoring for the same title. In any case, it's probably the cutest. With only six pews providing seating for 12 (24 can fit in a squeeze), the church measures 24' x 12' and was built in 1957-58 by Mr. and Mrs. P. L. Milkint. Over the years, it's caught on as a tiny tourist tradition, attracting hundreds of thousands of small-minded thrill seekers. Next door is the "Smallest Mailing Office," where you can dash off a postcard to all your envious relatives stuck at home. One likely message: "Wish you were here, but you wouldn't fit."

Krishna Kastle

Prabhupada's Palace

Palace Rd.
RD 1, Box 319
Moundsville, WV 26041
(304) 843-1600

Hours: Daily 9 a.m.- 9 p.m.
Admission: Requested donation to tour palace, adults, $5; children, $3
Getting There: Take I-70 to I-470 (near Wheeling) to Bethlehem Exit 2. Take Rte. 88 8 miles to U.S. 250. Turn left and follow 250 2 miles to palace signs; turn left and proceed miles to the palace.

Ever wanted to visit the Taj Mahal, b didn't have enough rupees? Well, We Virginia has got one that rivals that o Taj in everything from opulence to de adence. Built by the Hare Krishnas fo their spiritual leader, Srila Prabhupac (a.k.a. His Divine Grace A.C. Bhaktivedanta Swami Prabhupada), the Palace of Gold fairly glitters with e: cess and grandeur. A sign at the entrance should read "Your Airport Terminal Dollars at Work."

What the Krishnas have carved out this otherwise unremarkable corner o West Virginia is a startling paradise complete with lush gardens, manmad lakes, gushing fountains, a fine-feathered aviary, and, of course, the extrava gant Palace of Gold itself. New Vrindaban is the name they have give this exotic miniland, and indeed, it seems as if a little piece of imperial Indi has been slam-dunked into West Virginia.

At the reqest of Srila Prabhupada, a disciple by the name of Srila Bhaktipada founded New Vrindaban i 1968. The palace work began soon after, but Srila Prabhupada died in 197

before his new pad was finished. The palace the dedicated Krishnas had originally conceived as an earthly home for their leader turned into a spiritual shrine to his memory. By 1980, the palace was finished. Now they want the world to see it, enjoy it, and leave some tourist dollars behind in the health food restaurant and gift shop.

The oddest thing about the palace is its extravagance: Virtually every square inch, from floors to ceilings, is awash in deftly wrought gold work, inlaid mosaics, beautiful Far East-inspired paintings, stained glass, and intricate carving. All this to memorialize a religious leader who preached asceticism and the abandonment of worldly goods. The Krishnas' explanation for this seeming contradiction? "Although Srila Prabhupada always dressed in the traditional garb of an ascetic, living a renounced life, his devotees now wish to honor him in a manner befitting his actual position as a representative of God."

To this end, they have planted wax *murtis* (a Madame Tussaud-like replica) where Prabhupada would have spent his days had he lived. In the study, leaning over a heavy marble table, a gilt pen in his wax hand as he signs a spiritual document, Prabhupada lives on. Elsewhere, seated on a golden, jewel-studded throne, his paraffin head topped with an oversized crown and his body draped in an embroidered fur robe, Prabhupada endures.

How is it that the ultimate flower children came to build such a place in the heart of the Appalachian state? The freedom and openness of the West Virginia region, they say, was the ideal setting for their New Vrindaban. And it's getting newer by the year: plans are in progress for an amusement-park facility, and work has already begun on the proposed "Great Temple of Understanding," which, when completed in 1995, will be the "world's largest solid granite temple in the classic Vedic style."

WEIRD
WONDERFUL
AMERICA

South

Alabama

Rock Garden

Alabama Museum

201 Glen Ave.
Fort Payne, AL 35967
(205) 845-1646

Hours: Mon.-Sat. 8 a.m.-5 p.m.; Sun. 1-6 p.m.
Admission: Adults, $5; children, $2
Getting There: From I-59, take Exit 218 and drive south 1 mile on Hwy. 35 (Glen Ave); the headquarters is on the left.

Fort Payne, the self-proclaimed "Sock Capital of the World," has another legacy as well: it is the home of the musical group Alabama. In a huge headquarters complex that could easily house a K-Mart or two, the band's Fan Club, Mail Order Department, Conference Room, June Jam Offices, Promotion Department, Rehearsal Hall, and Truck Bay Area rub elbows with, you guessed it, the museum. The museum displays such not-to-be-missed items as the band members' early musical instruments, promotional photographs, personal memorabilia, and much more. Many of Alabama's 265,000 fan-club members have visited the museum to get a glimpse of musical history in the making; others just come to the headquarters to enjoy the fan club offices, where they can see the multitudinous gifts showered upon the band by fans everywhere. As a headquarters brochure points out, visitors who "Browse among the photographs, paintings, plaques, and other hangings" on display in the fan club will also discover, to their undoubted delight, "that they may purchase T-shirts, caps, record albums, and dozens of other Alabama souvenirs." They can rock, but can they buy socks?

Small Wonder

Ave Maria Grotto

St. Bernard Abbey
Cullman, AL 35055
(205) 734-4110

Hours: Daily 7 a.m.-sunset
Admission: Adults, $2; children, $1
Getting There: Located a mile east of Cullman, which can be reached from I-65, U.S. 31 and 278, and state Hwy. 69. Cullman i 50 miles north of Birmingham.

The little things in life really counted fo Brother Joseph Zoettl—they counted s much, in fact, that at last count there were 125 of them, almost all lovingly crafted by the hands of this monk min iaturist. Over a period of 60 years, the hunchbacked brother worked at his hobby: building miniature replicas of great religious and cultural sites. The result is a landscaped park filled with tiny versions of Jerusalem, Lourdes, S Peter's Basilica, the Pantheon, the Colliseum, and dozens of other famous places, along with the magnificent Ave Maria Grotto itself.

Brother Joe, as he was known at the abbey, was born in Germany in 1878. His dreams of becoming a priest were crushed in an accident that left him wit a hunched back, which put the rigorou duties of priesthood beyond his reach. Instead, he took the vows of a monk a the St. Bernard Abbey in 1897. He wa to spend most of his life shoveling coal in the abbey powerhouse, using what spare time he had constructing his sma world. By the time Brother Joe died in

62, his little hobby had turned into a
money-maker for the abbey, with
thousands of people pouring in every
year to view the grotto and its surrounding three-acre landscape of
minimonuments.

The first section of what has been
called "The Scenic Shrine of the South"
was put on display in an old rock quarry
adjoining the abbey in 1934. This portion, replicating the Holy Land, soon
became known in tourist circles as "Little Jerusalem," and news of its intricacy
and originality began to spread. People
from around the world began sending
him bits of broken jewelry, seashells, old
bricks, and parts of statues, which the
brother gratefully accepted and used to
build his miniatures.

Brother Joe saw beauty in other people's junk, and used everything from
castaway bird cages (for the dome of his
version of St. Peter's Basilica) to empty
cold-cream jars (in the "Temple of the
Fairies") to create his tiny tributes. His
masterpiece, a man-made cavern/
shrine, the Ave Maria Grotto, is decorated with bits of glass and seashells from
Florida, and even includes realistic-
looking stalactites that hang from the
ceiling. The grotto is 27 feet in width,
height, and depth, the largest structure
in the park.

You'll feel like Gulliver in Lilliput as
you stroll the grounds here, for around
every corner and on every hillside is another tiny miracle waiting to be seen.

Visitors to the Grotto park probably
figure that the builder was a well-trav-
eled man who made meticulous
drawings and notes while visiting each
place he planned to reproduce. Not so.
The only original sites Brother Joe ever
saw were those in his German birthplace, Landshut, and those at the ab-

bey. All others were recreated from
postcards and photographs.

A few of the structures came from
Brother Joe's own imagination. He built
the "Tower of Thanks" as a symbol of
his gratitude to all the friends who had
sent him materials (the tower is topped
with green glass balls that had been
floats for fishing nets in Ireland), and
constructed an American flag from colored marbles and cement as a memorial
to former St. Bernard College students
killed in World War II. His imagination
also took flight with the "Temple of the
Fairies," complete with a rosy-cheeked
visit from Hansel and Gretel, and a
dragon held back with a chain.

Brother Joe built himself a world of
his own, a world perhaps more pleasing
in its romanticism and embellishments
than the serious and sober places he
sought to recreate but would never see.
It may be a small world after all—but
the Ave Maria Grotto somehow makes it
feel a little bit bigger, and a little bit
brighter.

The Write Stuff

Bessemer Hall of History

1905 Alabama Ave.
Bessemer, AL 35020
(205) 426-1633

Hours: Tues.-Sat. 10 a.m.-4:30 p.m.
Admission: Free
Getting There: The museum is on Alabama
Ave. in the heart of Bessemer, which is 10
miles west of Birmingham, just off I-57/20.

What does sweet little Bessemer have in
common with Nazi Germany? They
share what might be called an elite
bond, in the form of Adolf Hitler's type-

writer. It's on display at the Bessemer Hall of History, a restored 1916 railroad station that serves as a local museum. So what is this ignominious machine doing in a museum that is mainly devoted to the town's history ("from fossils to foundries," according to the Hall's promotional material)? Mable Waits, the Hall of History's director, isn't sure herself, but she says, "We assume it was liberated by a local GI."

Weevil Overcome

Boll Weevil Monument

Enterprise Chamber of Commerce
P.O. Box 577
Enterprise, AL 36331
(205) 347-0581

Hours: Always visible
Admission: Free
Getting There: Enterprise is located on U.S. Hwy. 84, 90 miles south of Montgomery and 7 miles west of Fort Rucker. The monument is in downtown Enterprise, at the corner of College and Main Sts.

From afar, this site is quite pleasing to the eye. A concrete wall topped with a decoratively spiked iron fence encircles a fountain and statue of classical design. The statue depicts a lovely woman draped in robes, her arms in the air as she gracefully lifts a chalice-like object to the gods. But on closer inspection you notice that it's not a chalice, or even a Grecian urn the fair maiden proffers: it's a really big, really ugly black bug. *Anthonomus grandis*, to be entomologically precise. A Mexican boll weevil, to be nationalistically precise.

Has there ever been a more verminous tribute? Probably not. The Boll Weevil Monument is, as the chamber of

commerce proudly notes, "The Only Monument in the World Glorifying a Pest!" Talk about bragging rights.

Enterprise's adoration of the insect began back in the summer of 1915, when the Mexican boll weevil found i? way into the cotton crop of southeast A abama, as well as much of the rest of t? cotton-growing South. Despite valian? efforts by farmers, boll weevils had gob bled up more than two-thirds of the co? ton crop within two years. You wouldn? think this destruction would lead the citizens to dedicate a monument, espe cially one with a commemorative plaque that reads: "In Profound Appr? ciation of the Boll Weevil and What It has Done as the Herald of Prosperity." But there's more to the story.

The boll weevil infestation, althoug? a disaster of mammoth proportions fo?

e South, forced farmers to diversify
eir cash crops to include peanuts, po-
toes, corn, sugar cane, hay, and live-
ock. Almost immediately, Alabama
as lush with a variety of vegetation,
d the once-struggling Cotton Belt was
born with a silver ploughshare in its
and. Alabama's Coffee County (home
 Enterprise) produced a record-
eaking peanut crop in 1917, and is
ill considered a major peanut-growing
gion. Enterprise now touts itself—
ough not without dispute—as the
Peanut Capital of the World."

ound of Renown

oon Dog Graveyard

0 Main St.
.O. Box 1006)
scumbia, AL 35674
05) 383-4531

ours: Always visible
dmission: Free
etting There: Take Rte. 72 west of
scumbia for 7 miles and turn left on Hwy.
7. Go 12 miles and follow the signs to the
aveyard.

t first glance, this memorial park
ems like any other—green grass,
ady trees, headstones in polished
arble or rough granite marking well-
nded graves. At second glance,
ough, things don't seem quite right;
e names on the headstones are a little
dd, and the lifespans seem tragically
ort. If you think you'll find any pussy-
ts or parakeets among these dearly
eceased, you're barking up the wrong
ee.

The Key Underwood Coon Dog
raveyard is an elite cemetery where
ore than 100 of man's best friends

have been laid to rest. The graveyard
was founded on Labor Day 1937, when
Key Underwood and two of his buddies
buried his famed coonhound Troop in
this spot. Other furry friends have since
followed, but not just any mutt or mon-
grel can be interred here—only the
greatest coon-hunting dogs are so honored. Each has to be judged a true coonhound before it can be accepted for
burial in this hallowed hound ground.

Here in the Cumberland Mountain
Range area, raccoon hunting is nearly as
old as the forests themselves, and the
training and maintaining of a fine coonhound is a serious endeavor. Truly great
dogs are rare animals with intelligence,
instinct, and obedience; owners of such
dogs will spare no emotion or expense to
lay their coon dog companions to rest

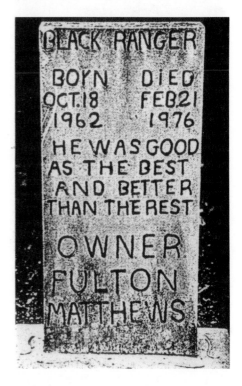

with dignity and honor. The headstones in the graveyard give silent testimony to this dogged devotion: Black Ranger (1962-1976), for instance, was "GOOD AS THE BEST AND BETTER THAN THE REST," according to the sentiments expressed in stone by owner Fulton Matthews.

The people of Tuscumbia hold a traditional Labor Day picnic here, complete with buck dancing (sort of like square dancing), a barbecue, and a liar's contest. During the rest of the year, the Key Underwood Coon Dog Graveyard is a hushed and serene memorial to the great hounds who have gone to those happy hunting grounds in the sky.

Arkansas

Bible Built

Christ of the Ozarks

Elna M. Smith Foundation grounds
P.O. Box 471
Eureka Springs, AR 72632
(501) 253-9200

Hours: Christ statue is always visible; hours for other facilities vary
Admission: Christ statue, free. Museums and galleries (admission price is per museum or gallery), adults, $2; children, $1. Holy Land (tour only), by donation. The Great Passion Play, prices range from $6.50 to $10; children, half-price. Other attractions have varying prices.
Getting There: The Elna M. Smith Foundation grounds are located east of Eureka Springs, just off Hwy. 62. Follow signs for "The Great Passion Play" to the complex.

There's a lot of religion going on just outside of Eureka Springs—the Elna M. Smith Foundation, founded in 1965, has seen to that. The foundation grounds are the site for a series of impressive and expensive projects aimed at preserving Christian legends, sites, and artifacts for the rest of the world. The foundation has set up an enormous complex filled with museums, galleries, statuary, life-sized holy places, a passion play theater, and lots more.

The most prominent attraction is Christ of the Ozarks, a stone super-savior standing seven stories high and weighing in at more than 2 million pounds. He looks out over Magnetic Mountain, where the foundation's famed Great Passion Play is performed nightly. The giant Jesus acts as a spiritual beacon for acres around, presiding over the whole religious region with outspread arms and a stern face.

Then there's the New Holy Land. For those who won't get a chance to travel to the original, this is the perfect place to get a glimpse of some holy replicas. Gerald L.K. Smith (Elna's husband) wrote that he woke up one night in a cold sweat, worried that the constant wars waged in the Middle East would destroy the historic shrines and temples there. So he and his wife set about building the New Holy Land—a project that involved creating life-sized structures identical to those in the Middle East.

Visitors to this Holy Land hop onto motor coaches, whiz through some impressive gates, and zip about the 50-acre site visiting the American versions of the Dead Sea, the Jordan River, the Sea of Galilee (complete with an appearance by the Apostle Peter), and Golgotha. Construction continues at a rapid pace, so if you return in a few years you may see more holy places than you ever imagined.

Next, you can visit the artwork dis-
ayed by the foundation. First there's
e Sacred Arts Center, featuring more
an 1,000 artworks depicting religious
emes, including some extraordinary
ld Masters. Next there's the Bible Mu-
um, with more than 7,000 volumes of
e Good Book in 625 languages, as well
another 3,000 Bible-related artifacts
d manuscripts. This is thought to be
at largest single Bible collection on
splay anywhere. A third collection,
atured in the Inspirational Wood-
rving Gallery, consists of religious
rvings by the late Cecil Mount. These
undant collections of religious mas-
rworks are well worth a visit alone,
d could fill a day or two of serious
ewing.

There's also the Noah's Ark Petting
ark, with real animals mentioned in
e Bible, and a variety of gospel con-
rts, one-person shows, and audiovisu-
productions. The Great Passion Play
probably the single biggest draw:

hundreds of thousands of visitors a year
come to experience this live action representation of the last week of Christ's
life.

There is a sweetness and spiritual de-
termination here that some religiously
themed parks don't have. It's probably
because there isn't a big push for tourist
dollars here, with admission charges remaining small or by donation only.

Hot Shot

Daisy Air Gun Museum
Hwy. 71 S.
(P.O. Box 220)
Rogers, AR 72757
(501) 636-1200

Hours: Mon.-Fri. 9 a.m.-5 p.m.
Admission: Free
Getting There: Located in the Daisy
Manufacturing Company building on Hwy.
71 S. Arkansas Hwy. 68 E. or I-40 W. will take
you to Hwy 71.

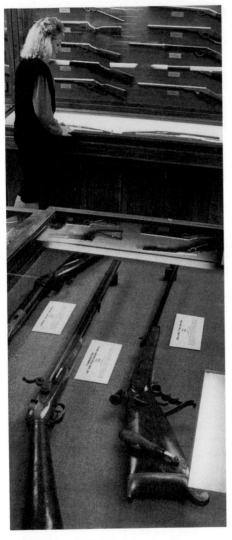

that the Daisy Air Rifle has stayed on store shelves for over 100 years.

In 1966, the Daisy Manufacturing Company set up a museum to display its collection of rare and exotic airguns. Here, in the 400-square-foot exhibit area, are 156 airguns that cover the range of the weapon's history from its eighteenth-century origins through its modern-day manifestations. One of the earliest airgun versions on display is a replica of a 1700s .45-caliber flintlock, which required a device that looks like a bicycle-pump to pressurize it. Another early airgun exhibited was designed to look like a walking cane, so that would-be poachers could stroll onto forbidden ground and hunt small game.

But the stars of this shoot-'em-up show are the Daisy Air Rifles. One of the very first is on display in a special show case, and a doozy of a Daisy it is (as far as history, if not looks, are concerned). This particular little airgun is an all-metal model with a bent wire stock, and was used as a freebie premium to stimulate sales of iron windmills for the Plymouth Iron Windmill Company. Although the windmill biz never churned up enough money to keep itself running, the demand for airguns created a windfall for the company.

Other models in the Daisy chain on display here include rare prototypes of the classic Model 25, handmade by its inventor Charles Lefever, and early versions of the Red Ryder, the gun that probably tops Santa's greatest-hits list. Other manufacturers' airguns are also on display, including unusual weapons created by the Upton Machine Company, the Benjamin Air Rifle Company, and the Markham Air Rifle Company. Probably the museum's hottest and fastest shot of all is a BB machine gun once used in military training.

Time was, parents could talk themselves blue in the face, stamp their feet, and hold their breath for as long as they wanted—but they still couldn't stop their kids from wanting a Daisy Air Gun. And, although the tide may have turned toward laser guns and other sci-fi gizmos, there are still enough kids with a taste for old-fashioned shooting

While the history of the airguns here s charming, the design of the museum is bit dull. The guns are displayed either hanging on the walls behind glass or in ree-standing cases, with plenty of documentation written on little cards plastered everywhere. While that's fine and dandy, one can't help wishing for a happier format.

Still, there is a genuinely fascinating history to be found here. For those grown-up kids who still remember the joy of unwrapping a shiny new Daisy for the first time, sliding on a coonskin cap, and heading out to the backyard to take potshots at horseflies, this museum gives plenty of bang for the buckshot.

Riveting

Frog Fantasies Museum
1 0 Spring St.
"Top of the Elmwood"
Eureka Springs, AR 72632
(501) 253-7227

Hours: Daily 9 a.m.-5 p.m.
Admission: $1
Getting There: On the upstairs of the three-ory, brick Elmwood House, which is on the Hwy. 62 business route (Spring St. as it runs through town), across from the Eureka Springs post office.

Two generations of the Mesa family have collected, cherished, and exhibited ogs. In 1986, they moved their 5,000-us collection, which has come to be known as the the Frog Fantasies Museum, to the top of Elmwood House, one Eureka Springs' most beloved little hotels. Museum business has been hopping since, and aside from the museum elf, with its thousands of frog statues, ys, baubles, carvings, and curios,

Louise and Pat Mesa have leapt into the festival fray. The Frog Fantasies Festival is now held every May with activities that include a contest for people to write about their own personal "Frog Fantasies."

Radio Daze

Lum 'N' Abner Museum
P.O. Box 38
Pine Ridge, AR 71966
(501) 326-4442

Hours: March 1-Dec. 1, Tues.-Sat. 9 a.m.-5 p.m.; Sun. 11 a.m.-5 p.m.; by appointment only during Dec., Jan., and Feb.
Admission: Adults, 50 cents; children, 25 cents
Getting There: Located in the heart of Pine Ridge, on "Lum 'N' Abner" Hwy. 88, approximately 55 miles northwest of Hot Springs (take Hwy. 270 to Hwy. 88) and 100 miles southeast of Fort Smith (take Hwy. 71 to Hwy. 88).

"Hello, Jot 'Em Down Store. This is Lum 'N' Abner" is the way folks from coast to coast were introduced to the "Lum 'N' Abner" show for almost a quarter century. What began as a local radio show in 1931 quickly blossomed into a phenomenally popular national event that had people waiting by their Zeniths week after week to hear the latest news from little ol' Pine Ridge. Aside from their hit program, Chester "Chet" Lauck (Lum Eddards) and Norris "Tuffy" Goff (Abner Peabody) also made 13 movies starring their home-cooked Arkansas characters, who related hometown tales and gossip about their semifictional roots.

The "Lum 'N' Abner" show recieved more fan mail than any other radio pro-

gram of its time—in one week alone, a million-and-a-half letters poured in. Oddly, the show hasn't been clutched to America's nostalgic breast as tightly as other radio programs of its era.

Fortunately, there's one place that will never forget "Lum 'N' Abner," and that's their adopted hometown. Although the two stars actually grew up in Mena, about 18 miles west, Pine Ridge was their claim to fame. So it is here that the Lum 'N' Abner Museum and adjoining Jot 'Em Down Store keep the memory of this downhome duo alive and kicking.

The museum is housed in Dick Huddleston's original general store, built in 1909, while the attached souvenir store is run out of the 1904 A. A. McKenzie store, memorialized as the Jot 'Em Down Store on the program. Both buildings have a rustic, Old West look about them, with high façades of wooden planking and deep porches fronting the

homey spaces within. Inside the museum, visitors discover a rich array of memorabilia from the "Lum 'N' Abner" show and films, including scripts, costumes, original taped programs, fan mail, and other bits and pieces of the Lum 'N' Abner legend. The Jot 'Em Down Store maintains the feeling of an old country shop, selling programs and premiums from the original show, as well as antiques and collectibles.

Pine Ridge was originally called Waters, but officially changed its name to match its radio counterpart in 1936, on the fifth anniversary of the show. Everyone made a big deal out of the name change, with the governor greeting Lauck and Goff in an elaborate ceremony on the steps of the State Capitol in Little Rock. The museum displays photographs taken at that time—and it's clear from all the attention given to the town that the semimythical Pine Ridge (Lauck and Goff changed the names be

ed their characters from residents of
ters) was a spiritual hometown for
ny Americans.

The legacy that "Lum 'N' Abner"
ssed down to future generations of ra-
listeners may not be apparent in the
rrent craze of "Golden Oldies" pro-
ms featuring shows like the "The
ne Ranger" and "The Burns and Al-
Show," but its reach can be felt deep
the psyche of modern radio. The most
minent example is Garrison Keillor's
g-running "A Prairie Home Com-
nion," which had millions of listeners
oked on its small-town tales.

Theory has it that America searches
a simpler heritage when it tunes in to
ows like "Lum 'N' Abner" and "A
airie Home Companion"—that some-
w in the rush and push of glitzy ur-
nization, plain folk have lost their
ace. But Pine Ridge hasn't changed
ach in the past century, and the Lum
Abner Museum proves that old radio
aracters don't really die either—they

just go back home and put their feet up
on the front-porch rail.

Instruments of Note

Miles Musical Museum
U.S. Hwy. 62 W.
(P.O. Box 488)
Eureka Springs, AR 72632
(501) 253-8961

Hours: May-Oct., daily 8:30 a.m.-4:30 or 5
p.m.
Admission: Adults, $4; children, $2
Getting There: The museum is in the
northern part of the state, outside of Eureka
Springs on U.S. Hwy. 62 W.

This collection of outrageous, beautiful,
and historic musical instruments was
started as a hobby more than 30 years
ago by Floyd and Martha Miles. Today,
visitors are taken on an hour-long, dem-
onstration-filled tour of the museum,
which is crammed with every conceivable musical instrument, from antique
cylinder and disk music boxes to a
hurdy-gurdy, a celestina, and a Mini-
Wurlitzer Rink Organ, complete with its
own tiny ferris wheel and merry-go-
round.

Although music is instrumental to the
museum, there are several other collections housed here, too, including a miniature animated mechanical circus, a
gallery of pictures made from buttons, a
display of onyx objets d'art created by
Ozark onyx artisan Charley Stehm, and
a collection of rare art and artifacts from
the Far East and other exotic spots
(highlights of the Borneo portion of this
particular collection: a "Cannible
Fork" and blowguns). The Miles Musical Museum is a lyrical collection of music and mayhem.

Florida

Ocean Crossing

Christ of the Deep

John Pennekamp Coral Reef State Park
(P.O. Box 487)
Key Largo, FL 33037
(305) 451-1202

Hours: 8 a.m.-sunset
Admission: 50 cents
Getting There: The park is on U.S. Hwy. 1 in
Key Largo.

Snorkeling through the crystalline waters in search of vibrant tropical fish and
tragic shipwrecks, divers at the John
Pennekamp Coral Reef State Park often
find themselves face to face with an un-
'isual underwater statue of Jesus Christ.
'Christ of the Deep" was cast in 1961
from the mold of a similar underwater
statue, "Christ of the Abysses," located
in the Mediterranean off the coast of
Genoa, Italy. The original was created
in 1954 by the Italian sculptor Guido
Galletti as a symbol of redemption for
the families and friends of those lost at
sea. The new "Christ" was commissioned by Egidi Crissi, a manufacturer
of diving equipment, and given as a gift
to the Underwater Society of America.
The society chose to install its statue at
the John Pennekamp Coral Reef State
Park, which was the first underwater
park in the world when it opened in
1962, and remains a favorite with
divers and glass-bottom boaters.
    "Christ of the Deep," located in the
White Bank Dry Rocks section of the
park, seems to rise out of the coral reefs
that surround it, arms held high as if to
catch and embrace the countless sailors
who have drowned along the treacher-
ous Key Largo coast. The nine-foot-tall

bronze statue weighs in at 2,000 poun∢
and stands in 21 feet of water, mount∢
on a 22-ton concrete base. Yet even
here, where amphibian tourists in scub
gear crowd the waters, the vastness an
silence of the ocean seems to engulf h∢
man endeavors.

For Art's Sake

Collection of Decorative and Propaganda Arts

Miami-Dade Community College
Third Floor, Building One
300 N.E. Second Ave.
Miami, FL 33132
(305) 347-3429

Hours: Mon.-Fri. 10 a.m.-5 p.m. (closed Fri.
summer)
Admission: Free
Getting There: The museum is on the
downtown Miami Campus of Miami-Dade
Community College, the entrance to which
two blocks from U.S. Hwy. 1 on N.E. Third ⊆

Miami seems a perfect setting for this
surprising and promisingly off-beat co
lection that opened its doors to the pul
lic in 1984. The Wolfson collection
holds more than 10,000 artifacts of
American and European design from
1855 to 1945. Sadly, the current quar
ters, upstairs in a building of the Miam
Dade Community College, are not nea
ly large enough to display the collectio
as a whole. Instead, various shows are
produced every few months to highligl
specific artistic movements or historic
events.
    The first show produced here concer
trated on visions of future life as seen b
designers of the 1920s and 1930s, an∢
included such eclectic pieces as the ori⍟

the style, design, and form of art and technology mesh with the cultural and social climate of the times. Miami is a living monument to just such a theory—it has risen almost suddenly out of the ocean foam, a vibrant new urban landscape of pink skyscrapers and green parks born from a renaissance of American business, housing development, and recreation. It is a natural home to the Mitchell Wolfson Jr. Collection, where art and life seem to imitate each other with an exuberant flair.

Heart of Stone

Coral Castle
28655 S. Dixie Hwy.
Homestead, FL 33030
(305) 248-6344

Hours: Daily 9 a.m.-9 p.m.
Admission: Adults, $6.75; children, $4.50
Getting There: The castle is on U.S. Rte. 1 (a.k.a. S. Dixie Hwy., or S. Federal Hwy., as it runs through Homestead). A block west, the Florida Turnpike Extension runs parallel to this section of Rte. 1.

l Scotch-tape dispenser, futuristical-curved pieces of furniture, and nu-rous artistic blueprints for a eamlined tomorrow. Other exhibi-ns have detailed British painting of Victorian era, the development of government-sponsored artists' pro-ams during the Depression, and the sence of style and function in lighting sign.

At any given time, a visitor might see ork Projects Administration posters, uvenirs from World Fairs, ashtrays corated with anti-Hitler slogans, or re portraits of the English gentry. hile the subjects seem disparate, they share the same basic premise: that

What drives a man to build a fortress, single-handedly, from tons of porous rock? In this case, it was a woman named Agnes Scuffs. The 16-year-old Latvian heart-breaker jilted her fiance, 26-year-old Ed Leedskalnin, on the eve of their wedding in 1913. The devastated groom-not-to-be packed up and left his tiny parish of Stramereens Pogosta in Latvia. In 1918, Leedskalnin settled in a log cabin in Florida City, where he began the first carvings for the Coral Castle. When Florida City became too populated, he moved his work and his dreams to an isolated 10-acre tract of land near Homestead.

Legend has it that Leedskalnin built this cozy, 1,100-ton estate in expectation of his beloved's eventual recapitulation. The Coral Castle is actually a fairly diminutive building surrounded by several acres of statuary and observation areas. Throughout the site, from the rocking baby cradle in the bedroom to the heart-shaped dining table in the open-air living room, there are sad reminders that the lonely Ed spent his entire life waiting in vain for the woman he called his "Sweet Sixteen."

The living quarters, where Leedsk nin dreamed of living in fairytale bli with Agnes and the family they wou raise, are filled with his-and-hers fur ture, including two 12-foot-long bed and giant twin rocking chairs. There many other monuments to amour, th most famous being the "Feast of Lo table, with its 5,000-pound heart-shaped surface (complete with a live flowering centerpiece), that's been called "The World's Largest Valenti by *Ripley's Believe It or Not.*

The castle grounds are likewise dot-
with intriguing items sculpted from
Ootilic limestone (a rock formed
m layers of calcite banded over coral
mations) that was Leedskalnin's pri-
ry building material. His fascination
th astronomy is apparent in the sun-
l and moon and planetary sculp-
es, as well as in the 20-foot-tall, 20-
Polaris telescope that can still make
curate calculations of the earth's rota-
n around the sun. Leedskalnin's oth-
coral creations on display run the
mut from a garden wishing well to a
ing table carved in the shape of Flor-
(complete with a water-filled section
presenting Lake Okeechobee).
Leedskalnin was a tiny man, who, at
nere 5'2" and 100 pounds, did a Her-
lean job of hauling and carving the
assive coral-based stones for his cas-
. Although it's known that
edskalnin used some pulleys and lers he fashioned from junked railroad
d auto parts, experts haven't quite
ured out how he managed the work
by himself. Although he never re-
aled his methods, Leedskalnin
imed to have learned the ancient sets of the Egyptian pyramid builders.
Living the life of a hermit for most of
Florida years, Ed Leedskalnin
rked on and off (mostly at night) on
castle, and spent much of his time
iting self-published books about his
ories of magnetism and cosmic
ces. He first openened the Coral Cas-
to visitors in 1920 (which makes this
oldest tourist attraction in Florida, if
u don't count the swamps). Leedskal-
died of stomach cancer in 1951, tak-
g the secret of his mystical building
ethods to the grave, leaving behind his
quiem in stone to a lost love.

The Knee Generation

Cypress Knee Museum
U.S. Hwy. 27
Palmdale, FL 33944
(813) 675-2951

Hours: Daily 8 a.m.-sundown
Admission: Adults, $2; children and senior citizens, $1
Getting There: The museum complex hops over Hwy. 27 (museum on one side of the road, gift shop and swamps on the other, bridged by a walkway in between), just north of the junction with State Rd. 29. Palmdale is west of Lake Okeechobee.

When you see the highway signs that read "LADY IF HE WONT STOP HIT HIM ON THE HEAD WITH A SHOE," [sic] it becomes instantly clear that a very special place looms ahead in this swamp country. Tom Gaskins' Cypress Knee Museum is quite possibly America's weirdest museum. Where else can you see cypress knees from 23 states ("Surprised?" asks Gaskins' brochure), walk over swamps where the knees still

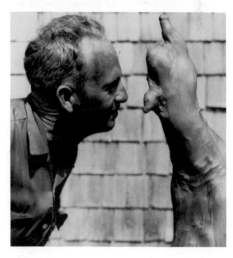

grow, watch a video of Gaskins explaining that he likes to lick wood fiber, and see the factory where exotic knee products, including vases and lamp bases, are created. Whew. The Smithsonian simply can't compete.

Tom Gaskins started out, a young self-proclaimed "Florida cracker" (poor and Florida bred), with an interest in turning a buck from the strange wood "knee" formations that grow around cypress trees like upwardly mobile mutant roots. He was foiled early on when he learned that the knees were solid wood, and that they rotted when uprooted. But he soon came up with a way to carve out the insides, got a patent for his knee-knacks, and went into the knee biz.

Gaskins' love for the knees

themselves—for their twisted and bi zarre formations, for that sweet way they sometimes grow up to look like Groucho Marx, for the almost indefi able air that separates a nice knee fi a knockout knee—led him to open a museum to show off his favorite spe mens. Since the Cypress Knee Muse opened in 1934 (first in Arcadia, m ing to Palmdale in 1937), hundreds thousands of visitors have been "bit by the knee bug" as Gaskins calls it. figures that as many as three-fourth the visitors who have signed the dicti ary-thick guest book are repeat atte ees, or those brought along by the a ready "afflicted."

What's so afflicting about these knobby pieces of wood? Like nimb clouds and Rorschach tests, they rep

at different things to different people.
me here bear an obvious resemblance
certain people or things—there's a
lipper" knee that looks like a portrait
the dopey dolphin, and there's a grin-
ng "Bona Lisa" ("Mona's brother")
at shares that secret Da Vinci smile
th the famous painting. Others' iden-
ies are reached by a certain stretch of
 imagination ("Hippo wearing a
rmen Miranda hat"). An added
arm is the chatty wooden placards
at describe and identify each knee.
ey have a good-natured colloquial
mor, a downhome common sense
at seems to speak directly to visitors in
 voice of Gaskins himself.

In fact, as stimulating as the knees
emselves are, Gaskins may well be the
ot of his museum's success. He is a
vagely independent person, with great
ide in his knee industry and with more
an a few choice words for and about
reaucracy and big business. A taste of

his delightfully combative personality is
carved into a large wooden sign that
stands in front of the museum entrance.
It reads: "The Cypress Knee Industry
Was Started By And This Museum Was
Built By A Selfish Reactionary, Without
Any Help Ever, From Any City, County,
State, Or Federal Government. No Price
Top, No Price Bottom, No Subsidy, No
Labor Union Protection. What You See
Here Can Never Be Duplicated. Souve-
nirs Of A Time Before Civilization Cov-
ered The United States." Enough said.

The museum is a low, cool place built
from white bricks with holes in the middle to let the breeze in. Were it not for
the "world's largest transplanted cypress tree" growing up from the middle
of the floor and out through the roof, the
building could almost be mistaken for a
cheap beachfront motel—except for the
lack of a beach and the proximity of a
swamp; visitors are warned to watch for
snakes. Gaskins can often be found in

his museum, willing and able to give a personal tour, which, aside from the indoor collection, includes a trip across a rickety $\frac{3}{4}$-mile catwalk over the swampland where cypress knees and other, creepier things grow.

Gaskins has been doing "controlled knee growth" experiments since 1938 to learn how knees develop, and some of his findings are on display in the museum. Other experiments are still growing in the swamp, visible from the catwalk. (You can tell an experimental knee by the bottles or other foreign objects stuck in its middle.) Gaskins says he hasn't figured out why the knees grow, but he thinks he knows how some of them got so funny-looking: the bumps and outgrowths that deform a once normal knee

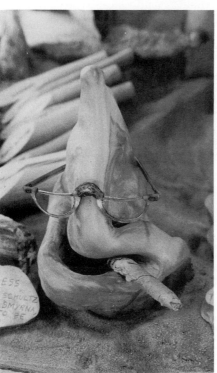

seem to be a reaction to a knee injury Like an oyster responding to irritatio by forming a pearl around the irritant cypress knee reacts to cuts and break by growing an excessive replacement part at the injury site. The most vivid example of this principle is a knee in which Tom Gaskins carved his initial the knee grew a pronounced "TG" bulge beneath the carving, giving the impression of raised lettering.

Another highlight of the complex is short film starring Gaskins, in which I demonstrates how to clean and polish knee by peeling off the outer layers o bark. From knee to shining knee, he takes the viewer through the whole process. The film also reveals Gaskin appetite for wood fiber, which he believes is a fundamental element of hu man survival through the ages. After you learn the background behind this unusual industry, you'll want to visit t factory and sales areas, where you ca see knee capitalism at work. In the fa tory, you can witness the actual peelin of knees, then take in the nearby Old Cypress Railroad, where loads of kne are dried and stored after harvesting. Next, you can shop, shop, shop at the knee outlet, where, aside from knee items like planters and other useful home furnishings, there are driftwood tables and clocks and a variety of oth unusual wood products.

After you've had your fill at the Cy press Knee complex, you can drive a mile south on Hwy. 27 to the Gatoram a huge alligator farm that Gaskins high ly recommends to visitors: "It's owne and run by Florida crackers who wer raised on alligators," he says, adding, "It's a great show." It figures that any one raised on alligators would be all right by a guy who licks wood fiber.

"BIG DADDY"

DON GARLITS

MUSEUM OF DRAG RACING
OCALA, FLORIDA

What a Drag

Don Garlits Museum of Drag Racing

6700 S.W. 16th Ave.
Ocala, FL 32674
(904) 245-8661

Hours: Daily 10 a.m.-5 p.m.
Admission: Adults, $5; children, $3
Getting There: Located 10 miles south of the central Florida town of Ocala, on I-75 (Exit for County Rd. 484).

The only thing about this museum that won't get your heart racing is the building itself—it looks like a corporate complex, and has about as much charisma as a shoe box. Once past this bland exterior, however, the revving, heartpounding, pedal-to-the-metal history of drag racing is presented in all its roaring glory. "Big Daddy" Don Garlits, a legend in drag racing for his speed records (he was the first to go 200 mph from a standing start in a quarter mile, and the first to hit 250 mph, and later 270 mph), and for his creation of the rear-engine drag car. In 1984, Garlits opened the museum he had spent eight years putting together. It was worth the wait. "Big Daddy's" cars are here, of course, including the infamous "Swamp Rat" vehicles that were the essential speed demons of their time. Among these is the restored "Swamp Rat-13,"

in which an accident blew off half of Garlits' right foot in 1970 (some slightly singed paraphernalia from the accident is on display). After his injury, "Big Daddy" set about building a less dangerous drag racing machine. At the time, the cars had open-air, front-end engines that would explode in drivers' faces on impact; "Big Daddy" solved the problem with a rear-engine car that has resulted in far fewer driver fatalities, making drag racing an (almost) safe sport.

But "Big Daddy" is only a small part of his namesake museum. There are also the cars and memorabilia of other famed draggers, including Shirley "Cha Cha" Muldowney, Craig Breedlove, Art Malone, Tom "Mongoose" McKewen, and Tommy Ivo. And there are some cars that are famous in their own right, including "The Bug," the first truly stripped-down dragster. Other exhibits include displays of racing uniforms, videotapes of great moments in drag history, and such spin-off sports cars as minidragsters and Go-Karts. A little bit off the subject of drag racing, but still on the subject of nostalgia, there is a large collection of restored 1930s and 1940s Fords, as well as a display of old slot machines and jukeboxes.

Drag racing got its start in the late 1940s on the California Dry Lakes, with a generation of drivers idling near the brink of the Greaser years to come.

JOHN GORRIE
STATE MUSEUM

Soon, the pursuit of the hottest wheels and the fastest times would consume a new breed of youth. Now, most of those revved-up rebels are driving station wagons and drinking wine coolers. But at the "Big Daddy" Don Garlits Museum of Drag Racing, the hot-rod heart still throbs.

Them There Ice

Gorrie State Museum
Sixth St.
Apalachicola, FL 32320
(904) 653-9347

Hours: Thurs.-Sun. 9 a.m.-5 p.m.
Admission: Free
Getting There: The museum is on Sixth St., one block off U.S. Hwy. 319/98.

The name Dr. John Gorrie may not mean an awful lot to most people, but without him, many of summer's simpler pleasures would be lost. Imagine a world with no iced tea, no dorm-room refrigerators, and (gasp!) no air conditioning. This museum is devoted—in name, if not in the entirety of its collection—to the memory of Gorrie, inventor of the ice cube machine from which many equally cool inventions were developed.

Gorrie arrived in Apalachicola in 1833 as a young doctor, and it was he: that he developed a device to cool the rooms of his suffering yellow-fever pa tients. This invention led to his creatic of an ice-making machine, which he patented in 1851. Gorrie died four yea later and never witnessed the crop of r frigeration units and air conditioners born of his technology. The John Gori State Museum has a replica of the orig nal 1851 patented machine, along wi other memorabilia of this chilling mar life, and various artifacts from the town's history and growth as an indu trial center for seafood production— and ice cubes.

Future Schlock

Home of the Future
Intersection of U.S. 192 and S.R. 535
P.O. Box 2286
Kissimmee, FL 32741
(305) 396-1992

Hours: Daily 10 a.m.-10 p.m.
Admission: Adults, $4.75; children (4-17),
$3.50; children 3 and under, free
Getting There: Xanadu is about 4 miles

Disney World and the Epcot Center, at the ersection of U.S. 192 and S.R. 535. You can't iss it.

ow will we live in the twenty-first cen-ry? If the creators of Xanadu are ght, we can look forward to a bubbly yrofoam house filled with a "sensori-n," a "waterfall spa," and (now here's cozy thought) an "electronic hearth." his Xanadu purports to be the model me of the future; unfortunately, if is is home, none of us will ever leave r living room. After all, once we've ttled down in our solar-powered mas-ige chair with a tape of a good book id a relaxing video of a fire roaring in e hearth, how could we pull ourselves vay?

Xanadu is basically constructed of ructural polyurethane sprayed all over uge hemispheric balloons. Talk about

energy efficient—this place is solid in-sulation. And how does it look inside? Perhaps the Xanadu folks, with their mod-speak, say it best: it's a "warm, hospitable environment with curvi-linear walls."

Once inside this roly-poly castle, you can experience all the ultramodern con-veniences that await us someday. With more than 6,000 square feet to fill, not a gadget or gimmick has been spared. The only problem is that this stuff isn't really all that unusual. Anyone who's seen "Lifestyles of the Rich and Famous" knows about bathroom spas and com-puterized kitchens. Xanadu would be a whole lot more fun if its creators had gone off the deep end and given us, as suggested, a prototype George Jetson home of tomorrow, instead of an Adnan Kashoggi present-day dream house.

Brands Across America

Oldest Store Museum

4 Artillery Lane
St. Augustine, FL 32084
(904) 829-9729

Hours: Mon.-Sat. 9 a.m.-5 p.m.; Sun. noon-5 p.m.
Admission: Adults, $2.50; children, $1
Getting There: The museum is on Artillery Lane, a block south of King St. between St. Georges St. and Avilles St.; St. Augustine can be reached by taking Exit 95 from I-95.

The name may sound generic, but the products lining the shelves are anything but. This old general store recreates the sights, sounds, and scents of a nineteenth-century general store with endearing gusto.

Not everything here is history, per se. There are ads for still-available Welch' Grape Juice and "First on the List" Hill Bros. Coffee, as well as early renditions of Hershey chocolate and Smith Brothers Cough Drops. There are shelves of nostrums and cure-alls (some as much as 90 percent alcohol) and bins of different-sized lima beans (baby lima, large lima). Baskets and lamps dangle from the rafters, a red Union suit is modeled by a mannequin, and a section of a rough-hewn wall has been devoted entirely to deer antlers.

There's something eerily familiar about all this; you may feel as though you've stepped into a scene from "Here Come the Brides" or onto the set of some spaghetti western. This sense of pseudo nostalgia can be as much of a curse as

ssing in a museum. But original arti-
ts and settings are the best weapons
ainst media-made misconceptions,
d the Oldest Store Museum is winning
e battle.

resting

olice Hall of Fame

600 S. Tamiami Trail (U.S. Rte. 41)
orth Port, FL 33596
05) 891-1700

ours: Daily 9:30 a.m.-4:30 p.m.
dmission: Adults, $1.50; children, 50 cents;
lice officers, free
etting There: Located on U.S. 41, just
uth of Sarasota.

pened in 1960, the American Police
all of Fame and Museum remains the
ly memorial to police officers killed in
e line of duty. Within the low, ranch-
yle building of brick and glass, the
all of Fame lists 2,614 slain American
lice officers, and the Police Memorial
ernal Light shines like a beacon, day
d night.

Despite the mournful tribute of the
all of Fame, the museum portion is
ely enough to make people think that,
en if crime doesn't pay, it sure is excit-
g. The original Dick Tracy cartoon
acing the entrance to the museum is
st about the only benign thing in the
hole place; after you make it through
e door, the criminal elements are ev-
ywhere. Among the more violent ex-
bits are a real electric chair (you can
t in it if you want—but who wants
?), a guillotine used in France, a vari-
y of tear gas canisters, and a "crime
ene" complete with the outline of the
dy drawn on the floor (visitors are

challenged to figure out "who done it").

On the lighter side, there's a super cop
car of the future, complete with gull-
wing doors and plenty of James Bond
gadgetry. (It also comes equipped with a
$20,000-plus price tag, so police de-
partments will have to dig deep into
their pockets to make this future a reality.) For thriftier tastes, there's a glistening motorcycle that visitors can mount
and pretend to live out their traffic cop
fantasies. Other displays include a case
filled with badges and stars, a retrospective of the FBI's Ten Most Wanted posters, and a variety of changing exhibits.

Despite the downright fun people
have here, it's sobering to realize that
the same violence and danger depicted
in the museum exhibits contributed to
the deaths of the officers memorialized
in the Hall of Fame. The cost of fighting
crime is expensive indeed.

Soak It Up

Sponge Museum
Spongeorama
Dodecanese Blvd.
Tarpon Springs, FL 33589
(813) 942-3771

Hours: Daily 9 a.m.-5 p.m.
Admission: Free
Getting There: Tarpon Springs is on
Florida's West Coast. Take Hwy. 19 to Alt.
Hwy. 19 and follow signs to Tarpon Springs;
the Spongeorama is on the edge of town, at
the docks.

Spongeorama—you've got to come
here, if only for the name. Aside from
housing the little Sponge Museum, this
sprawling shop overflows with Florida
souvenirs and sponge products. The

museum consists of more than 50 exhibits depicting the history of the sponge-diving industry. Only here can you learn in such vivid detail how Tarpon Springs became a leading sponge center in the first half of the twentieth century. By 1910, a wave of Greek immigrants had swept into the town, bringing with them their Mediterranean sponge-diving know-how. Dozens of sponge boats worked out of the port, creating an international trade from their harvest within the 10,000 square miles of sponge beds in the Gulf of Mexico.

But in 1947, a crippling sponge disease wiped out most of the crop. Tarpon Springs never quite recovered; the devastation of the sponges, combined with the rapid growth of the artificial sponge business, left little room for the now-quaint profession of sponge-diving. Nevertheless, several sponge boats still work out of Tarpon Springs, and the town continues to soak up tourist dollars because of its unusual industrial history. There are some terrific sponge buys here, and the museum's really quite absorbing.

Pool Hall

Swimming Hall of Fame

1 Hall of Fame Dr.
Fort Lauderdale, FL 33316
(305) 462-6536

Hours: Mon.-Sat. 10 a.m.-5 p.m.; Sun. (Nov. May only) 11 a.m.-4 p.m.
Admission: Adults, $1.25; students, military and senior citizens, $1; families, $3
Getting There: From U.S. Hwy. 1, take Sunrise Blvd. east to A1A and drive south to its intersection with Hall of Fame Dr., where the museum is located.

If the exhibits here are any indication, the "wet look" never went out of style.

Take a peek, for instance, at the "Swimming Presidents Wall," which naturally includes a retrospective of Ronald "Dutch" Reagan's lifeguard career and a photo of Gerald Ford accepting a "Nation's No. 1 Swimmer" plaque. Other exhibits depict the lives and victories of past Olympians, including heavy-medal winners Mark Spitz, Buster Crabbe, and Johnny Weismuller.

There are also life-sized wax figures and caricatures of famed water lovers, displays of aquatic art, and "The Old Swimming Hole of Fame," a theater shaped like a boat that exhibits comical photos and memorabilia from the days when swimsuits looked like knickers. The trophy room is an aquatic fanatic's dream display of gold medals, cups, awards, and plaques, as well as the world's largest trophy (try to hold this one up for the cameras, and you'll probably fall through the floor) and the world's smallest trophy (a tiny loving cup made from a gold thimble mounted on a collar button). For those who prefer laps to cups, the Olympic-sized pool is open to the public for recreational swimming, with special lessons available for a fee for brushing up on rusty strokes. You may walk in the door, but you'll leave with a good crawl.

Stranger Than Paradise

Tiki Gardens
196th Ave. and Gulf Blvd.
P.O. Box 8)
Indian Shores, FL 33353
813) 595-2567

Hours: Adventure Trail, daily 10 a.m.-7:30 p.m.; hours for shops and restaurant vary.
Admission: Adventure Trail, adults, $2;

**AN EXOTIC WORLD
Polynesian Adventure Trail**

children, $1; access to shops and restaurant is free
Getting There: Indian Shores is on Florida's West Coast. Take Hwy. 699 and follow the signs to Tiki Gardens.

Tiki Gardens actually fills only 12 ½ acres on an island ("a romantic bit of transplanted Polynesia") located between Clearwater and St. Petersburg. For a small fee, you stroll down Tiki's "Adventure Trail," complete with lagoons, and bright flowers that float around in the water, and lots of wooden bridges, stone footpaths, trickling waterfalls, thatched-roof "missionary cottages" and even a "Pagan Sun Temple."

And let's not forget the "strange gods" planted strangely here and there, including wooden replicas of Easter Island statues and an angry-looking concrete rendition of the "Lono Tiki God." There's also a "Trader Frank's Restaurant," some shops that sell reproductions of Polynesian crafts, and plenty of tropical birds and "natives" (including "lovely wahinis") to give the place that lived-in look. It's actually almost kinda lovely here, in a transplanted sort of way. If only they could get rid of all those camera-toting tourists.

We Saw PRESIDENT KENNEDY'S CAR

ST. AUGUSTINE, FLORIDA

Tragic Magic

Tragedy in U.S. History Museum

7 Williams St.
St. Augustine, FL 32084

Hours: Daily 9 a.m.-dark
Admission: Adults, $3.50; students, senior citizens, military, and "local people," $3; children, $1
Getting There: St. Augustine is on Florida's upper East Coast on Rte. 1, 5 miles east of I-95 (Exit 95). Once in town, take San Marco St. to Williams St. and follow the signs to the Fountain of Youth. The museum is located several blocks past the fountain on Williams St. on the right side of the street, next to the Old Jail.

Don't go asking the St. Augustine Chamber of Commerce how to find this eccentric museum; they'll say they've never heard of it. You won't find it on city maps, either. For years, L. H. "Buddy" Hough has been embroiled in a bitter battle with local tourism agencies to have his Tragedy in United States History Museum put on the maps as a tourist attraction, alongside such local favorites as the Fountain of Youth and Ripley's Believe It or Not Museum. But the authorities have refused him at every turn, invoking an ordinance that says museums have to exhibit items relating to St. Augustine history. Besides, they think it's too morbid.

Too morbid? Absolutely. And there lies its rather disarming charm. This i museum for rubberneckers and ambu lance chasers, soap opera fans and as sassination historians—a group that, added together, probably represents most of the American populace. Who could resist a peek at the car Jayne Mansfield was decapitated in, or Lee Harvey Oswald's bedroom furniture (along with the very comb he used to keep his part straight)? From the sig promising "Inside . . . See Things You'll Never Forget" and the manne quin dressed as Oswald in the display window out front, you know this is go ing to be a special, if weird, experienc

Hough got the idea for a museum d voted to brutal American tragedies when he heard that President Kenned had been assassinated. Within a matt of weeks, he was in Dallas wheeling an dealing to buy as much assassination memorabilia as he could cart back to Florida. Among his booty: the car in which Oswald rode to the assasination point, the ambulance (stretcher and al in which Oswald rode following Jack Ruby's fatal attack (a framed glossy photo of the ambulance driver hangs near the vehicle), and the aforemen tioned bedroom suite. "I believe he planned the assasination . . . on this very furniture," reads an accompanyin statement by Mary Bledsoe, owner of e Dallas rooming house where Oswald ayed.

Hough also wanted, but couldn't buy, e theater seat Oswald was sitting in at e time of his capture and the window rough which he shot Kennedy. But he oes have a replica of Oswald's rifle and frame-by-frame exhibit of the famous apruder film showing the Kennedy nooting. (Hough does go a bit far at mes—a description of the Zapruder lm on a museum flyer promises it hows "each bullet as it struck the resident.")

Still not enough tragedy, you say? Vell, this museum's four rooms and ully stocked backyard come complete ith antique torture equipment, includng a whipping post and a "neckbreakr;" the whistle, speed recorder, and lead engineer's watch from the famous rain "Wreck of Old '97"; a real slave ill of sale; and a 1718 Spanish jail cell eaturing human skeletons. There are lso a few things related only indirectly o tragedy, including a convertible limo hat Hough says was one of President Kennedy's favorite cars, although it's lot the one in which he was killed. The nuseum's version of the bullet-riddled ar Bonnie and Clyde couldn't "getway" from fast enough was used for heir cinematic deaths, not their real nes. But the museum is back on the ragic track with Jayne Mansfield's leath car, complete with a copy of the accident report.

Although the Kennedy assassination, along with a few other choice tragedies, s the focal point of the museum—in act, the walls are practically papered with newspaper accounts—Hough seems to think the greatest tragedy of all s the local government's denial of his museum's existence. He even exhibits

accounts of the fight in his museum. Thanks to this major slight, Hough says, the museum doesn't get as much business as it should. But he believes his collection will catch on someday, despite the city's cold shoulder. If it doesn't, it will be a tragic loss.

Plastic Fantastic

Tupperware Gallery

Tupperware International Headquarters
P.O. Box 2535
Orlando, FL 32802
(305) 847-3111

Hours: Mon.-Fri. 9 a.m.-4 p.m.
Admission: Free
Getting There: Located between Orlando and Kissimmee, 5 miles south of the Florida Turnpike (U.S. 192) on Orlando's South Orange Blossom Trail (U.S. 441, a.k.a. 17 and 92).

The burping of plastic bowls at Tupperware parties is an American domestic tradition akin to the call of the "Ding-Dong" Avon Lady. So what better place to stop and get a taste of homeland culture than the Tupperware International Headquarters? Just a short drive from the big-buck attractions like Disney World, it is home to an exhibit center that traces the history of food-storage containers, while treating visitors to a sort of never-ending Tupperware party.

It's a murky history at best, but there are theories that it all began back in prehistoric times: as civilization evolved, food container get-togethers probably did, too—from clay pot luncheons, to woven basket shindigs, to Grecian urn galas, and so on. While there's little evidence of the actual social gatherings, the containers remain, and some of them are on display at the Tupperware Gallery of Historic Food Containers.

The whole range of food-container history virtually sprawls before the visitor in this long gallery, with porcelain pitchers, earthenware jugs, clay vessels, and glass goblets nicely displayed on pedestals in well-lit display cases. One of the earliest pieces in the collection is a stunning Krater container, circa 300 B.C., with slip decoration painted in Italo-Greek. It's a truly lovely piece, with figures in flowing robes, mystical symbols, and the ever-popular leaf pattern wrapping around the body of the vessel. There are many other pieces on display in the gallery; but don't forget, even while you're seeing the food containers of the past, that all around you the future of food containers is being made. Which is why, after the gallery, you must visit the exhibit center's other pièce de résistance: the Tupperware Home.

Among the exhibits in this home-away-from-home are a child's play area (filled with plastic toys and craft supplies) and a photomontage of the Tupperware design and manufacturing process. But the most exciting part is the model kitchen, which acts as sort of a running Tupperware party, complete with "burping" demonstrations and other soft-sell amenities. Tupperware products are neatly arranged throughout the model kitchen—model refrigerator shelves are stacked with model pitchers and bowls, the model counters display model cooking tools, and the model breakfast table is set with model juice cups, toast plates, salt-and-pepper shakers, and even model food. All that's missing is a model family, but the Tupperware people are probably working on that in their model laboratorie

Georgia

Yankee Blow Home

Double-Barreled Canon

on lawn in front of City Hall
Athens, GA 30601
(404) 549-6800

Hours: Always visible
Admission: Free
Getting There: City Hall is in downtown Athens, at the corner of College and Hanco Aves.

The South has an endearing habit of clinging to the tragedies and injustices of the Civil War like a burr on a jackrabbit's behind. But every now and then, there's a flash of good-natured humor about an otherwise horrible conflict. The case of the double-barreled canon i among the liveliest. Advertised by the city as "One of Athens' most cherishe memorabilia . . . a totally unique failure," the canon was originally conceived as a secret weapon to aim a one two punch at the advancing Yankee forces. It was designed by a local housebuilder, John Gillebrand, and manufactured to his specifications in 1862 at the Athens Foundry and Machine Works.

The idea was to have an eight-foot-long chain connecting the cannonballs in the twin chambers; when the canon was fired, the enemy would be flattene by the chain that was stretched betwee the soaring cannonballs. A fine theory.

But, according to an account written at the time the contraption was tested, all was not well on the southern front. After the canon was fired, the cannonball/chain missile went in a "kind of circular motion, plowed up an acre of ground, tore up a cornfield, [and] mowed down saplings." At this point, the chain between the cannonballs snapped, sending them flying apart to separate but equally ignominious destinies: "One killed a cow in a distant field, while the other knocked down the chimney from a log cabin." It was further reported that bystanders "scattered as though the entire Yankee army had been turned loose in that vicinity."

Put out of commission (and its misery) before it was ever used on the battlefield, the double-barreled canon is now the centerpiece of the lawn in front of the Athens City Hall. The weapon points northward, perhaps as a warning to the Yankees that the South has its own share of homespun ingenuity—and self-effacing humor.

Barn Raiser

Georgia Agrirama

Exit 20 and I-75
(P.O. Box Q)
Tifton, GA 31793

Hours: Labor Day-May 31, Mon.-Sat. 9 a.m.-5 p.m. and Sun. 12:30-5 p.m.; June-Labor Day, daily 9 a.m.-6 p.m.
Admission: Adults, $4; children, $2
Getting There: The Agrirama is at Exit 20 on I-75.

Some world travelers are undoubtedly lured to this museum complex by the promising kitsch of the term "Agrirama" (which seems to evoke images of giant silos painted with wraparound wheat-threshing murals in dayglo colors). Such dreamers should seek their heart's desires elsewhere. The Georgia Agrirama is actually Georgia's official museum of agriculture, and it consists of a grouping of recreated farms, rural towns, and industrial sites. Anyone looking for a good, solid, no-

nonsense, seat-of-the-pants lesson in rural southern agricultural history will find the visit worth the effort.

Displays include a real barnyard complete with real animals (and with real, um, barnyard smells), a sawmill, a blacksmith shop, and all those other educational-type restorations that seem to spring forth, fully preserved, in history-minded towns like Tifton. Depending on the time of year you visit, various authenticated events are held: come in May and you'll catch the "Turpentine Still Firing." If you're here in January, you may enjoy the "Traditional Hog Killing." Then again, you may not.

Monumental Mystery

Georgia Guidestones

State Hwy. 77
Elberton Granite Association
1 Granite Plaza
(P.O. Box 640)
Elberton, GA 30635
(404) 283-2551

Hours: Always visible
Admission: Free
Getting There: Located 7 miles north of Elberton, on State Hwy. 77, in a field on the farm of Mildred and Wayne Mullenix.

It's got the earmarks of a classic mystery: who done it, and why? All that anyone in Elberton knows (or says they know) is that one day in 1979, a man who called himself "Mr. Christian" walked into the office of the president of the Elberton Granite Finishing Company and commissioned a giant stone monument to be placed in a nearby field. Less than a year later, the Georgia Guidestones were unveiled to a baffled crowd of 400 people. The true identity

of Mr. Christian and the group he sa planned and financed the expensive guidestone project was never reveale

The huge granite stones stand alo in the middle of a field, bearing a me sage of hope to future generations th is, at the same time, a strange and di turbing warning to this generation. T purpose of the monument is to provi guidance for preserving a threatened civilization, or rebuilding a destroyed one. Only 10 "commandments" are g en, but they are etched in 12 languag including the modern tongues of Eng lish, Russian, Hebrew, Arabic, Hindi Chinese, Spanish, and Swahili, as we as the archaic languages of Sanskrit, Babylonian cuneiform, Egyptian hier glyphics, and classical Greek.

The stones measure 19′3″ tall, wei a total of 119 tons, and radiate like fo giant, symmetrical tablets with a slin

er stone in the center and another cap-
ng the top of the structure. They are
nfigured to provide astronomical
ignment with solar and celestial
ovements, as well as the summer and
inter solstices. The comparisons with
ngland's Stonehenge are already le-
on, and the resemblance was probably
anned from the start by its mysterious
at savvy creators.

The message the guidestones send to
ture generations also appears to have
en the product of wise and thoughtful
anning. Here, verbatim, are the words
ched in the granite monoliths:

Maintain humanity under
00,000,000 in perpetual balance with
ature.
Guide reproduction wisely—improv-
ig fitness and diversity.
Unite humanity with a living new
nguage.
Rule Passion—Faith—Tradi-
on—and all things with tempered
isdom.
Protect people and nations with fair
ws and just courts.
Let all nations rule internally resolv-
ig external disputes in a world court.
Avoid petty laws and useless officials.
Balance personal rights with social
uties.
Prize truth—beauty—love—seeking
armony with the infinite.
Be not a cancer on the earth—Leave
oom for nature—Leave room for
ature.

It's a message that humanity could
enefit from these days, but it is meant
or a time when there is nothing left of
ur civilization but the cryptic remnants
f a people who may have brought
bout their own destruction.

Cookie Connection

Girl Scout National Center

142 Bull St.
Savannah, GA 31401
(912) 233-4501

Hours: Mon.-Sat. 10 a.m.-4 p.m.; Sun. 11 a.m.-4:30 p.m.
Admission: Adults, $2.50; children (under 18), $1.75
Getting There: The birthplace and scout center is at the corner of Oglethorpe Ave. and Bull St., in the heart of Savannah's Historic District.

The most amusing and provocative thing about this place is the woman whose history is preserved here. Juliette Gordon Low, founder of the Girl Scouts, was an eccentric and daring woman known to wear real fruit as adornment and deliberately drive on the wrong side of the street. Low financed the birth of her wholesome girl's club with money she won in a nasty court battle with her dead husband's mistress over rightful inheritance of his estate. Now her birthplace and childhood home is a mecca for more than 10,000 Girl Scouts a year as well as some 40,000 other tourists. The home is restored to its original Victorian splendor, and the collection of Girl Scout memorabilia, from badges to uniforms, will instill a sense of pride in any current or former cookie pusher who happens to tag along.

The Hard Stuff

Granite Museum

Elberton Granite Association
1 Granite Plaza
(P.O. Box 640)
Elberton, GA 30635
(404) 283-2551

Hours: Jan. 15-Nov. 15, daily 2-5 p.m.; Nov. 15-Jan. 15, Mon.-Fri. 2-5 p.m. (Closed weekends, holidays, and the day before and after major holidays during this time.)
Admission: Free
Getting There: Elberton is in northeast Georgia, between I-85 and I-20. The museum is adjacent to the Elberton Granite Association center, situated a half-mile west of downtown Elberton on State Hwy. 17/72.

Everybody takes Elberton for granite—or at least they take granite from Elberton. This Georgia town has chiseled its name in the rock of ages by becoming "The Granite Capital of the World." In fact, in the last hundred years since Elberton really hit the jackpot, 35 granite quarries and 110 monument manufacturing plants have opened in and around the town. About a third of all monument granite used in America comes from around here, where some 200,000 markers, mausoleums, and monuments are produced every year. With these hard statistics, it's not difficult to imagine why there's a granite museum in Elberton as well.

The Granite Museum was opened in 1981 to give all the granite artifacts around town a central location. Unfortunately, this central location happens to be an incurably ugly, pre-fab building that looks from the outside as if it should be storing airplane parts. The building and the chunky sign out front (carved in glorious granite, of course) belie a love of the subject matter contained within.

The large, open museum space has been broken up with a two-tiered design that includes a gallery walkway and corner displays, and there is plenty of room to move through the exhibits without feeling cramped. The displays themselves are a bit meager, albeit informative, and range from an early black-and-white photomontage titled "Quarrying Granite" to an exhibit case of "Granite Working Tools of the Past" that shows off some clumsy-looking mallets and chisels.

One of the more interesting exhibits is a short film and miniature model depicting the "Mysterious Georgia Guidestones," the giant, Stonehenge-e monoliths that stand in a field just tside of Elberton. The real uidestones were designed in 1979 us- g astronomical coordinates and rved with a message to future genera- ns about how to promote civilization d save humankind. The museum's m and miniature display reveal the erall design of the structure and tell e story behind the guidestones, pro- ding valuable insight for those who an to see the strange memorial.

The most amusing item on display is e giant figure known as "Dutchy," the st statue made of Elberton granite. he almost comically round and squat utchy was unveiled in 1898 in the wn square as part of a Confederate ldier memorial. But Dutchy (who got s name when a townsperson said he oked like "a cross between a Pennsyl- nia Dutchman and a hippopotamus") as not a hit with the Elbertonians. hey thought he looked suspiciously ke a Union soldier—his billed cap was ore common with the Yankee soldiers, d his long coat was far from standard onfederate issue. Actually, Dutchy's eator was an immigrant sculptor who new little of the dress style of the sepa- te factions, and merely formed his sol- er as a composite Civil War veteran. egardless of the lack of intended mal- e, a "lynch" mob pulled Dutchy off his edestal in 1900 and buried him face own (a sign of military dishonor) in a allow grave.

In 1982, the Elberton Granite Associ- tion exhumed Dutchy, drove him rough a car wash to clean the rich, red eorgia soil from his crevices, and put im on display in the museum. Now, the nce-despised Dutchy stands revered as e firstborn son of Elberton's granite dustry.

Feather in Their Cap

Poultry Park

Triangle at Broad, Church, and Grove Sts.
(P.O. Box 763)
Gainesville, GA 30501
(404) 532-0473

Hours: Always visible
Admission: Free
Getting There: The park is in the triangle at the intersection of Broad, Church, and Grove Sts. in downtown Gainesville, just west of I-985.

Gainesville has a lot to crow about, giv- en its reputation as the "Poultry Capital of the World." So, counting its chickens after they hatch (some 2,650,000 broil- ers are produced here weekly) and com- ing up with a major industry, the locals shelled out some money to build Poultry Park. The centerpiece of this midtown retreat is a 25-foot-tall Geor- gia marble monument topped with a three-foot bronze rooster. Six bronze plaques detailing the history of poultry production in Georgia and Gainesville are mounted on the monument as well. The rest of the park is a peaceful oasis, with landscaping and ornamental shrubs that reflect the overall chicken theme.

Landed Gent Tree

Tree That Owns Itself

corner of Dearing and Finley Sts.
Athens Area Chamber of Commerce
P.O. Box 948
Athens, GA 30603
(404) 549-6800

Hours: Always visible
Admission: Free
Getting There: The tree is at the corner of Dearing and Finley Sts. in Athens, which is in central Georgia on U.S. Hwy. 129/441.

Everybody's heard of the loony or lonely people who leave their estates to a favorite Persian pussycat or Pekingese pup—but leaving it to a tree? That's just what the late Professor W. H. Jackson did. For many years he nurtured and enjoyed the shade of the magnificent white oak tree on his property, and he wanted to ensure that it would grow on after his death. Logically enough, he willed the tree the land on which it grew, so that no one could ever cut it down or build too closely around it. As legend has it, Jackson's wishes were worded thus: ". . . for and in consideration of the great affection which he bears this tree, and his desire to see it protected, [he] has conveyed . . . [to the tree] entire possession of itself and of the land within eight feet of it on all sides."

The people of Athens, never ones to turn down appearances in "Ripley's Believe It or Not" or the *Guinness Book of World Records*, took fine care of the leafy landowner. They surrounded it with granite posts and chains and carefully tended the enclosed area. But a storm blew the oak down in 1942, so the inheritance was passed on to a strapping young sapling, grown from an acorn of the original tree and replanted in 1946.

Now this new branch of the oak clan towers 50 feet above the intersection, carrying on the legacy.

Briar Conviction

Uncle Remus Museum

Turner Park
Eatonton, GA 31024
(404) 485-6856

Hours: Mon.-Sat. 10 a.m.-noon and 1-5 p.m.; Sun. 2-5 p.m.
Admission: Adults, 50 cents; students, 25 cents
Getting There: Eatonton is about 50 miles south of Athens and 40 miles north of Macon. From I-20, take U.S. Hwy 441 S (Exit 51) through town. The museum, located in Turner Park, can be found at the far end of town on Hwy. 441.

Eatonton is the hometown of Joel Chandler Harris, the "father" of that famous storytelling slave, Uncle Remus. The tales told by Uncle Remus of Bre'r Rabbit, Bre'r Fox, and "all de critters" became a part of folk legend and literary history during the bitter years of the South's reconstruction following the Civil War. They also served to virtually obliterate the name of their real author in favor of his black alter-ego, Uncle Remus.

In the center of town is a rather clumsy statuary rendition of Bre'r Rabbit, complete with coat and tie. After laughing a bit (and be warned: the kids could be frightened by the bunny's enormous haunches), head to the more subdued and even strangely profound Uncle Remus Museum in Turner Park. The museum provides a glimpse of the fictional storyteller, "de critters," and their shy creator, who spent his early teens working on a plantation newspaper and listening in awe to the stories told by old slaves.

The museum building is a log cabin created from two actual Putnam County slave cabins and looks a lot like Uncle Remus' home as described by Harris. A rustic fireplace at one end of the cabin is the setting for slave-era pots, pans, chairs, and other household items, all assembled to resemble the corner in which Uncle Remus might have told the Little Boy his famous animal tales. The windows of the museum are filled with plantation-life scenes, while shadow-boxes reveal wooden carvings of Bre'r Rabbit and the whole furry gang.

It's probably a tribute to Joel Chandler Harris that, although he wrote many other stories and articles during the late nineteenth century, the ones for which he is best remembered are the ones that have made him anything but a household name. Ask anyone who's seen the Disney film "Song of the South"—or who was weaned on the sly tales of Bre'r Rabbit—who the storyteller was. They'll all answer Uncle Remus. "Joel Chandler who?" will be their only question.

Shell Shock

World's Largest Peanut

Turner County Chamber of Commerce
121 College St.
Ashburn, GA 31714
(912) 567-2541

Hours: Always visible
Admission: Free
Getting There: The peanut is visible from I-75 just outside of Ashburn, which is in north-central Georgia.

So, there you are, tooling happily along I-75 in Ashburn; maybe you're going to Grandma's for dinner, or maybe you're just passing through town, another anonymous tourist looking around. Suddenly, as you cruise the interstate, "it" looms ahead of you like an enormous chrysalis, its snubby brown body planted firmly atop a brick pedestal and giant tilting crown. Yes, you've stumbled upon one of North America's most majestic peanuts. Standing 10 feet high in stocking feet, this peanut behemoth was the gift of the Turner County Chamber of Commerce, in acknowledgment of the lowly legume's lofty status in Georgia's economy. "Georgia 1st in Peanuts" screams the bold lettering on the crown-topped pedestal supporting Super Peanut. Ashburn, where the county's chamber of commerce officially resides, calls itself the "Center of the Peanut Belt." Small wonder; not only does Ashburn boast this hefty peanut, but it's also the hometown of Gold Kist, "the Largest Peanut Shelling Plant in the World." At last, an entire town that will work for peanuts.

Louisiana

Matchless

Brimstone Museum

800 Picard Rd.
Frasch Park
Sulphur, LA 70663
(318) 527-7142

Hours: Weekdays 9:30 a.m.-5 p.m.
Admission: Free
Getting There: From U.S. 90 as it runs through Sulphur, take Picard Rd. heading south. The museum is just off Picard Rd., in Frasch Park.

Where else but in a town called Sulphur would you find a museum devoted to the history of brimstone (a.k.a. sulphur) manufacturing? The museum is housed in Sulphur's 1915 Southern Pacific Railway Depot, which was moved to Frasch Park in 1975 and renovated for use as the Brimstone Museum, which was opened a year later.

The main focus of the Brimstone Museum is the Frasch Process of mining sulphur, which gave the park its name and the town its major industry. Herman Frasch (1851-1914) was a German-born inventor and scientist who created the method of melting below-the-surface sulphur deposits and then pumping the liquid to the surface, thereby saving workers from the dangers of shaft mining. At the time, Europe had the monopoly on the sulphur market; Frasch's simple and ingenious method opened the market to lesser-developed mining regions, including the area around Sulphur.

The history of Frasch's discovery and the development and implementation of his system is documented in the museum with a short film, diagrams, old tools, artifacts, and even a one-ton block of brimstone from the sulphur mines. Other exhibits include a full-sized replica of the Liberty Bell, old railroad spikes, a railroad lantern, and stuffed examples of local wildlife.

Sulphur doesn't have a sulphur business anymore—the industrial market for sulphur had largely died out by 1925, so the mines were converted for oil and natural gas production, and are now used for storing crude oil—but it's still got its history.

odoo You Trust?

oodoo Museum

Dumaine St.
w Orleans, LA 70116
4) 523-7685

urs: Daily 10 a.m.-dusk
mission: Adults, $3; students and senior
zens, $2; children, $1
tting There: Located in the heart of New
eans' French Quarter on Dumaine St.
ween Bourbon and Royal Sts. Jackson
uare is three blocks to the southwest of the
seum.

ecommended for the entire family" is
w Charles Massicot Gandolfo, the
oprietor of this creepy museum, ad-
rtises his voodoo collection. Well, it
pends on how strong your family's
rves are; this place could be a little too
ird for some squeamish kids or older
ks. But anyone else with a fascination
th the occult, and especially the an-

cient religion of voodoo, will enjoy it.

In its earliest form, voodoo originated
in West Central Africa and was brought
to the French West Indies with African
slaves in the midseventeenth century.
The Roman Catholicism taught to the
slaves was integrated with their homeland religion, and the traditional form
of voodoo—Christian beliefs blended
with African rituals—was born. It
spread throughout the West Indies, taking firm hold in Haiti and Martinique,
and then moved to North America with
the French colonization of Louisiana.
Through the centuries, the rituals were
banned in many areas, forcing a secrecy
among practitioners that to this day is
an important part of the religion's self-
sustained mystique.

It is this history, along with illustrations and artifacts from voodoo rituals,
that the New Orleans Historic Voodoo
Museum celebrates. Gandolfo's strange,
hypnotic-yet-cartoonish oil paintings
depicting voodoo rituals make up a
large part of the collection, along with
portraits and drawings by Gandolfo and
other artists of famous voodoo practitioners. Marie Laveau, considered the
queen of voodoo—visitors came from all
over the world to request her services or
to watch her rituals—is a major focus of
the museum.

Other exhibits explain the variety of
voodoo rituals and their related paraphernalia, including the infamous voodoo doll; the Gris-Gris bag, a charm created from the mixture of black-and-
white magic (*gris* is French for "grey");
and ritual candles, potions, and amu-
lets. Visitors will also learn how zombies
are "made" by giving the victim a poisonous potion that causes him to fall
into a death-like trance.

Ritual shows, as well as tarot-card

readings and lectures, are produced at the museum, but for those wanting an even more in-depth look at the religious practices, a three-hour tour of New Orleans' historic voodoo sights departs from the museum Tues.-Sat. at 1 p.m. ($15 per person). Among the sites are Marie Laveau's tomb, a voodoo drugstore, a voodoo church, and a witchcraft shop. The museum also offers ritual tours and swamp tours for the truly strong of stomach and spirit (call for times and prices).

The New Orleans Historic Voodoo Museum may not be for everyone, but it's a good place to learn about voodoo magic and rituals without getting personally involved.

Mississippi

Only Game in Town

Checkers Hall of Fame

Chateau Walker
Lynn Rae Rd.
(Drawer A)
Petal, MS 39465
(601) 582-7090

Hours: By appointment
Admission: Free
Getting There: The 20-acre Chateau Wa estate is centrally located in the town of Pe in the suburban outskirts of Hattiesburg.

When Charles C. Walker, an insuran executive with a love of checkers, dis

vered there was no official hall of
me for his favorite game, he didn't go
pieces—instead, he turned his home
to a checkered palace. Walker, a one-
ne Mississippi checkers champion,
ilt the International Checkers Hall of
me and Museum as a living monu-
ent that's also a lived-in monument.
Walker has filled his extravagant
hateau Walker estate with every
ape, form, function, and spirit of
eckers he could find. The "official"
rt of the Hall of Fame and Museum,
dicated in 1979, is a 20,000-square-
ot wing that features a seven-story
wer filled with artifacts ranging from
re and outrageous boards (including a
ndmade jade playing surface worth
ousands of dollars) to memorabilia of
eat checkers players. (Did you even
ow there were great checkers play-
s?) Even the living quarters are
eckered—an ornate bed in the main
est suite is topped with a fanciful,
t-checker king's crown. Throughout
e hall of fame and into the residential
rt of the chateau, many of the wind-
g hallways, arched walkways, and
g, sunny rooms are decorated with
eckerboard rugs, wallpaper, and ceil-
g tiles.
The biggest thing going for the Inter-
tional Checkers Hall of Fame and
useum is an enormous 16-square-foot
eckerboard, which covers part of the
e floor of the tower's basement gallery
om. The playing surface is created
th green and white linoleum tiles, and
e playing pieces are actually round
d and white cushions. When checkers
urnaments are held here, the oppo-
nts play on a regular-sized checker-
ard, and their moves are mirrored on
e giant board for spectators, who
tch from an observation gallery

above the floor. The walls of the gallery
are hung with photographs of champs
past and present, which add a sense of
history to the tournament games being
played below.

Although checkers is the name of the
game here, Walker's museum also displays mementos, knickknacks, and art
that have more to do with his personal
taste and memories than with the game
of checkers. There are childhood toys,
paintings by his father-in-law (who first
lit the flame under Walker's checker
passion), and a collection of eighteenth-
century Bibles. The exhibits reveal a
collector who moves comfortably from
the whimsy of impulse-bought gewgaws
(old bottles, space toys) to the wisdom
of an art connoisseur (the price of one of
the rare Salvador Dali prints on display
appreciated tenfold over three years).

But checkers is what people really
come here for. After all, it's not whether
you win or lose, it's how big a game you
played that really matters.

North Carolina

Way of the World

Belhaven Museum

Main St.
(P.O. Box 220)
Belhaven, NC 27810
(919) 943-3055

Hours: Daily 1-5 p.m.
Admission: Free; donations appreciated
Getting There: Belhaven is near the North
Carolina coast, south of Albemarle Sound, on
Hwy. 264. The museum is in the second floor
of the City Hall office building on Main St.

"This knife was inserted to the handle in
a north Belhaven native's back . . . .

Native is still working every day, believe it or not, so says Dr. Wright," reads a card next to a wicked-looking knife on display in the Belhaven Memorial Museum. Not too far away, an electric drill on exhibit is described as having electrocuted a fellow named Sam Richard Repress in 1974, when he turned it on while standing in a puddle of water. But wait—if you think *that's* morbid, you should see the 10-pound tumor yanked from the belly of a local woman. And then there are the jars and bottles that hold, among other anomalies, an eight-legged pig and a four-legged chicken.

Now don't get the wrong idea about the Belhaven Memorial Museum. It's more than just a selection of life-and-death traumas. This little jumble of a museum is also home to a universe of delightful oddities, curios, artifacts, and just plain stuff. It is also a lively memorial to a lady named Eva Blount Way, who never threw anything out. Ever.

By all accounts of locals who still remember her, Way was a remarkable woman. She would break into a jig as she walked down the street, often gathered neighborhood kids around her for stories and songs, and loved to kill (and can) rattlesnakes and bears. She came from one of the oldest families in North Carolina, which traces its lineage back 13 centuries to royalty and soldiers. She ran her farm with an iron hand and a sharp hoe, and raised five children with the same delightful sensibilities and respect for the oddities of life that she herself espoused.

Way had several different explanations as to why she started taking in the oddities of the world. One story was that her mother-in-law once let her keep any buttons she wanted from a sewing box, and a newfound fascination with rhine-stone buttons soon spread to virtually every item and object that landed in her possession. The other story is that, as a young bride newly settled in a barren Belhaven farmhouse, Way immediately set about finding things to fill the empty rooms—and she never stopped.

Whatever her reasons, Way's passion for the eccentric was soon legendary throughout Albemarle County. Up until her death in 1962, strangers and friends would drop by at all hours to give her this or that odd thing they'd come across. Neighborhood boys gave her a human skull they'd found on the beach, an old sea captain handed over his prized 100-million-year old petrified walrus tusks, and a cousin donated a pin from his hip. Even after Way died, the streams of unusual and delightful objects continued to show up on her door step, taken in by her daughter and added to the collection. To this day, the word around North Carolina is, if you don't know what to do with it, take it to the Belhaven Memorial Museum.

Way's Museum, as it was originally called, was simply Eva Way's home, which she opened up to curious tourists in 1940 to earn money for the Red Cross. A few years after her death, some Belhaven residents banded together to save the collection from being sold and disposed of. The Belhaven Memorial Museum was incorporated in 1965 and spent two years in a small storefront location before moving into its present quarters, upstairs in the city office building.

The building is an angular, red-brick structure that still shows its firehouse roots with a high, gabled roof and arched doorways in front. An unassuming little door on the left side of the building is marked simply "Museum,"

iving no hint to the amazing and outra-
eous exhibits inside. It is just as well,
ecause part of the collection's charm is
ts element of surprise. Standing on tip-
oe to peek into a foggy jar, bending
own to examine an exotic carving, or
eering into a dusty display case evokes
hrill upon shock upon laugh in this
mile-a-minute monument to eclecti-
ism.

History is the key here. Everything
om that deadly drill to the dress of a
00-pound woman has a story to tell.
he joy of the objects on display comes
s much from their givers as from their
wn nature, with the ridiculous and the
ublime sharing the same crowded shelf
ace, ennobled by the local lore that
urrounds the entire collection. Every
quare inch of this upstairs area is
ammed with items that literally spill
ver the shells and onto the floors,
imbingup the walls. Only the ceiling
anages to evade the show.

Way's addictive buttons are here—
0,000 of them, framed and displayed
a mirage of patterns that covers a
ng section of wall. And the ever-popu-
r "Dressed Fleas—Bride and Groom,"
op a tiny wedding cake (visible only
th a magnifying glass), is prominently
splayed. There are six jars with hu-
an fetuses, aged one to six months,
d another jar holding twin deer fetus-
. The cans of food that were on Way's
elves when she died (everything from
rn and peas to "possum and taters")
e displayed, and so is a set of spoons
ade from silver dollars. Also here are
eglasses for chickens and horses, hu-
an hair in bottles (her sister-in-law's
sses) and formed into flowers, a rat-
snake-skin tie, and a lightbulb that
anaged to survive an American bomb-
g raid.

This is a collection of nature, humanity, and love of all things ordinary and
extraordinary. If a thing exists, then its
very existence gives credence to its
worth: this is the lesson of Eva Way's
museum. If all of life itself were
crammed into one little room, it might
look a lot like this.

Gourd Vibrations

Gourd Museum
N.C. Hwy. 55 W.
(P.O. Box 666)
Fuquay-Varina, NC 27526
(919) 639-2894

Hours: Daily sunrise-sunset
Admission: Free
Getting There: Located on Hwy. 55 W., a
mile north of Angier, opposite the Kennebec
Airport.

The humble gourd is about as common
in households of the tropical climes as
nonstick cookwear is in the homes of
America. With uses ranging from serving bowls to wine flasks, the gourd is the
container of choice for the rain-forest
set. So if there were going to be a museum celebrating the versatility and beauty of gourds, it would probably be off in
a grass hut on some island paradise,
right?

Wrong. It's on a North Carolina
highway.

Mary and Marvin Johnson loved
gourds, and whenever they traveled,
they hunted for unusual or delightfully
decorated specimens. They were gourd
hoarders of the first degre , collecting
carved gourds, painted gourds, gourd
figures, gourd banks, gourd vases, and
gourd instruments. The Johnsons

opened this tiny museum in 1966 to show their gourds to the rest of the world, and what a gaudy gourd collection it is. Most of the time it is left unattended, and the solitude within this little roadside museum somehow makes the exhibits even more amazing—you just walk in, and the place is empty except for all these gourds.

There are shelves and shelves of them, in all shapes and sizes. Some are gourd conglomerations—bunches and bits of the giant fruit shells glued together in the shapes of mice and elephants. Others are handpainted with American Indian symbols or African patterns. There are gourds encased in woven-bead sheaths and gourds crudely carved with floral designs. The overall effect is stunning, charming, and illuminating. It's a shame that the gourd never caught on in American kitchens, for the beauty and elaborate artistry of the pieces on display here make our own stainless steel implements seem barren in comparison.

Oklahoma

You-Do Economics

Enterprise Square, USA

2501 E. Memorial Rd.
Oklahoma Christian College
(Rte. 1, Box 141)
Oklahoma City, OK 73111
800-522-9203 (in state); 800-654-9245 (out of-state); 478-5190 (local)

Hours: Mon.-Sat. 9 a.m.-4 p.m.
Admission: Adults, $3.50; students and senior citizens, $2.50
Getting There: Enterprise Square, USA is the southeast corner of the Oklahoma Christian College campus, located in the f: north side of Oklahoma City; take I-35 to E Memorial Rd., and follow signs to the building.

Enterprise Square, USA has the uniq privilege of being the only museum-*cum*-theme-park devoted to the stud and glorification of the American ecc nomic system. Small wonder. But, w:

ppets and video games, talking heads
d moving parts, this Disneyesque
eme park takes on the subject of mon-
with a multimedia gusto usually re-
ved for more trivial pursuits.

When you enter the lobby to join a
ur group, you are greeted by a video-
ed Bob Hope. "Why Bob Hope?"
u might wonder, and with good rea-
n. But before you get a chance to pon-
r this mystery of life, Ed McMahon
ts in with an annoucement that
ens have crash-landed nearby. Wow!
From this point on, the tension
unts. The "aliens" (whose cute little
ange faces, pie-plate-wide grins, and
or-coordinated uniforms are more
miniscent of Willy Wonka's Oompa
ompas or Jim Henson's Muppets than
y space creatures likely to land in
lahoma City—even at the Oklahoma
ristian College) must join the tour
up to learn the wonders of capitalism
hey can get respectable jobs, buy the
ff they need to fix the ship they just

totaled, and zoom home again.

So off you go, aliens in tow. And what
do you know? You soon find yourself
moving through a series of interactive
exhibits, shows, and theme displays.
There's never a dull moment—which in
itself is a miracle, considering that eco-
nomics, not a pirates' cove or the world
of tomorrow, is the focus here.

Among the many thrills awaiting you
in this monument to moola is the "Great
Talking Face of Government," which
has video screens strategically placed at
the eyes, ears, nose, mouth, etc., to tell
you all about the evils of government in-
tervention. Another show stopper is the
"Great American Market Place," where
huge dollar bills sport mechanized faces
that chat about the free market system,
and even do a barber shop quartet number or two.

If giant bills and faces are your cup of
tea, you'll also enjoy the "World's Largest Functioning Cash Register," a display of jumbo soup cans, and, of course,

the "Hall of Giants." The latter has a series of huge figures illustrating the lives and memorabilia of some of America's great entrepreneurs, including Alexander Graham Bell, Henry Ford, Helena Rubinstein, and George Washington Carver. Also not to be missed is the "Remarkable Doughnut Shop," where the concepts of market demand and diminishing returns are illustrated—how else?—with the help of interactive video and friendly robots.

Then there's the time tunnel and the occupation video gameroom. Throughout the day, starting with the first tour at 9 a.m., time marches on from the turn of the century to the present at the rate of a year every six minutes. You get to choose your occupation (from lemonade seller to United States President, and a few jobs in between) on one of six terminals, pitting your economic survival skills against the trials and tribulation of the year currently being explored. (Try to avoid being here in 1929, if you can.) The good news is that if you manage to keep your business afloat despite flood, famine, dust bowl, Pearl Harbor and Watergate, you can earn bonus points redeemable for discounts at the Enterprise Square gift shop.

How did this marriage between Mickey Mouse and Adam Smith come to pass? Big business donated big bucks to help create this $10 million, 60,000-square-foot homage to capitalism. Every year thousands of visitors from the United States and abroad are painlessly economically indoctrinated—oh, and a few space aliens, too.

Gene Autry's O.K.

Gene Autry, OK

Gene Autry Chamber of Commerce
P.O. Box 158
Gene Autry, OK 73436

Hours: Always open (though they may roll up the sidewalks at dusk)

Admission: Free

Getting There: Gene Autry is located halfway between Dallas and Oklahoma City, on I-35, about 6 miles east of Hwy. 53.

This town, with its population of 200, has had almost as many name changes as residents. When first established in the 1800s, the town was called Lou; over the next half-century, it would be called Dresden, Dresden Flats, and Berwyn, until finally settling on the name of the singing cowboy, Gene Autry. Autry's "Flying A Ranch" was located just outside of town, so it was a publicity stunt made in heaven for a tiny town that didn't mind changing its name one more time if it would earn a place in the newsreels. And indeed it did, with 35,000 tourists on hand in November 1941 to witness the historic event.

Gene Autry is purportedly the first town named for a living Hollywood star, which was part of the reason for the big fuss in 1941, when screen stars were closer to godliness than even cleanliness. And Autry, the swell fella with a guitar and a horse, was cleaner than most, so his star was shining as bright as a sheriff's badge. Unfortunately, the town's glory days are long since past, though it does come to life every summer, when the Gene Autry Cowboy and Indian Day Celebrations are attended by as many as 5,000 people.

The Gene Autry Chamber of Commerce (which claims to be the largest per-capita chamber in the world, with a global membership in numbers that dwarf the town's population) has been trying for years to get enough money to turn Autry's ranch into a museum, to no avail. But it keeps trying to raise the funds, and distributes a brochure offering money-raising souvenirs of the town and the man—$17 polo shirts, a $45 Gene Autry satin show jacket, and, of course, a bargain basement $10 membership in the ever-growing Chamber of Commerce.

So far, however, the stables that once housed Champion, "The World's Wonder Horse," and the fields where the Flying A Rodeo Company once practiced still stand unattended amid the blowing tumbleweeds and hot Oklahoma dust storms—a sort of ghost ranch of lost dreams, on the outskirts of a dream town filled with ghosts.

You Really Got a Hold On Me

Wrestling Hall of Fame
405 West Hall of Fame
Stillwater, OK 74075
(405) 377-5242

Hours: Mon.-Fri. 9:30 a.m.-4:30 p.m.; Sat.-
Sun. by appointment only
Admission: Free; donations encouraged.
Getting There: From I-35, take Exit 174 east
to Stillwater and follow the signs to the
museum.

Wrestling fans flip over this hotbed of
wrestling remembrances. The National
Wrestling Hall of Fame pays homage to
the oft-forgotten *sport* of wrestling,
rather than to the blood-curdling entertainment form performed by the likes of
André the Giant and Hulk Hogan, who
strut their stuff (and probably stuff
their struts) before throngs of crazed,
beer-slurping fans. Indeed, this hall of
fame takes visitors on a tour of the more
gentlemanly sport, showing off such artifacts as uniforms, trophies, and even a
derby hat. Guys like Hugh Otapalik,
Frank "Sprig" Gardner, and Arnold
"Swede" Umbach get the recognition
they struggled to earn on the Wall of
Champions, which displays plaques
honoring more than 3,500 national

wrestling champions and members of
United States international teams. It's a
great place to learn the real ropes of
wrestling—and you thought Stillwater
didn't run deep.

South Carolina

S.C. Law

Criminal Justice Hall of Fame
5400 Broad River Rd.
Columbia, SC 29210
(803) 737-8600

Hours: Mon.-Fri. 8:30 a.m.-5 p.m.
Admission: Free
Getting There: From I-20, take Exit 65 to U.S
Hwy. 176 (Broad River Rd.) heading NW
toward Irmo. The museum is at the Criminal
Justice Academy, about 5 miles up the road.

Where else will you find the Melvin
Purvis gun exhibit? Nowhere but here.
The South Carolina–born Purvis was
the G-man who tracked down—and
gunned down—gangster John Dillinger
and he is remembered in this Hall of
Fame with displays of his guns, accounts of his good-guy exploits, and
memorabilia from his life. Other exhib
its include an old jail cell that must have
been punishment enough for any crime
and the moonshine stills that helped pu
a few people away in some of those nas
ty cells. There is also a memorial room
with plaques bearing the names of slain
South Carolina law enforcers, and a
granite monument to their memory.
The South Carolina Criminal Justice
Hall of Fame works pretty well as a
crime-deterring facility; visitors here
will think twice before breaking the law

is museum isn't quite as fun or excit-
; as the American Police Hall of Fame
North Point, Florida, but then again,
me doesn't pay as well in South Caro-
a, either.

storic Plaque

ental History Museum

dical University of South Carolina
Ashley Ave.
arleston, SC 29403
3) 792-2288

urs: The museum does not have regular
urs; entrance can be gained through the
iversity's Waring Historical Library, which is
en Mon.-Fri. 8:30 a.m.-5 p.m.
Imission: Free
tting There: Located on Ashley Ave., near
e St., at the Medical University of South
rolina's campus.

Anyone who hates going to the dentist
will love going to the Macaulay Museum
of Dental History. One look at this assortment of sharp, hooked implements,
old drills, and early X-ray equipment
will send nervous patients into near ec-
stasy over the advances in dental tools
and technology in recent years. The museum, which has one of the world's largest collections of antique dental equipment, is the result of Dr. Neill
Macaulay's decades-long dental-col-
lecting passion. Macaulay, who donated
his collection to the Medical University
of South Carolina in the early 1970s, received his dental degree from Emory
University in 1926 and went on to pub-
lish and lecture extensively on the history of dentistry until his death in 1983.

The Macaulay Museum reveals its
collector's love for all things
dental—from the gallery of dental
chairs to the quackish electro-surgical

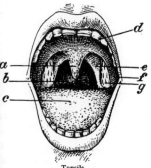

Tonsils.
a, uvula ; *b*, pharynx ; *c*, tongue ; *d*, palate ; *e*, posterior, and *f*, anterior pillar of
the fauces, between which is *g*, the tonsil.

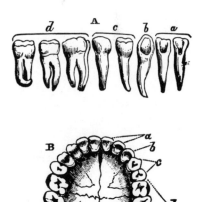

unit bought during the late 1800s by gullible dentists in the belief it could cure all oral diseases. One of the collection's earliest pieces has a doubly historic significance: this early instrument was designed by Paul Revere for use by Dr. Josiah Flagg, the first American-born fulltime dentist. Other items in the collection include the first dental X-ray in South Carolina, instruments used during the Civil War by Macaulay's grandfather, and a gold mill, a small dental instrument, dating back to the nineteenth century. It's a toothsome treasure, to be sure.

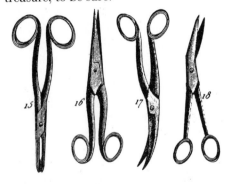

Grain Expectations

Rice Museum

Front and Screven Sts.
(P.O. Box 902)
Georgetown, SC 29442
(803) 546-7423

Hours: Mon.-Fri., year-'round, 9:30 a.m.-4:30 p.m.; Sat., April-Sept, 10 a.m.-4:30 p.m. and Oct.-March 10 a.m.-1 p.m.; Sun., year-'round, 2 p.m.-4:30 p.m.
Admission: Adults, $2; military, $1; students, free
Getting There: Front and Screven Sts. meet near the Sampit River waterfront in Georgetown, which is located in South Carolina's "Low Country" and can be reached from U.S. Hwys. 17, 701, and 521.

Rice has been nice to Georgetown. In fact, during much of the 1700s, this region produced more than half of the entire United States rice crop. But Georgetown eventually lost its grip on the rice market after the Civil War scarred the land, scattered the population, and left the southern plantation economy struggling to catch up with a rapidly industrializing world. Today, history is probably the richest crop of this third-oldest city in the South, and the Rice Museum is the product and the benefactor of this heritage.

The Rice Museum is a housed in several southern-sun-washed brick buildings that date back to the 1840s, which provide a genteel setting for the museum displays. Inside the hospitable exhibition rooms are all the illustrative maps, dioramas, and sundry paraphernalia—from harvesting tools to sales receipts—a student of the rice industry would ever want to see. For the visitor who has a more general interest in the history of the area, there is also a gallery with changing exhibits that explore other aspects of the region's culture and development.

This isn't exactly a thrill-a-minute museum, but it does provide an unusual glimpse into the growth and demise of an agricultural society built around a single crop. There is an undertone of lost glory throughout, and you may feel a bit like you've just walked through the ruins of Rome rather than the Rice Museum of Georgetown. But step outside again into that warm southern breeze, stroll through the surrounding waterfront park with its lush, bright gardens and you'll realize that nature has not deserted this corner of South Carolina. It's just as civil as it ever was—albeit less lucrative.

Tennessee

; You War

onfederama

32 Tennessee Ave.
ıattanooga, TN 37409
▌5) 821-2812

ɔurs: June-Labor Day, daily 9 a.m.-9 p.m.;
bor Day-June, daily 9 a.m.-5 p.m.
ɪdmission: Adults, $3; children, $1.50
etting There: Confederama is at the foot
Lookout Mtn., reached by taking I-24 or I-
into downtown Chattanooga and
lowing Broad St. through town to the
ɔuntain.

ʌer wished you could go back in time
ɪd see what the Civil War was really

like—without getting blood on your
shirt, that is? Well, Confederama has
the answer. With 5,000 realistic miniature soldiers waging war on a realistic
miniature set, with realistic miniature
puffs of "cannon" smoke poofing up
here and there, and a realistic light show
strobing the whole scene into psychedel-
ic pandemonium, what better way to get
a feel for that horrible conflict?

The display's narration takes viewers
through the decisive battles of Chattanooga and Chickamauga, boom by
boom, as 650 lights flash around the
480-square-foot terrain. It's great fun
for the whole family, and worth the trip
even if only to see Confederama's exterior: a bright white "fort" facade that
looks like something out of "Ivanhoe
meets General Lee," with square turrets
bearing huge confederate flags and a
genteel red and white canopy over the
entrance. All the southern comforts.

Woofers and Tweeters

Field Trial Museum
Dunn's Supply Store
Hwy. 57
(P.O. Box 449)
Grand Junction, TN 38093-0449
(800) 223-8667 (in Tenn.: (800) 325-0051)

Hours: Mon.-Sat. 9 a.m.-5 p.m.; Sun. 1-5 p.m.
Admission: Free
Getting There: The museum is housed in
Dunn's Supply Store, which is on Hwy. 57 just
as you enter Grand Junction.

Dunn's Supply Store has been giving
L.L. Bean a run for its money for quite
some time, and Banana Republic has
probably felt a touch of competition,
too. This huge retail and mail-order

sporting business in the tiny town of Grand Junction sells everything from duck calls to elephant guns. And one entire room of the store is devoted to a subject close to the Dunn empire's home and heart: field trial champions.

The National Field Trial Championships, which pit the finest field-hunting bird dogs against each other, are held every year in Grand Junction. The museum displays portraits of every winning woofer since 1896, from setter to pointer, along with trophies, equipment, and other memorabilia of Grand Junction's hometown sport. Dunn's claims to have outfitted and/or trained almost every one of the last 44 champion dogs, so this museum is also the store's way of wagging its own tail.

high and 70 feet long, this guitar is big enough to make even a cello fret a little. In great big letters underneath the neck (which, by the way, has windows for sound holes) is the none-too-surprising statement: "World's Only Guitar-Shaped Music Museum." And if you think the building is a mere knock-off, think again: it carries the logo (and endorsement) of C.F. Martin, one of the finest acoustic guitar manufacturers around.

Within the chambers of this monument to music are some 200 rare string instruments, from beautiful banjos to vibrant violins, all lovingly displayed and described. There are dulcimers, dobros, mandolins, and ukuleles galore—and, of course, guitars—with a strong emphasis on folk, country, and mountain music instruments. This

Strum Major

Grand Guitar Museum

535 New Kingsport Hwy.
Bristol, TN 37620
(615) 968-1719

Hours: Call for hours of operation
Admission: Free
Getting There: Located near the Virginia-Tennessee border, off I-81 (Exit 74A) on Hwy. 11W (New Kingsport Hwy.).

Some museums are housed in boring buildings that look more like banks or airplane hangars than exhibit centers, but not the Grand Guitar Museum. Its home is a giant guitar. Three stories

downhome theme recurs throughout the small but noteworthy museum, especially on a wall map pinpointing the local birthplaces of great country and bluegrass performers.

Some of the collection, which includes numerous rare and beautiful pieces, is displayed in free-standing glass cases, but many of the instruments are mounted on the wall or on stands, giving the feel of a music shop. A re-

ling studio and real instrument shop
he building reinforce this sense of
'ing music."

t a Load of This

useum of Ancient Brick

23
). Box 3547 CRS)
nson City, TN 37602
5) 282-4661

urs: Mon.-Fri. 8 a.m.-4:30 p.m.
mission: Free
tting There: Located in a giant, round
k office building of the General Shale
ducts Corporation, which is on the
skirts of Johnson City on Rte. 23. I-81 runs
hin 15 miles of the museum.

ck has almost mythical qualities.
e of the three little pigs thwarted the
bad wolf with a brick house; the
losseum in Rome was built with
cks, the museum folks point out, and
l stands today; brick came over on
Mayflower as ballast. It seems that
ck legends are legion. Yet there are
ne who might call brick boring. Such
ckbatters should hasten to the Gen-
l Shale Museum of Ancient Brick,
l learn the exciting and glorious his-
y of brick.
The museum displays bricks that
te back 10,000 years, when we first
ured out how to make a strong build-
; material just by leaving hand-
med clumps of clay to dry in the sun.
hibits include mud-and-straw bricks
m ancient Egypt, early sun-dried and
n-fired bricks from Babylon and bib-
al Israel, and a variety of rare bricks,
m medieval England to colonial
erica. Aside from the actual bricks,
re are also displays explaining an

cient versus modern brick-making
practices, photographs of bricklayers,
and other items relating to brick history.
But it is the bricks themselves that are
this museum's chief attraction.

Who could gaze at a brick from the
city of Jericho and not be moved just a
little—especially when the brick still
bears the finger indentations of its maker? Or how about the paw print that is
inexplicably imbedded in a brick from
the original White House foundation?
Such imprints are fossils of societies
long past, the everyday remnants of
people and creatures who were left out
of the legends that preserved a few great
figures and forgot the rest.

There are other, equally compelling
legacies from the artisans of the past—a
stamp imprinting the brick maker's
name can be clearly seen on a 1,600-
year-old flat brick from ancient Byzan-
tium. Another brick, found in Jerusalem, bears part of the inscription "LEG
X FR," revealing that it was made under
Rome's Tenth Legion of Frentises—the
same legion that destroyed Jerusalem in
70 A.D.

Many of the bricks in the museum
come from momentous times or places,
including a specimen from the Cairo
(Egypt) Opera House, dedicated in
1869 on the same day the Suez Canal
was opened. (Verdi's *Rigolleto* was presented on the Opera House's opening
night, a last-minute substitution for

Aida, which he had not finished writing in time for the premier.) There is an original brick from George Washington's house of worship, Christ Church, in Alexandria, Va., built in 1773. There is a brick from the portion of the Great Wall of China built in 1584, and another carved with a round, jolly figure before firing, from an eighteenth-century Hindu temple near Calcutta.

The museum is housed in the offices of the General Shale Products Corporation, one of the largest brick manufacturers in America. The building itself is quite an exercise in brickwork, with 16 of its sides inscribed within a 100-foot circle, giving it the appearance of a giant brick cylinder rising out of the ground. Although the displays won't win any awards for scintillating design—just simple glass cases and neatly written explanations throughout—it's a fascinating look at the foundations of ancient and modern civilizations. With so many museums filled with smattered scatterings of bric-a-brac, it's nice to find one that just has brick.

Pop Art

Museum of Beverage Containers

Ridgecrest Dr.
Goodlettsville, TN 37072
(615) 859-5236

Hours: Mon.-Sat. 9 a.m.-5 p.m.; Sun. 1-5 p.m.
Admission: Adults, $2; children, $1
Getting There: Despite its Goodlettsville address, the museum is in Millersville, just north of Nashville on I-65 near Exit 98.

Soda makes you wonder, doesn't it? Well, it certainly makes the Bates family wonder—and wander, too. In fact, they've spent the better part of 14 ye wandering all over the place in the search for soda and beer bottles and cans. Now they've put their collectio on display in a a museum that lavish high-tech attention (a computer data base keeps track of the holdings) on what many people consider throwaways.

It was throwaways that first got th family started—in 1973, Tom Bates b gan picking up empties from the side the road on his way home from scho While some parents might have been less than kind about their son's trash hobby, Tom's let him keep on rumm ing. He housed his growing collectior his room for a while, until it spilled o into the family's den, backyard, and finally its first "real" headquarters i Millersville, which was opened in 19 By this time the whole Bates clan was volved: Tom Bates and his dad, Paul run the museum; while mom, Karen the "glue" of the crew, keeping reco and running the gift shop.

Visitors will marvel at the collectio of 25,000 cans and 5,000 bottles. Th *Guinness Book of World Records* has tested that this museum has the worl largest can collection; the bottles can claim the same record for their catego yet, but the Bateses are working on i The collection also includes exhibits advertising art (including those neon signs that flash in bar windows) and other paraphernalia related to the be erage industry.

But it is the bottle and can designs and sometimes their contents—that the most intriguing element of the m seum. Along with the familiar contai ers, old and new, there are some unus collectibles here, including camoufla

er cans used by American soldiers
ring World War II and a batch of
hi bottles used on the TV sit-com
Iappy Days." Also on display are
me examples of a product that falls
o the "Gee, I'm glad I didn't think of
at" school of beverage invention: soda
p for pets. According to the labels,
ver can quench his canine curiosity
th "K-9 Cola," while Tigger can in-
lge in feline fantasies with "Pussy
p" (although the taste just might
ock off a few of her nine lives). The
d adage about one man's trash being
other man's treasure is put to a de-
htful test at this museum. See it if you
n.

the Pink

ink Palace Museum
50 Central Ave.
emphis, TN 38111
01) 454-5600

ours: Tues.-Fri. 9:30 a.m.-4 p.m.; Thurs. 9:30
m.-8:30 p.m.; Sat. 9 a.m.-4 p.m.; Sun. 1-5

p.m. Call for information on extended
summer hours
Admission: Adults, $2.50; children/students
with ID/senior citizens, $1.75
Getting There: Located near the intersection
of Central Ave. and Lafayette, and is most
easily reached by driving north on Central
Ave. from the western side of the I-240 loop
through Memphis.

Out of much silliness, great things may
come. Someone famous probably said
that once, and it certainly holds true for
the Piggly Wiggly grocery empire that is
memorialized in the Pink Palace Museum. Charles Saunders got the silly name
for his revolutionary retail idea after
watching his children play "Piggly Wiggly" games with their toes as they lolled
on the lawn of his home one day. Soon
after, he opened his first Piggly Wiggly
in Memphis in 1916, and by 1922 the
innovative chain of self-service grocery
stores had spread to 1,200 locations
across the South and West. A walk-
through replica of the original Piggly
Wiggly is a focal point of the Pink Palace Museum, which also displays a vast

array of other permanent and changing exhibits.

The museum is housed in a spacious modern building, located next door to the glorious pink marble mansion that Saunders was constructing when he went broke in 1923 after trying to corner the grocery market on the New York Stock Exchange. The city eventually finished the project and turned the building into an earlier version of the Pink Palace Museum. Now the mansion is used as an education center with study laboratories and classrooms.

Although Saunders made a killing in the stock market, only the name of his Piggly Wiggly chain was silly; the rest was a serious departure from retailing practices of the time, which eventually spelled disaster for the mom-and-pop brand of corner grocery store. The concept of self-serve groceries made the stockboy's job obsolete, thereby freeing up much of the store's funds to reduce prices or build innovative displays. Saunders can also be credited (or blamed?) for the early science of marketing—that is, displaying items and laying out the store in such a way that the customer has to wind his or her way through aisles of sugared cereal and TV dinners before coming to the milk, eggs, and other staples.

The Piggly Wiggly replica in the Pink Palace is delightfully true to the original store, down to the four-aisle layout and authentically price-stamped goods. Campbell's Soup sold for 6 cents and 8 cents a can, while beans and corn ran to 10 or 12 cents. For the big spender, a can of asparagus could be purchased for a hefty $1.23. Antique cash registers, cracker barrels, and produce bins also help recreate the flavor and feel of an authentic 1916 grocery store.

If you happen to be in the museum o a weekend, you might also catch a glimpse of Clyde Parke's minicircus, animated extravaganza hand-built by Parke from household objects. The minicircus is a delicate, intricate show that the museum runs for just two hou a week, on weekends only. Call in ad vance for the showing schedule.

Pipe Dreams

Tobacco Museum
800 Harrison St.
Nashville, TN 37202
(615) 242-9218

Hours: Tues.-Sat. 10 a.m.-4 p.m.
Admission: Free
Getting There: The museum is in the U.S Tobacco manufacturing facility at the corn of 8th Ave. and Harrison St. From downtov Nashville, take the James Robinson Parkwa to 8th Ave. and drive north.

The Museum of Tobacco Art and Hist ry traces the story of the flammable le from 2000 B.C. to the present, with cc lections of antique pipes, snuff contai ers, cigar store figures, advertising de vices, and plenty of other fuming fascinations.

The history of the tobacco industry Tennessee and Kentucky is also ex- plored in depth, with special attentio to the early role of tobacco in making this part of the south a self-sufficient farming region. What started in Virgi ia in 1612, when John Rolfe successfull harvested his first tobacco crop, quick became a goldmine for southern planta tions that began producing a finer to- bacco than their Spanish and Portu- guese competitors. And as the tobacco

dustry billowed, so too did the adver-
sing and marketing businesses that
rew up around it.

This museum takes a serious ap-
roach to the history and impact of to-
acco in cultural development, and tells
any matchless tales, including the sto-
y of how the sixteenth-century French
ueen, Catherine de Medicis, had a pen-
hant for snuff that caused an entire so-
ety to take up the habit. Pipes came
ong later, when the peaceful puffing of
ew World Indians became all the rage
s soon as Columbus brought the habit
ack home. There are some rare and
vely examples of early pipes, includ-
g an enormous European meer-
haum pipe, intricately carved with the
e figure of Diana, the Roman goddess
the hunt, that dates back to the
idnineteenth century.

Such artifacts make one long for the
ys before prepackaged cigarettes,
en the habit of smoking was at least

cloaked in a veneer of artistry. Then
again, a Surgeon General's warning
would have been pretty hard to carve on
all those pipes.

A Wrenching Experience

World O' Tools Museum

Rte. 1
(Box 180)
Waverly, TN 37185
(615) 296-3218

Hours: By appointment
Admission: Free
Getting There: The museum is 2 miles south
of Waverly, on Hwy. 135. From I-40, take Exit
143 and drive 13 miles north on Hwy. 135;
there is no museum sign, but look for the
owner's mailbox, marked "Pilkington."

This is Hunter Pilkington's own personal collection of tools and tool technol-

ogy. But it got so unwieldy that he moved it to a building 300 feet away from his house and decided to call it a museum. A museum it certainly is, with more than 15,000 tools and tool-related items, along with a vast research library that includes books, catalogs, and reference material on tools from the 1870s to the present. Pilkington has a special place in his heart for adjustable wrenches, and he's got more than 1,500 of them in the museum. The rest of the collection includes tools and other equipment used in blacksmithing, coopering (barrel making), wheelwrighting, tinsmithing, and woodworking.

The owner has chosen not to open his museum to the "general public" (i.e., those who walk in for a free-for-all tour) because, he says, "It is a whole different ball game . . . some of the general public are inconsiderate and destructive, as well as capable of liberating small goodies." That said, he is willing to show the

museum to anyone with a real interest the world of tools. Although he'd pre a call in advance, he can show the co lection whenever he happens to be hor (there's no museum sign up, but just look for his name on the mailbox), so those tooling around nearby might wa to drop in for a visit.

Texas

Horns of Plenty

Buckhorn Hall of Horns Lone Star Brewery
600 Lone Star Blvd.
San Antonio, TX 78204
(512) 226-8301 (226-8303 weekends and holidays)

Hours: Daily 9:30 a.m.-5 p.m.
Admission: Adults, $2.25; children, $1; ser citizens, $2

tting There: The brewery and museum s can be reached from several major tes: from IH-37, take Florida to S. St. Mary's, left, and turn left onto Lone Star Blvd; from . 90/10, take a left onto Probandt, Mission, Roosevelt to Lone Star Blvd.; and from IH-35, take S. Alamo to a right onto Probandt, n left onto Lone Star Blvd.

e Lone Star Brewery is almost as mous for this eclectic collection of xas and animal artifacts as it is for its er. There are actually several collec- ns here, ranging from hilarious and ird mutant deer horns in the Hall of rns to the graphic and somewhat uesome wax figures in the Hall of story.

First, the horns. It all began back in 81 when the Buckhorn Saloon first ened in San Antonio. Proprietor Al- rt Friedrich displayed his collection of usual cattle antlers and related mem- abilia in the establishment, and his patrons liked the decor so much that they began adding to it. Eventually, the Buckhorn collection became a tourist draw in San Antonio, with curious cow- pokes and city folks going out of their way to see the well-appointed display. The Friedrich family sold the collection to the Lone Star Brewery in 1956, and soon the Buckhorn Hall of Horns was officially ensconced at the brewery headquarters along with a growing col- lection of other area oddities.

It's hard to know how to describe the items in the Buckhorn Hall—first off, aside from the actual Hall of Horns, there's the Buckhorn Hall of Feathers, the Buckhorn Hall of Fins, and the ever- alive Buckhorn Bar itself. The Hall of Horns is sort of a hornucopia of mutant, rare, and beautiful horns, horn arts and crafts, and stuffed animals big and small. There are horns mounted on the walls, and horns left on the original ani- mal's head (one mounted deer's head

has one horn growing up normally, and the other growing down the side of its face). There's a chair made of cattle horns created by Albert Friedrich's father, and a display of intricately carved scrimshaw horns. There are also stuffed caribou, moose, giraffe, and deer, along with hornless beasts including polar bears, anteaters, and that local favorite, the armadillo.

The Halls of Feathers and Fins have equally impressive collections of birds and fish, while other, less-well-defined exhibit areas and much of the brewery grounds spill over with odd objects and kooky collections. Walk around enough, and here are some of the other things you'll run into: a Texas star made out of rattlesnake rattles, framing a portrait of Friedrich; a giant white shovel (thought to be the world's largest), stuck in the ground, with a welcoming "Bienvenidos" painted on the handle and the Lone Star beer symbol emblazoned on the shovel; a collection of more than 200 Lone Star and other beer bottles, old and new; a leathery, stuffed gorilla that once stood in the original Buckhorn Saloon; and O. Henry's "house," a building transplanted from its original location on South Presa St., where the great short-story writer often visited, although he never really lived here. Last but not least, there's the Hall of Texas History, with 14 dioramas depicting in sometimes gory detail the winning of the West, and particularly the battle for Texas (in one scene, an Indian scalps a settler, with plenty of waxy blood dripping everywhere).

The collections of the Lone Star Brewery are every bit as savage, disparate, and off-the-wall as the state this beer is named after. This is a lone collection, a star collection, a downright eccentric group of horns and beasts and wax pioneers that will make you feel as though you've had one beer too many—or one too few.

Toro, Toro, Toro

Bullfight Museum

Del Camino Motor Hotel and Restaurant
5001 Alameda Ave.
(P.O. Box 10200)
El Paso, TX 79993
(915) 772-2711

Hours: Daily 7 a.m.-2 p.m.
Admission: Free
Getting There: Located in the Del Camino Hotel, on U.S. Hwy. 80 East (Alameda Ave. as it passes through town); from I-10, take the Raynolds exit, drive four blocks south on Raynolds and one block east on Alameda to the hotel and museum.

There's some bullfight memorabilia in this museum that might make some collectors see red, if only because they'd do anything to own them. The collections sprawl all over the main entry building of the Del Camino Motor Hotel and Restaurant—behind the reservations desk hangs a Spanish tapestry of a bullfighter, in the lobby are several antique *Capotes de Paseo* (the ornamental vest worn by bullfighters), the hallway to the lounge is hung with nineteenth-century prints depicting bullfights, and the lounge lobby displays the head of "El Firmador," an infamously fierce Chihuahua bull. The "Corrida Room" exhibits an elaborate and expensive bullfighter's costume, along with a display of the swords and other articles used in the fight. The "Barrera Taurina Room," entirely devoted to the collection, displays the costume of a picador (the bull

Getting There: Take Rte. 385 through to the northern end of Hereford and follow the black-and-white signs to the museum, located one block from Rte. 385.

ghter's sidekick) along with other styl-ed costumes and accoutrements of various caped crusaders. Portraits of famous bulls and bullfighters, photo-graphs of fights, the trophies awarded brave fighters (bull ears, tails, and feet), and written accounts of the sport's great moments are also displayed throughout the museum, which opened in 1973. Be warned that many of the exhibits, par-ticularly paintings and photographs (not to mention bull parts), are gory and sometimes downright shocking. It's an eclectic but fascinating gathering of me-mentos from a savage spectacle that continues to pack in herds of spectators despite the modern predilection for tamer sports.

Lovely lassoing ladies like Sydna Yokely Woodyard are honored in this hall of fame, but so are women who won the Wild West with words, including Willa Cather and Laura Ingalls Wilder. Other inducted Westerners (who just happened to be women) range from ranchers and missionaries to singers and bootmakers. The National Cowgirl Hall of Fame and Western Heritage Center was founded to honor the women who have prevailed in, profited from, and promoted the heritage of the great American West.

While the only chaps in this collection are the ones the women wore on their legs, the common denominators that usually color male tales of the West—courage, perseverance, inde-pendence, and ingenuity—are here in force. From Annie Oakley, one of the finest shots ever and the only woman to ride with the Buffalo Bill Cody Wild West Show, to Georgia O'Keefe, the New Mexico artist who painted sensual portraits of the desert and a lot more,

Lasso Lassies

Cowgirl Hall of Fame
515 Ave. B
(P.O. Box 1742)
Hereford, TX 79045
(806) 364-5252

Hours: Mon.-Fri. 9 a.m.-5 p.m. (closed noon-
p.m. daily)
Admission: Adults, $2; children under 12,
free

the women honored here are as varied and lively as a day at the rodeo. Aside from portraits of the inductees, there are displays of cowgirl memorabilia, including some decorative chaps and a few rare sidesaddles. There are also collections of priceless photographs (notably an extraordinary set depicting Annie Oakley, donated by her niece) and a permanent exhibit of artwork relating to the American West. The Hall of Fame gives proof plenty that some women are more at home riding the range than cooking on it.

What a Kick

National Mule Memorial
Main St. (Hwy. 84)
Muleshoe Chamber of Commerce
(P.O. Box 356)
Muleshoe, TX 79347
(806) 272-4248

Hours: Always visible
Admission: Free
Getting There: Muleshoe is in northwest Texas, on U.S. Hwys. 70 and 84, and state Hwy. 214. The monument stands on the town's Main St. (Hwy. 84).

Where else would you expect to find the National Mule Monument but in a town called Muleshoe? The memorial to the unsung mule stands proudly at one en of Main St., a mule on a pedestal lookir out over the West it helped to win wit nary a whinny. The monument, dedicated in 1965 as a tribute to the untirir farm work done by the humble beast, was erected with the enthusiastic support of more than 700 contributors to the memorial fund. A wrinkled old dol lar bill was sent in by a widow who wa still taking care of the two faithful mule who had worked her farm for years, an a large sum was kicked in by a New York oil company executive "in memo ry of his boyhood experiences with mules," according to the Muleshoe Chamber of Commerce.

"Building a Better Muleshoe" is the Chamber of Commerce's motto, and they certainly got the mule part of thei slogan right when this memorial was built. The statue has a regal, if snubnosed, bearing—it is a perfect remembrance of mules past. A plaque at the monument states the simple and solid legacy of the mule thus: [sic]

> The Mule, without ancestral pride or hope for offspring; the mule—along with buffalo, hound, and longhorn—made Texas history. In war he carried a cannon on his back. Because he was available freight, forts rose on frontiers. Indians ate horses hitched to cart or coach, but let tough mule meat go by. His small hooves scaled rock and steep trails untrod by horse or ox. But big ears endangered him in lake or river. He went fast, endured much, ate sparingly. Since the beginning of Christian era, he has helped all over the world to bear the burden of mankind.

...ming Through the Rind

...range Show

...1 Munger St.
...). Box 13760)
...uston, TX 77219
...3) 552-1767

...urs: March-Dec., Sat., Sun., and selected ...lidays, noon-5 p.m.; weekdays by ...pointment only
...mission: Adults, $1; children, free
...tting There: Located on Munger Rd., just ...the Gulf Freeway IH-45. From the Freeway ...uth, take the Tellepsen exit, turn left, and ...n left again to go under the underpass. ...er the underpass, take a left and go three ...ocks to Munger. From the Freeway North, ...:e the Telephone Rd. exit, then go right and ...two blocks to Munger.

...ff McKissack had a vision: he wanted ...build a monument to his favorite ...od, the orange. So, for 26 years, he ...llected odd and ends and bits and ...eces of other people's discarded be-...ngings, and slowly built a strange and ...ondrous world devoted to this succu-...nt citrus.

...McKissack believed the orange was ...he perfect food," being a clean and ...holesome source of nutrition. He even ...rote a book, *How to Live 100 ...ars—And Still be Spry*, about the or-...nge's super-food properties. Unfortu-...ately, he didn't practice what he ...reached—at least not absolutely. He ...ied from a stroke in 1980 at the age of ...8; but from all accounts he was still ...ory at the time. Fortunately, ...IcKissack completed the final work on ...ie Orange Show in 1979 and opened it ...the public that same year. After his ...eath, a foundation was set up to pre-...erve and promote the Orange Show, .../hich is now also the site for cultural

activities ranging from films and concerts to picnics and festivals.

From the instant you arrive at the Orange Show, you're in for a juicy treat.
The entrance gate is an ornately sculptured construction made from railroad
spikes and machine parts. Inside, there
are a variety of exhibits and shows, including a weird maze that leads you on a
journey through the history of the orange and its nutritional benefits. There
is also a museum with elaborate sculptures and scenarios that incorporate the
ever-present orange into the stories of
such American favorites as "The
Woodsman" and "The Indian." Other
sections feature a "Monument to the
World's Orange Growers," and an array
of lively mosaics and sculptures.

The Orange Show is considered by many to be one of this country's finest "folk art environments"—a rather ostentatious label for outrageous places like the Orange Show that are born of junk and dreams—monuments to wild ideas, built in backyards and open fields. What makes the Orange Show a slice above the rest is its cohesive and thoughtful, if wacky, design. An almost Victorian lavishness—ornate ironwork and elaborate, offbeat ornamentations—combines with a Texas sunshine stylization of low hacienda buildings and brick pathways to create a thoroughly delightful fantasy land. Done in shades of white and, of course, orange, the Orange Show is an appealing landscape of junk art, with the look, feel, and essence of a whimsical creamsicle calliope.

Green With Envy

Popeye Statue

Zavala County Chamber of Commerce
101 E. Dimmit St.
Crystal City, TX 78839
(512) 374-5565

Hours: Always visible
Admission: Free
Getting There: Crystal City is in central Texas on Hwy. 83. The statue stands in front of the City Hall building in the middle of town.

For more than half a century, Crystal City has had a clear-cut mandate as the "Spinach Capital of the World." Aside from the area's hefty spinach crop, there is a week-long spinach festival and a "life-sized" statue of Popeye the Sailor Man to help keep the title fresh year after year. In 1987, the city celebrated the fiftieth anniversary of its mascot statue, and although he's no spring chicken, Popeye looks pretty good. The middle-aged salt stands in front of City Hall, with one hand raised to his pipe, a winsome grin on his still-youthful face, and his tattooed forearms bulging from as much spinach-induced muscle as ever. Must be the sea air that keeps him looking so young.

But 1987 was more than just a year for celebrating in Crystal City—it was also a year for defending its title. A contender, in the form of the town of Alma, Ark., sprang up like a weed in a spinach patch. Alma, which also grows a large spinach crop, proclaimed itself the world's spinach capital, held a spinach festival, and even planned a dedication of its own Popeye statue. A leafy food fight ensued between the two salad citizenries, but since Crystal City had a full 50-year head start on the little Arkansas town, for the moment at least the spinach laurels remain planted firmly in Texas.

Playing Posse

Texas Ranger Hall of Fame

Fort Fisher Park
(P.O. Box 2570)
Waco, TX 76702
(817) 754-1433

Hours: Sept.-May, 9 a.m.-5 p.m.; June-Aug., 9 a.m.-6 p.m.
Admission: Adults, $2.50; children, $1.50
Getting There: The hall of fame is located just off I-35 at the Ft. Fisher exit.

Ah, the Texas Ranger, that he-man of the rootin'-tootin' set who bit the bullet

and died with his boots on. These guys were the ultimate law enforcers for lawless times, shooting bandits, killing Indians, and generally trying to tame the Wild West with methods as savage as the adversaries they faced. The Texas Ranger Hall of Fame and Museum documents their violent and courageous history with multimedia presentations, dioramas, memorabilia, and art. There are saddles, rifles, boots, and hats used by these range-roaming lawmen, and sculptures and paintings immortalizing their showdowns with gunslingers and lone-star sojourns. Dioramas of famous shoot-outs and manhunts are also on display, along with such artifacts as arrest warrants, Bowie knives, and well-worn gunbelts.

The Texas Rangers were founded in 1823 as a private army for the protection of early settlers, and soon became the arbiters of war and peace on the Texas range. While the ways of the Old West disappeared into the sunset years ago, the Rangers still sit tall in the saddle.

Virginia

A Sleeper

Bedrooms of America Museum

9386 Congress St.
New Market, VA 22844
(703) 740-3512

Hours: March 1-June 1, daily 9 a.m.-5 p.m.; June 1-Sept. 1, daily 9 a.m.-9 p.m.; Sept. 1-Dec. 31, daily 9 a.m.-5 p.m.
Admission: $2
Getting There: Located on Congress St., two blocks east of I-81 on Rte. 11 (take exit 67), in the center of New Market at the only traffic light in town.

True to its name, the Bedrooms of America Museum is filled with Ameri-

can bedroom furniture. There are 11 rooms of complete bedroom sets, ranging from the William and Mary style to art deco. In between, there are bedrooms done in a variety of styles, including Chippendale, Queen Anne, Sheraton, and Victorian.

To be honest, it's about as much fun as visting a "fine furniture" showroom. But then again, this is the only museum devoted solely to bedroom furniture in the entire country. And as such, it's the only place to witness the progression of bedroom furniture styles from the early English pieces brought across the ocean by settlers to the twentieth-century, purely American forms that changed the shape of the boudoir forever. It's a journey from heavy, dark, ornately carved wooden suites to light, airy pieces with streamlined curves and crushed-velvet upholstery. You can see such designs as canopy beds and caned

chairs as they go in and out of style.

Since we cannot live on beds alone, there is also an exhibit of antique dolls in the museum, along with a pottery store, ice cream parlor, basket and silk flower shop, and reproduction furniture store. It's sort of a one-stop history lesson and shopping mall. The museum and stores are housed in the Lee-Jackson building, which had been the Civil War headquarters for General Jubal Early and later became a popular country inn from the 1880s to the 1940s. Parts of it are said to have been built by John Strayer, whose wife was Dorcas Lincoln, Abraham Lincoln's first cousin. There's a lot of peripheral history in and around the building, so it seems somehow appropriate that it now houses a bedroom museum—the boudoir being one historic meeting ground that rarely finds its way into the history books.

mb with a View

ders Mortuary
useum

E. Main St.
. Box 106)
yville, VA 22611
) 955-1062

urs: Mon.-Fri. 9 a.m.-5 p.m.; Sat. 9 a.m.-
n.

mission: Free

ting There: Berryville is in the
andoah Valley near Skyline Drive.
ning from the west, take I-81 to the
yville/Virginia Rte. 7 exit, which leads to
in St. (Those coming from the east can
Rte. 7 all the way from the Washington,
., area). The funeral home, which also
uses the museum, is a two-story brick
ding with blue shutters.

ere's a different kind of visitation go-
on in this valley-town mortuary, and

the folks filing through are more likely
to ask questions than to offer their con-
dolences. While you probably need a
certain fascination with the macabre to
really enjoy this museum, the name of
its resident funeral home, "Enders,"
and its location, "Berryville" (say it out
loud), will lighten the spirits of even the
gravest of characters. Morbid jokes
aside, the Enders Mortuary Museum
brings to life the world's third-oldest
profession as it was practiced during the
late nineteenth century.

It all started in 1984 when Reggie
Shirley, owner and operator of the Enders Funeral Home, purchased an 1889
Crane & Breed Horse-Drawn Hearse at
an auction. After having the hearse restored to its original splendor, Shirley
turned the funeral home's garage into a
sunny exhibition space, added a collection of antique mortuary paraphernalia
he'd found on the property, and opened

it all to the public. Along with the mortuary material, the museum houses memorabilia from Berryville's first volunteer fire department, founded in 1900 by the funeral home's original cabinetmaker/mortician, John Enders. Although Enders' fire hat is charming, you're bound to be more intrigued by the mortuary collection.

Because the mortician's craft is shrouded in well-deserved mystery, most of the items on display have a certain ghoulish glamour. After all, practically every history museum in America has old guns and tools and pots and pans; but how many have jars of cosmetics for prettying up the dead? Or an iron used to crease casket linings? In a country where we've all been bored to death by the sameness of typical historical objects, these tools of the funeral trade are genuinely fascinating.

That's not to say the items on display aren't somewhat disturbing. More than a few spines will be chilled at the sight of a tiny wooden casket, built for a child, with a sliding door on top for viewing the face; and some of the embalming implements look like they crawled out of a Vincent Price movie. Among the many other items on display are a cooling board, a wicker casket, a machine for engraving plaques on caskets, and a hand-crank printing press for churning out funeral bulletins. A modern, working crematorium was recently installed—an eerie juxtaposition with all the antique funerary equipment on display.

And then there's the hearse—the restorers paid special attention to such details as the peg-board floor, which is dotted with silver-plated coffin pins to hold the casket in place during the ride. This hearse looks almost like a fancy

puppet theater on wheels, its glass-sid oak carriage draped with fringed cur tains, its buckboard upholstered in ri Brazilian leather and illuminated on ther side by shining oil lanterns. Ove all, it's a glorious cart, much more cei monial and beautiful than the long, or inous station wagons we call hearses day. How could death be not proud when transported in such a way?

General Principals

George C. Marshall Museum and Library
Virginia Military Institute
P.O. Box 1600
Lexington, VA 24450
(703) 463-7103

Hours: Mon.-Sat. 9 a.m.-5 p.m.; Sun. 2-5 p.
Admission: Free
Getting There: From I-64, take Hwy. 11 ir Lexington and follow Main St. to the Virgi Military Institute Parade Grounds, where th museum is located.

This museum, founded in 1964, is a forcefully educational tribute to the l

d times of Gen. George C. Marshall,
nner of the Nobel Peace Prize in 1953
d creator of the renowned Marshall
an for the recovery of Europe. Exhib-
include memorabilia from Marshall's
nnsylvania childhood, an entire room
voted to the Marshall Plan, and an
ctronic map illustrating key events in
orld War II. Other generals' memora-
lia abound as well: Patton's helmet,
d the Best Picture Oscar the film
'atton" won in 1970 are on display, as
General Gerow's operation map of
maha Beach. And there's a "Try on a
ece of History" program that lets chil-
en don army get-ups, etc. Wary par-
its should expect a lot of Rambo-esque
bber on the way home if they let the
ds partake.

riner's Shrine

eorge Washington
lasonic Memorial

llahan Dr. at King St.
O. Box 2098)
exandria, VA 22301
03) 836-3713

ours: Daily 9 a.m.-5 p.m.; tower tours
heduled daily 9:15 a.m.-4 p.m.
dmission: Free
etting There: Take the George
/ashington Memorial Parkway (Rte. 1A) into
wntown Alexandria and turn west onto
ng St., the major thoroughfare that runs
rough the center of town. After you pass
der the train/Metro tracks, the memorial
uilding is directly ahead.

's pretty hard to miss the George
/ashington Masonic National
1emorial—the 333-foot-tall building
ses up like a giant, square wedding
ake from the multiterraced Shooter's

Hill, a prominent mound once considered for the U.S. Capitol building. The
hill didn't make the final cut, though
you can still get a fine panoramic look at
Washington, D.C., directly across the
Potomac River. But there's more than
just a pretty vista here—inside the memorial building is an eccentric assortment of objects, dioramas, furnishings,
and models.

This building is an explorer's dream.
In almost every nook and cranny (and
there are hundreds), you can find
strange and intriguing things. Start in
the basement, and you'll come across
the world's largest Persian rug, a 357-
year-old masterpiece that measures almost 30' x 50'. The rug covers part of

The GEORGE WASHINGTON
MASONIC NATIONAL MEMORIAL

the floor of the Memorial Room, which features a series of dioramas depicting George Washington's military and political careers, and cases filled with memorabilia from the International Order of Job's Daughters (a cape worn by Junior and Senior Princesses is prominently featured) and the Legion of Honor.

Another basement chamber, the Parade Room, has a glittering display of 181 temple fezzes, each with a temple's name and the Masonic symbol (a five-pointed star dangling from a crescent with the sphinx's face in the center, which in turn dangles from a scimitar) emblazoned in rhinestones and sequins. The Parade Room also offers a delightfully gawky mechanical Shrine parade, with a racetrack of tiny Shriners—some in their famous little cars, others marching—careening around a central field (where stand more little Shriners and tiny elephants) and past a Taj Mahal-replica reviewing stand. March music blares into the room as the parade commences, and the clickety-clack of the circling figures adds a nice counterbeat.

And that's all just in the basement. On the second floor, there's a tiny museum that feels more like a broom closet but has such treasures as a limestone horseshoe bearing the Masonic symbol and a china plate "said to have been used by George Washington at a banquet in Alexandria in 1718," according to a descriptive card. Just outside the little museum, in a room hung with paintings of General Lafayette and Martha Custis, stands a leather-topped table with a glass case in the center. The table is odd enough in itself, but the contents of its case are even odder: the pen used by President Taft to sign the register at Alexandria's Lodge 22, a signed copy of Harry Truman's book, *Mr. President*, a padlock with masonic symbols, an envelope with postage stamps commemorating George Washington's 200th birthday, and, the pièce de résistance, John Brown's handcuffs "worn just prior to his execution." It's quite an assembly of offbeat Americana.

While casual visitors are allowed free run of the first two floors, they have to take a tour to see the rest of the memorial. It's worth sticking around for this guided trip, because that's the only way to see the George Washington Museum on the fourth floor, which has the largest known collection of Washington memorabilia on public display. It's a gathering of artifacts of the first president that is both impressive and amusing. The centerpiece of the collection is Washington's family Bible, but there are other items here that are much more enthralling, if less historically important—such as the instruments used to bleed the dying President, and the clock that was stopped at the exact moment he died (10:20 p.m., for trivia buffs).

Alexandrians had conflicting emotions about the Masonic Memorial when it was completed in 1932. Many said it was an eyesore, an embarassingly ugly

ndering of the Lighthouse in Alexan-
ia, Egypt, that made Alexandria, Vir-
ia, look downright silly. But for the
ys who ride around in little cars, wear
nny hats, and build hospitals for crip-
d children, this place is a mecca; for
yone else, it's an eccentric piece of ar-
itecture filled with odd collections.
ther way, you can't lose.

ried Treasures

luseum on Americanism

01 E. Boulevard Dr.
ount Vernon, VA 22121
3) 765-1652

urs: Mon., Wed.-Sat., 10 a.m.-4 p.m.; Sun.
4 p.m.
dmission: Free; donations appreciated
tting There: The museum is in the
llingwood Estate, just east of the George
ashington Memorial Pkwy. between
ount Vernon and Alexandria; look for the
ns on the parkway.

is small museum is located at an es-
te once owned by George Washington,
w the headquarters of the fraternal
der called the National Sojourners,
rt of the Shriners. It's situated half-
y between Alexandria and Mount
rnon, just off the George Washington
rkway, and the impressive white
llingwood manor house and expan-
ve grounds, stretching down to the Po-
mac River, would be lovely enough for
visit even without the museum's
esence.
The museum itself is upstairs in the
ain house, in a long dreary room. The
llection consists mainly of a few cases
ed with some poorly labeled arrow-
ads, commemorative coins and

plates, and some other less-than-com-
pelling patriotic and historical
remnants.

There are two exceptions to this otherwise unstimulating exhibit. One is a
framed copy of Abraham Lincoln's
1863 proclamation for a day of Thanksgiving (originally set for Thursday, August 6); the other is purportedly the
world's smallest Bible. That's right—it's
a teensy, sturdy tome, with a text just
big enough to read with a magnifying
glass. If the size isn't enough to pique
your interest, the orginal owner adds
some spice: this was the family Bible of
Scottish poet Robert Burns. In fact, the
registry of family events is written in
Burns' own hand. It just goes to show
that even the littlest museums sometimes have a tiny treasure or two tucked
away.

Shell of a Place

Oyster Museum

Maddox Blvd.
(P.O. Box 4)
Chincoteague, VA 23336
(804) 336-6117

Hours: Memorial Day-Labor Day, daily 11
a.m.-4:45 p.m.; fall and spring, most
weekends 11 a.m.-4:45 p.m. (call ahead to
verify which weekends)
Admission: Adults, $1; children, 25 cents
Getting There: Take Hwy. 175 into
Chincoteague and take a left at the (only)
traffic light onto Main St. Continue north on
Main, following the signs to Assateague
Island. The museum is on Maddox Blvd.
(a.k.a. Beach Rd.) just before the bridge.

When most people think of Chincoteague Island, they imagine the water of
the Chesapeake Bay churning with wild
ponies (remember *Misty of Chinco-*

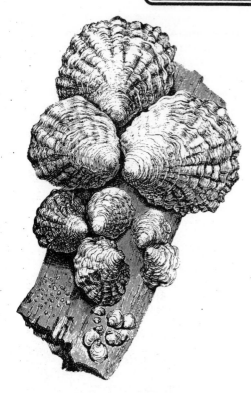

the National Aquarium in Baltimore, f‹
the unusual history this tiny museum
tells, it's a pearl of a place.

Smokes and Cloaks

Tobacco-Textile Museum

614 Lynn St.
(P.O. Box 541)
Danville, VA 24543
(804) 797-9437

Hours: Mon.-Fri. 10 a.m.-4 p.m.
Admission: Adults, $1.50; children, 75 cer‹
senior citizens, $1.20
Getting There: The museum is on Lynn S‹
five blocks east of U.S. Rte. 29N Business J‹
in downtown Danville

teague?) swimming across from nearby
Assateague Island. But the island's
livelihood comes from something else in
these waters—seafood. And oysters in
particular.

This tiny museum, opened in 1972,
traces the history of the Chincoteague's
oystering industry with exhibits showing marine artifacts from early oystering days, shell specimens, and (aw,
shucks) the implements of the trade. A
diorama shows the whole process from
catch to cash, and running films depict
the oystermen at work. There are also
live marine exhibits, with samples of
oysters and other sea life, including
starfish, seahorses (not the ponies who
cross the bay), clams, and crabs. While
the Oyster Museum doesn't have the
money or design flair of a big place like

Smoking and spinning are two of the
great and lucrative pastimes that com‹
out of Danville. This museum has tw‹
lively collections that reflect not only t‹
historic and economic significance of
the Virginia tobacco and cotton crops
but also their social, artistic, and cultu‹
al impact. The tobacco part of the mus‹
um has exhibits that range from the
"Gallery of Worldwide Cigarette
Packs" and "Plug Cutters of Yesteryear" to displays of of cigar box label‹
and rare tobacco advertisements. The‹
is also an exhibit of 3,100 cigarette
lighters and a "Gallery of World Fam‹
ous Pipes" that includes the personal
pipes of such world leaders as Gerald
Ford and Anwar Sadat. The textile pa‹
of the museum takes the visitor on a co‹
ton-picking adventure, detailing the
process by which a bale of cotton end‹
up as a piece of cloth. Here, visitors ca‹
examine spinning frames, a knitting
machine, madras plaid table cloths, an‹

enormous brass bell once used to call
eteenth-century textile workers to
: factory. There's also a three-story-
 model of a textile finishing plant
t explains, once and for all, how we

get such modern luxuries as stain and
wrinkle-resistant polyesters and flame-
retardant fabrics—which is a good
thing, too, considering the collection
next door.

WEIRD
WONDERFUL
AMERICA

Midwest

Illinois

Preacher Feature

Billy Graham Museum
Wheaton College
Wheaton, IL 60187
(312) 260-5157

Hours: Mon.-Thurs. and Sat. 9:30 a.m.-5:30 p.m.; Fri. 1-9 p.m.; Sun. 1-5 p.m.
Admission: Free, though a voluntary donation is requested: adults, $2; children, 50 cents
Getting There: The museum is on the campus of Wheaton College, 25 miles west of Chicago, just off Main St. in Wheaton.

This high-tech, high-concept museum traces the history of evangelism from its early, Bible-thumping, town-stumping roots to today's multimedia, multi-million-dollar industry. Along the way, visitors can see films of the excitable early twentieth-century preacher Billy Sunday and "Walk Through the Gos-pel" into a convoluted room meant to represent the crucifixion and resurrection. Along the way are displays of the memorabilia and methods of famous evangelists, artifacts from such Christian organizations as the Salvation Army and the YMCA, and, naturally, a great deal of Billy Graham memorab

including humorous letters ("Mr.
~~ly~~ Grayam") and videotapes of his
~~l~~atest moments. This is a classy, well-
~~d~~igned museum that somehow con-
~~s~~ts with the often gritty roadside re-
~~al~~ tent history contained herein.

~~a~~ Snap

~~C~~ookie Jar Museum

~~Stephen St.~~
~~m~~ont, IL 60439
~~2)~~ 257-5012

~~Ho~~urs: Daily 10 a.m.-3 p.m.
~~Ad~~mission: Adults, $1.50; children, 50 cents
~~Ge~~tting There: The museum is in Lemont,
~~wh~~ich is to the southwest of Chicago on Rte.
~~__~~. From I-55, take Lemont Rd. (Exit 271) and
~~go~~ south into town.

~~Lu~~cille Brumberek must have gotten
~~her~~ hand caught in the cookie jar once
~~too~~ often as a kid, because she's got
~~qu~~ite a fixation on those ceramic sweet
~~ho~~lders. From fat little piggies to ladies
~~in b~~all gowns, Howdy Doody to Dumbo,
~~the~~re are more than 2,000 cookie jars
~~lin~~ing the shelves of her museum.
~~Bru~~mberek opened the lid on her collec-
~~tio~~n in 1975 and continues to seek out,
~~buy~~, and display cookie jars whenever
~~she~~ can.

~~Sup~~ermaniacs

~~M~~etropolis

~~Ma~~ssac County Chamber of Commerce
~~__~~ Market Street
~~(P.~~O. Box 188)
~~Me~~tropolis, IL 62960
~~(61~~8) 524-2714

~~Ho~~urs: Always visible
~~Ad~~mission: Free
~~Ge~~tting There: Metropolis is on U.S. Hwy.
~~45~~ in the southernmost part of Illinois as it

borders Kentucky. Take Exit 37 from Hwy. 45
and head west about 3 miles into town.

In 1972, Metropolis officially claimed
the title of Superman's hometown for its
own, and the Man of Steel's cape has
blanketed the town in the form of tourists and publicity ever since. Although
Metropolis's new image had a less-than-

super launching in the early '70s when
its carnival-atmosphere "Amazing
World of Superman" exhibition center
failed to fly (it closed down and plans
for a museum were scotched), Superman is enough in evidence around the
city to make a side-trip worth any less-
than-Herculean effort.

Among the representations of Clark
Kent's better half to be found here are: a
giant building mural of Superman as we
know and love him best (in his famous
horizontal flight pattern), and a rather
unflattering statue that has become a
mecca during the Metropolis Superman
festival held every June. But the Chamber of Commerce holds the true key to

the city's lock on the comic hero's legend: a display featuring Superman's own official phone booth, into which visitors can leap for a chat with the big guy himself. Also exhibited here are the Superman Awards that the chamber has issued to outstanding Americans. Friendly tourists may even be given a piece of Superman's deadly foe, Kryptonite. Granted, it bears a striking resemblance to a mere spray-painted pebble with specks of glued-on glitter, but then again, Superman is disguised as a nerd himself most of the time. In other words, avoid ducking into phone booths when you've got that rock in your pocket.

Dial M for Museum

Parks Telephone Museum

529 S. Seventh St.
Springfield, IL 62721
(217) 753-8436

Hours: May-Sept., daily 9 a.m.-4:30 p.m.; April and Oct., Mon.-Sat. 9 a.m.-4:30 p.m.; Nov.-March, Mon.-Fri. 9 a.m.-4:30 p.m.
Admission: Free
Getting There: From I-55, take the Sixth St.

exit to the corner of Seventh and Edwards S the museum is at the intersection in the ground floor of the Illinois Bell building.

Oliver P. Parks wanted to reach out a touch someone—a lot of people, in fa So, in 1975, the retired lineman donated his collection of 79 antique tele phones, switchboards, and related iter to the Illinois Bell Company, with the stipulation that it create a free museu to display his telephonic treasures. A the phone company did just that, buil ing an innovative and appealing exhil space right on the ground floor of the Springfield District Headquarters.

Thanks to the exhibit's circular, wi dow-encased design, you can see mos of the collection by walking around tl outside of the building. Inside, a close look at the history of Ma Bell's telephones and their offspring awaits. Th museum loop starts with the "Alexander Graham Bell Story" (complete wi a replica of the famed one-way model that transmitted the first words ever spoken over the telephone) and ends with a display of "Old Telephone Pictures." In between, there are exhibits about everything you ever wanted to

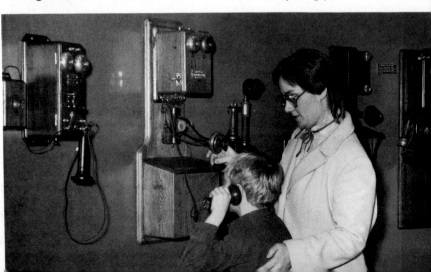

ow about telephones, but didn't
ow who to call for information.
One display exalts the bravery of line-
n (including Parks) and includes an
ibit of open-wire insulators, lined
p miniature telephone poles that
ve been lovingly arranged amid
asses and big rocks. Another shows a
nnequin operator plugging away at
turn-of-the-century Stromberg-
rlson switchboard. But the stars of
show are the telephones, old and
v—from candlesticks and pay
ones to high-tech telecommunica-
ns systems.

Especially evocative are the Picture-
one sets—futuristic phones with
eens, similar to those premiered at
1964 New York World's Fair, that
ame stock sci-fi film props, but nev-
actual consumer items. Funny, senti-
ntal reminders of the future of the
st, these phones with screens gently
se our dialtone dreams.

Fighting War

Peace Museum

430 W. Erie St.
Chicago, IL 60610
(312) 440-1860

Hours: Tues.-Wed. and Sat.-Sun. noon-5
p.m.; Thurs. noon-8 p.m.
Admission: Adults, $2; students and senior
citizens, 50 cents
Getting There: The museum is in the upper
west end of the city, on W. Erie St., which runs
between W. Ontario and W. Huron Sts., just
north of I-90/94.

Here is a museum that wants to give
peace a chance. In 1982, the founders of
this unusual collection gathered together the memorabilia and works of peace
activists and put them on display.

Peace is a difficult subject to
illustrate—there aren't any "weapons"
other than petitions, any "heroes" other
than the marchers and volunteers. This

museum approaches its subject through the philosophy of peace, through the art and paraphernalia of antiwar movements past and present. One particularly moving tribute to peaceful protest (and to the tragedy and irony of violence) is the display featuring a guitar once owned by John Lennon. Other exhibits tell the stories of famous marches and protests and display the writings and teachings of great nonviolent activists. Also housed in the museum are portions of "The Ribbon," a strip of cloth made from sections embroidered with anti-nuclear statements and the names of loved ones by people from around the world, which was wrapped around the Pentagon in a 1985 protest; it was a rare case of people sewing for peace rather than suing for it. While the ribbon didn't disarm the world, the delightful and emotionally charged sections here will certainly disarm museum-goers,

both as examples of international fol art and as personal appeals for peace

Famous Amish

Rockome Gardens
Rte. 2
(Box 87)
Arcola, IL 61910
(217) 268-4216

Hours: May 2-Oct. 25, Mon.-Fri. 10 a.m.-5 p.m.; Sat.-Sun. 9 a.m.-5:30 p.m. (Closed or some Mon. and Tues.—call ahead to verif
Admission: Adults, $4.25; children, $2.75; senior citizens, $3.25. (Add $1.50 per admission price for access to attractions ar rides.)
Getting There: Arcola, in central Illinois, c be reached by taking to I-57 to Arcola (Exi 203). Turn right at the top of the exit ramp a follow signs to Rockome Gardens.

ockome Gardens is the closest thing
e Amish and Mennonites have to an
nusement park. It started out a series
strange, sprawling rock and flower
rdens in 1939, built on the estate of a
cal industrialist, Arthur Martin, who
as looking for a way to keep his work-
s employed during the Depression.
hen former Amishman Elvan Yoder
rchased the gardens in 1959, he set
out building a wholesome tourist at-
ction around them, complete with
rm rides and gift shops. The resulting
-acre park is a combination of
hmaltzy tourist shrines, family restau-
nt dining experiences, and tame,
rse-drawn rides, the combined effect
which makes the place pretty darned
arming.

The gardens themselves, which cover
out three acres of the park, are a mix-
e of chunky, funky rock statuary and
chitecture (oversized bird cages,
py arches) built from bits and pieces
rock, and meandering flower beds
t explode with color and foliage.
ewhere on the grounds, visitors can
lore a house made from old Fresca
tles. It comes complete with a bottle
ghouse (for a soda pup, no doubt)
the "Haunted Barn" (it's probably
really haunted, but the exhibits of
tant animals will send a chill down
r spine). There are also lots of shops,
ging from "Das Kandy Haus" to the
rist Mill/CheeseShop." In fact,
re's a whole recreated frontier town,
d Bagdad Town," filled with quaint
ps and craftspeople. And then there
the horse-and-buggy and hayrides
he machine shed, which also has dis-
ys on how horsepower was used in
automobile days.

ockome Gardens is located in the
rt of the Illinois Amish country, and
many of the people employed at the
park are Amish. It's a pleasant enough
family place, infused with a wholesome
exuberance. Considering the hair-rais-
ing, money-melting nature of most
amusement parks, Rockome Gardens is
a tamer alternative.

Calling All Phones

Telephony Museum

225 W. Randolph St.
Chicago, IL 60606
(312) 727-2994

Hours: Mon.-Fri. 8:30 a.m.-4 p.m.
Admission: Free
Getting There: *The museum is in the Illinois Bell building on W. Randolph St., one of the major arteries that heads toward City Hall and crosses I-90/94.*

Illinois Bell is no phoney when it comes
to preserving the history of telecom-
munications. Along with the personal,
witty collection represented in the Oliver P. Park Telephone Museum in
Rockford, the company also has a Chi-
cago-based Telephony Museum. This
museum is filled with phones, from the
old, cranky variety to more modern con-
veniences, like early direct-dial instruments. An old switchboard is on display
for a bit of play, and there's an informa-

ve collection of Alexander Graham
ell inventions. There are also plenty of
nsulators, cable ducts, and wires and,
or a change of pace (or a piece of
hange), there's a bunch of coin tele-
hones. E.T. would have a blast here.

very Second Counts

ime Museum

ock Tower Inn
01 E. State St.
.O. Box 5285)
ckford, IL 61125
15) 398-6000

ours: Tues.-Sun. 10 a.m.-5 p.m.
dmission: Adults, $3; students over 18 years
d senior citizens, $2; children, $1
tting There: The museum is in the Clock
wer Inn at the Clock Tower Resort and
nference Center, at I-90 and U.S. Hwy. 20
usiness) on State St.

nis timely collection traces the history
timekeeping devices from 3,000 B.C.
the present, and it's a bright and sur-
isingly varied history. The Time Mu-
um, housed on the premises of the
ock Tower Inn, is divided into 14 sec-
ns that turns visitors into time travel-
s. Each section ushers in a new era or
velopmental theme: early instru-
nts (including water clocks and sun-
als), the Middle Ages (when mechani-
l clockmakers had their hands full),
e "leap to precision" in the 1600s,
d on up to today's atomic and quartz
cks. Group tours arranged in ad-
nce are treated to demonstrations of
rforming clocks with singing birds,
llet dancers, and even a German beer
zzler by the name of Gambrinus.
me is truly of the essence in this enter-
ning museum.

Victorian Principal

Tinker Swiss Cottage

411 Kent St.
Rockford, IL 61101
(815) 964-2424

Hours: Viewing by tour only, Wed.-Sun. 2
p.m., 3 p.m., and 4 p.m.
Admission: Adults, $2; children, 50 cents;
senior citizens, $1
Getting There: From U.S. Hwy 20 (Business),
take the S. Main St. exit heading north, turn
right at Kent St. Go one block and turn right at
the cottage sign.

Within shouting distance of bustling
downtown Rockford, this chalet,
perched upon a limestone bluff, looks
like a set for a hot-chocolate commercial. But no, the Tinker Swiss Cottage is
a real place complete with a preserved
collection of furniture and primitive art,
just like other historic homes. What

makes this place a lot livelier than most
is its funky architecture. The outside
has all the curlicues, angles, and twists
that any alpine skier could ever dream
for. With lots of winding staircases and
intricately wrought wooden thises and
thats, the inside is considered one of the
15 finest remaining examples of Victorian interior design in America. The
cottage also houses some interesting collections and items, notably a variety of
Hawaiian artifacts from the
premissionary era and a rare square
Steinway piano.

Light Fantastic

Way of Lights
9500 W. Illinois, Rte. 15
Belleville, IL 62223
(618) 397-6700 or (314) 241-3400

Hours: Shrine open daily; call for hours of
specific events and exhibits. Way of Lights
open from the day after Thanksgiving to the
Sun. after New Year's; nightly, 5-10 p.m.
Admission: Free; donations encouraged
Getting There: The shrine is on Hwy. 15, ju
outside Belleville. There are directional sign
at the appropriate exits on I-64, I-70, and
I-255.

The National Shrine of Our Lady of th
Snows is the largest outdoor shrine in
the United States. It's quite a place any
time of the year, what with its nearly ex
act (²⁄₃-scale) replica of the grotto at
Lourdes, its sight-and-sound show,
"The Power," and its various and sun
dry contemplative spots, such as the Ag
ony in the Garden statue, the
Annunciation Garden, the Father's
Prayer Wall, and the Mother's Prayer
Walk, to mention a few. But the finest
exhibit is on display for only a few
months of the year and draws people
from distant states. The Way of Lights
a mile-and-a-half-long, 150,000-
lightbulbs-strong extravaganza that
must turn the local electric company o
ficials into believers.

As far as the eye can see and the fo

1911 Packard Eighteen Landaulet

 walk, the trees and fields are aglitter
h "electro-art" shepherds, animals,
 twinkly stars that lead the way to
at may be the ultimate life-sized na-
ty experience. For the weary travel-
halfway through the Way, there's the
Joseph's Visitor's Center, complete
h a gift shop, the Shrine Restaurant
th its all-you-can-eat smorgasbord
ner), and the Pilgrim's Inn Motel.
s is a heck of a plugged-in prayer
, but don't bother trying to find the
 North Star—it can't compete with
those bulbs.

ja Vu, All Over Again

heels O' Time Museum

23 N. Knoxville Ave.,
nlap, IL 61525
9) 243-9020

urs: May-Oct., Wed.-Sun. noon-5 p.m.
mission: Adults, $2; children, $1
tting There: Located on Rte. 88, 8 miles

north of downtown Peoria.

This collector's paradise, located just
minutes from downtown Peoria, was the
creation of John Parks. Parks, an antique-car buff and clock restorer,
dreamed of opening a museum to show
off his treasures, and he knew other collectors who had similar yearnings. The
group combined their private passions
and put them on public display as the
Wheels O' Time Museum. Aside from
old cars and clocks, the museum has big
trains and tiny trains, antique tools, a
full-scale reproduction of the Red Baron's Tri-Wing Fighting Airplane, and a
picturesque display of Caterpillar Trac-
tors. A replica of a country kitchen,
complete with potato mashers and cherry pitters, is another big crowd pleaser.
And for anyone who loves a big band
now and then, there's a 1937 juke box
that'll spin the disks of Glenn Miller,
Artie Shaw, and Tommy Dorsey for a
mere nickel. The only question is, will it
play in Peoria?

Real Troopers

Zitelman Scout Museum

708 Seminary St.
Rockford, IL 61108
(815) 962-3999

Hours: Wed. 9 a.m.-5 p.m.; Sat. 9 a.m.-3 p.m.;
or by appointment
Admission: Free; donations appreciated
Getting There: From I-90, take the Hwy. 20
bypass west to Hwy. 2 (S. Main St.), turn right
and drive north on Main to the second traffic
light, turn right (drive over the bridge), and at
the second traffic light turn left onto Seminary
St. Drive half a block to the museum.

When Lou Zitelman gave her husband
Ralph a reprint of a 1911 Scout Hand-
book, his historical interest in scouting
was piqued and the Zitelman Scout Museum was born. It opened in 1974, and
now exhibits the handbooks, badges,
flags, uniforms, and paraphernalia of
Boy Scouts, Explorers, Girl Scouts, and
Brownies, as well as their illustrious
Scoutmasters, Cubmasters, and Troop

and Den Leaders. There are also uniforms from 15 countries and several d
play cases filled with such scouting st
as neckerchiefs and knots. Ralph
Zitelman says he'd be delighted to giv
guided tour of his spiffy collection to
anyone who calls in advance—scout'
honor.

Indiana

Oldies But Goodies

Bird's Eye View Museum

325 S. Elkhart St.
Wakarusa, IN 46573
(219) 862-2367

Hours: Weekday evenings and Sat. by
appointment only
Admission: Adults, $2.50; children, $1.25
Getting There: The museum is in Wakarus
12 miles south of Elkhart, just west of Rte. 1

is collection of miniatures has a more
mey feel than most. There are no
ndiose attempts at seashell Sistine
apels or bottle-cap Westminster Ab-
ys here. Instead, there are toothpick
d popsicle stick renditions of
akarusa landmarks and the nearby
nneville Mill. While the prospect may
t incite non-Wakarusans to a mass
grimage, the models on display are as
e an example of basement craft as
u'll find around the country. So what
hey're sort of outdated (many of the
oleaux are strictly 1950s vintage,
m the tiny, tail-finned cars on the
ads to the super-suburb architecture);
is timewarp adds a certain innocence
the collection. It may have been a
all-scale dream, building a miniature
akarusa, but the result is a larger-
an-life feel for an America long lost to
rome and glass.

ur Gang

ohn Dillinger Museum

ite Rte. 46
O. Box 869)
ishville, IN 47448
2) 988-7172

ours: March-Nov., 10 a.m.-6 p.m.; Dec.-
b., 1-5 p.m.
dmission: Adults, $2.50; children, $1.75
etting There: Located in a frame house in
wntown Nashville on Rte. 46. Nashville is
out 50 miles south of Indianapolis,
tween Columbus and Bloomington.

deference to the Dillinger clan, the
rators of this collection opened their
useum not in John Dillinger's home-
wn of Mooresville, but in the nearby
wn of Nashville. That, apparently, is
here the deference ended. Barton

Hahn and Joe Pinkston, the museum
owners, surely couldn't have thought
Dillinger's family would be relieved to
see wax figures of their naughty boy's
corpse on a morgue slab or in an open
casket.

The legendary 14-month reign of terror that Dillinger enjoyed before he was
gunned down outside a Chicago movie
theater was one of the bloodiest and
most profitable in gangland history.
The stories of his death at the hands of
G-men (Melvin Purvis, et al.) and the
treachery of the "Woman in Red" who
betrayed his whereabouts to agents
have become, if anything, more legendary than his actual criminal exploits. A
gleefully macabre fascination for
Dillinger's death is played out in two of
the four rooms of this museum, and visitors often hurry through the earlier sections ("The Early Years, Mooresville
1903-1933," depicting Dillinger's
childhood; and "Banks and Bullets,
1933-1934," illustrating his short, violent crime spree).

To heighten the tension, a red light
flashes outside the door of the first of the
death rooms, warning away any faint-
hearted, weak-stomached tourists. Inside is the "Chicago Morgue, July 22,
1934," where Dillinger's sheet-covered
"body" (a wax dummy) is laid out on an
autopsy table. Nearby, display cases exhibit artifacts of the slaying, including
the trousers Dillinger was wearing when
he was killed and newspaper accounts
of the event. There are also some horri-
fying photographs of the blood-covered
gangster. The next room, "The Harvey
Funeral Home—Mooreseville," is a
recreation of Dillinger's funeral, complete with his actual funeral coach and a
wax body in a casket.

Other deathly items on display here

include Dillinger's second tombstone (people keep vandalizing and stealing the headstone at the Indianapolis graveyard where he's buried; it has had to be replaced four times) and two death masks. Mementos from his life include the wooden gun he used in a famous jail break, and a rabbit's foot he gave to William "Tubby" Toms, a journalist who had covered the gangster's career. The museum also has wax figures and brief descriptions depicting the careers of other notorious gangsters, including Bonnie and Clyde, "Ma" Barker, and "Pretty Boy" Floyd.

Museum owners Hahn and Pinkston are retired lawmen with an interest, so they say, in preserving this exciting period of American history without condoning it. "Offered without social or moral comment it is dedicated to the genuine loss and sorrow on both sides of

the law during Dillinger's 14 months the headlines," reads a brochure they hand out at the museum. But a plaqu on display in the funeral room belies sentiment that is hardly lacking in soci or moral comment: "May the shock a horror of this true-life scene serve as reminder that for the 14 months of ex citement, John Dillinger paid a terrib price."

Bats Incredible

Slugger Park
Hillerich & Bradsby Co., Inc.
1525 Charleston-New Albany Rd.
Jeffersonville, IN 47130
(812) 288-6611

Hours: Mon.-Fri. 8 a.m.-noon and 1-3:30 p.m. (closed last three days in June, first tw

eeks in July, Christmas week, and holidays)
dmission: Free
etting There: Located just east of I-65.
ke the Clementsville-Clarksville exit (Exit 4),
oss Rte. 31-E and the railroad tracks, and
low the signs.

d you know that it takes 200,000
es a year to supply the bats for just
e major league season? Or that Mick-
Mantle's bat measured 35 inches long
d weighed 32 ounces—a full 10
nces lighter and an inch shorter than
be Ruth's? Such scintillating sports
via and much more awaits you at
illerich & Bradsby's Slugger Park.
arting with a baseball and golf memobilia museum, and ending with a tour
the bat- and club-making facilities in
e manufacturing plant, there's plenty
information about players and their
raphernalia.
Hillerich & Bradsby got its start in
ouisville, Kentucky, during the mid-
800s, as "J. F. Hillerich, Job Turning."
illerich's job was turning wood into
dposts, bowling balls, and porch col-
ans. That all changed in 1884 when
s 18-year-old son, John "Bud"
illerich, crafted a bound-for-glory bat
r Pete "The Old Gladiator" Browning
the Louisville Eclipse baseball team.
en years later, the company's famed
ouisville Slugger bat hit the market,
d a batting legend was born. Custom-
ed bats for players like Ty Cobb and
ickey Mantle assured the company a
lace in the annals of sports history,
hile their mass-produced line of bats
ld through hardware and sporting
ods stores kept the company's books
the black. In 1911, an aggressive
orting goods promoter, Frank
radsby, was hired to boost business; he
rned out to be a key player. In 1916,
e same year Bradsby's name was add-

ed to the company's name, a line of golf
clubs, eventually known as Powerbilt,
was added to the company's repertoire.

The history of this bat-and-club company is evident throughout the museum, where early models of bats (some
the original prototypes) and clubs are
displayed, as well as uniforms, records,
and other memorabilia of the athletes
outfitted by Hillerich & Bradsby. Later
additions to the company's product line
displayed here include mitts and batting
gloves.

After seeing the company's past, you
may be surprised to find during the
hour-long plant tour that manufacturing methods haven't changed much in
the past century. You can see the bats
being turned, smoothed, and "brand-
ed" with the company logo, and witness
the crafting of golfing woods and irons.
If you are blessed with good timing, you
may even get a chance to see a bat being
hand-turned for a major league player.
This is an enormous place—about seven
acres in all, and the sheer volume of
bats, clubs, and other products pouring
out of the plant is a true sporting-goods
spectacle.

Iowa

Semi Precious

Antique Truck Museum

Hwy. 65 N.
Mason City, IA 50401
(515) 423-0550

Hours: May 25–Sept. 22, Mon.–Sat. 10:30
a.m.-4 p.m.; Sun. 11 a.m.-6 p.m.
Admission: Adults, $3; children, $1.50
Getting There: The museum is on Hwy. 65
N., 2½ miles north of Mason City. Look for the
Autocar truck-mounted museum sign.

Sometimes, it seems as though every big
city, little town, and shopping mall has
its own antique-car museum. If you're
lucky, there might just be a truck or two

on display as well. But here's a museum
devoted entirely to that workhorse of
the four-wheel set, and a dandy collection it is.

Lloyd Van Horn's auto salvage business eventually led him to collecting and
restoring old trucks, and in 1984, Van
Horn and his wife, Margaret, opened a
museum to display their collection of 60
trucks dating from 1909 to 1930. Most
of the trucks in the collection are rare,
but Lloyd Van Horn says almost 90 percent of them can still go chugging down
the street. Among the trucks on display
are a Winthur-Marwin model used during World War I, a preprohibition
Pierce Arrow whiskey truck, and a 1919
Oldsmobile gasoline truck. The museum also houses a display of old mechan-
ic's tools and gas pumps. Even the sign
identifying the truck museum is unique;
it's mounted on a 1922 Autocar truck.

Flights of Fancy

Balloon Museum

11 N. E St.
P.O. Box 149)
ndianola, IA 50125
515) 961-8415

Hours: Mon.-Fri. 9 a.m.-4 p.m.
Admission: Free; donations accepted
Getting There: Located in Indianola, 20
minutes south of Des Moines on Hwy. 65-69.

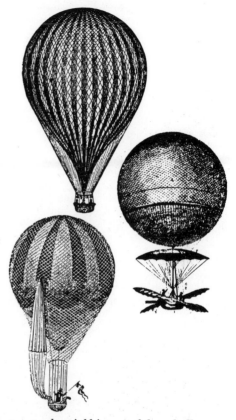

At last, a museum that's full of hot air
and proud of it. (No, it's not a presidential library.) The million-dollar National Balloon Museum has alighted only recently in Indianola, bringing with it the
excitement and beauty of ballooning's
great moments. Balloons were the first
successful and remain the most graceful
of flight methods for earthbound humanity. In keeping with ballooning's
tradition of wonderment, this museum's
collection is filled with enough eye-popping balloons, blood-stirring accounts,
and awe-inspiring memorabilia to make
even jaded museum-goers feel light-
headed.

The National Balloon Museum was
the product of years of memorabilia ac-
cumulation by the National Balloon
Federation, which stored as much as it
could at its own headquarters. Eventually, the federation needed a larger
place to put all the baskets, balloons,
uniforms, and flight logs that kept landing on its doorstep, courtesy of generous
collectors and balloonists. Thus, in
1987, the current museum was born.

Among the rarities in the collection
are ballooning artifacts dating back as
early as 1800, including old gas balloons and baskets. Accounts of record-
setting rides and heart-stopping races
abound, as do artifacts from the mili-

tary and social history of these balloons.
But the most popular exhibit is one that
should logically strike terror in the
hearts of all balloonists: Pins! Lapel
pins, actually, belonging to the pilots
who participate in the Nationals (*the* big
United States balloon competition). The
pins, created in the colors of each balloon, are given to the pilots by the federation; following the race, they are tradi-
tionally donated to the museum. The
collection of lapel pins and other artifacts grows yearly as more and more afi-
cionados contribute their air-looms—
which makes this one of the only museums in the world where inflation keeps
the place afloat.

Rocky Redemption

Grotto of the Redemption

West Bend, IA 50597
(515) 887-2371

Hours: Always visible
Admission: Free; suggested donation of $2 per adult
Getting There: West Bend is in upper central Iowa, northwest of Fort Dodge and midway between Hwy. 18 (to the north) and Hwy. 20 (to the south). Signs for the Grotto abound; it is the town's main industry and attraction.

When Father Paul Doberstein caught a nearly fatal case of pneumonia while a seminary student, he made a promise to the Virgin Mary that if she saved his life he would repay her with a shrine to h memory. He lived, graduated, came t West Bend as a pastor, and, in 1912, s about keeping his promise. He spent 4 years building an enormous grotto-filled shrine out of rocks and semi-precious stones.

The Grotto of the Redemption (fans call it "The Eighth Wonder of the World") is said to be the largest grott in the world. It is actually composed o nine grottoes and has an estimated (b them) geological worth of more than $2.5 million. The grottoes are enormo structures, crusty and sharp-surfaced from the millions of stones and rocks used in the construction. They are fanc ful and jutting tributes to the tenets o the Catholicism that Doberstein contin ued to preach to his congregation fulltime, despite the arduous, year-

round building schedule he set for imself.

The nine grottoes trace the history of Christianity from the Garden of Eden through the life of Christ, with scenic tops along the way at Christ's birth, childhood, adulthood, crucifixion, and resurrection. Each grotto illustrates its theme with a combination of stone statues and rock mosaic backgrounds. Gold-leaf inscriptions throughout add to the aura of ornate jewel artistry that the mixture of stones and rocks projects.

Adjacent to the grotto grounds stands St. Peter and Paul's Church, where Father Doberstein led the congregation until his death in 1954. His finest work is visible here, in the form of the Christmas Chapel, a gem-encrusted nativity scene of intricate and sparkling artistry.

Brazilian amethyst incorporated into the chapel is one of the largest in the world, weighing more than 300 pounds. The amethyst is just one of the truly rare and precious stones that Doberstein gathered or was given, and most of them ended up in the chapel. He chose to preserve the chapel indoors because he feared the delicate jewels would not weather the elements, which, if anything, have given a burnished glaze to the outdoor grottoes.

Father Doberstein traveled extensively to collect the materials for his grotto, which include carbuncle (a red garnet), bloodstone (a green jasper with red spots), amber, emeralds, sapphires, and jade, as well as such natural formations as stalactites, stalagmites, and fossils. His goal in building this giant set of glittering stone grottoes was to leave behind a piece of religious devotion that would last for all time; as he wrote when he was building the Grotto of the Redemption, ". . . IMPERISHABLENESS is the outstanding feature of the Grotto."

Duke's Place

John Wayne Birthplace
224 S. Second St.
(P.O. Box 2)
Winterset, IA 50273
(515) 462-1044

Hours: Dec.-March, daily noon-4 p.m.; April-Nov., daily 10 a.m.-5 p.m.
Admission: Adults, $1; children, 50 cents
Getting There: The birthplace is on S. 2nd St. in Winterset, which is on Rte. 92, just east of Hwy. 169.

It's hard to imagine John Wayne as a squawling infant, but this is where the baby Duke made his first stand. On May 26, 1907, Clyde and Mary Brown Morrison welcomed their bouncing baby cowboy into the world in this little house, commonly known as a "miner's cottage." The home has been restored to its original, turn-of-the-century appearance, complete with authentic fur-

nishings and knickknacks. But if you'd rather not imagine a diapered Duke, there's also a large collection of Wayne memorabilia and photographs on display, including the eye patch he wore in the film "True Grit."

All Washed Up

Maytag Museum
1700 S. 15th Ave. W.
(P.O. Box 834)
Newton, IA 50208
(515) 792-9118

Hours: May 1-Oct. 1, daily 1-5 p.m.
Admission: Adults, $1; children, 50 cents
Getting There: Located at the junction of I-80 and Rte. 14. Take Exit 164 N. and turn right onto Frontage Rd.

If Newton were permanently pressed for funds, this tiny Iowa town could always call on its title as "Washing Machine Center of the World" to pull it through the wringer. Thus, the Maytag Exhibit holds a special place of honor in the up stairs of the Jasper County Historical Museum.

The Maytag Company, long a local Newton business, began churning out its washing machines in 1907. The museum traces the company's history from washboards to modern home appliances; but the strong point of the exhibit is the large collection of early models, most of which bear a striking resemblance to giant ice-cream makers or overturned washtubs. Many of these machines look well-tended, despite their age: their wooden barrel bodies are still smooth and glossy, the metal crank handles still shine a little, and the fancy gold script of the Maytag name against creamy white background has a nostalgic gentility that puts modern logos to shame. Other items from the early twentieth century (candlestick 'phones, a framed newspaper page declaring the end of World War I) are placed here and there to add a sense of technological and historical perspective. Advances in the

shing machine industry over the past
years or so are also explored in the
hibit, as are the birth and growth of
er Maytag products, including
thes dryers, dishwashers, and other
chen appliances.

There was a time when Newton truly
s the Washing Machine Center of the
rld (a fading red banner in the exit room proclaims this fact); aside
m the Maytag Company, there were
ch industry leaders as "Woodrow,"
utomatic," and "One Minute" head-
artered here. But these companies
re washed up years ago; only Maytag
ayed around. When the Jasper County
storical Museum was opened in 1979,
aytag's collection of old washers was
ansferred to the new exhibit facility.
ide from the Maytag displays, the
useum offers other bits of local histo-
, including the registration desk from
e Grand Hotel in Colfax (the center of
sper County's once-booming mineral-
ater vacation industry) and a 40-foot-
ng bas relief of the county's history,
om Indians to industrialization. All
ld, this museum is good, clean fun.

through La Crosse. The museum is in the
Chamber of Commerce building, on the east
side of Main St. Free street parking is
available.

The small town of La Crosse, Kan.,
(population 6,000) has a big reputation
for being the "barbed wire capital of the
world." This unusual claim was staked
in 1971 when the Kansas Barbed Wire
Collectors Association opened the
world's only barbed wire museum in the
heart of this heartland community.

For the estimated 10,000 barbed wire
collectors in the United States and
abroad, as well as the casually curious,
this one-room museum is a treasure
trove of every conceivable kind of
barbed wire and related memorabilia:
500 different types of wire, post-hole
diggers, fence stretchers, and oddities of
nature incorporating barbed wire.

The barbed wire samples, displayed
as mounted 18-inch lengths, include
Nadelhoffer's Parallel barbed wire, pat-

Kansas

Making Points

Barbed Wire Museum

14 Main Street
La Crosse, KS 67548
(913) 222-3116

Hours: Open all year, Mon.-Fri. 1-5 p.m.;
closed weekends and holidays

Admission: Free.

Getting There: U.S. Rte. 183, which cuts
across Kansas, becomes Main St. as it runs

ented in 1884, Stubby's Small-Plate
barbed wire, patented in 1890, and
M.M. Mack 2-Strand, patented in 1875.
Also on display are the tools of the
barbed wire trade, including splicing
gloves and other paraphernalia, as well
as samples of the post rock for which
this region of Kansas is famous.

If a celebration of barbed wire sounds
a bit esoteric in our modern world of
high-tech electronic surveillance and se-

curity systems, consider the importance of barbed wire in the Wild West. The cattle industry created a need for a form of deterrent fencing to keep cantankerous Texas Longhorns contained. The first patents for barbed wire were issued in 1867 to two ingenious easterners, Lucien B. Smith and William Hunt. Although Smith and Hunt never managed to turn a profit on their invention, a herd of other wire designers soon followed. By the 1880s, more than 400 patents had been issued for barbed wire. Barbed wire buffs believe that without the security of these prickly fences, the winning of the West might have been a losing battle.

But all was not quiet on the western front. Indeed, the fencing of the plains led to countless range wars between cattlemen and farmers. The fences

the creation of battlefield and prison camp wires, a legacy that puts some barbed wire collectors on the defens An information flyer created by the Kansas Barbed Wire Collectors Asso tion addresses this problem squarely "Many people dislike barbed wire intensely."

There's also a lighter side to the seum's collection. Indeed, if you ha only a few minutes to view the muse Marlene Woods, Secretary Treasure the La Crosse Chamber of Commer insists that "The one thing in the co tion you've just got to see to believe" 72-pound crow's nest made almost clusively of barbed wire. The nest w

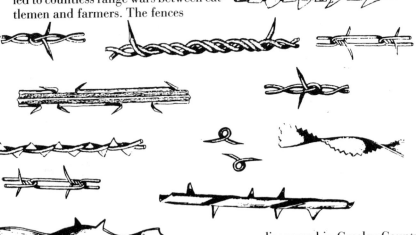

blossomed, turning what had once been open grazing and planting land into the divided domains of a chosen few.

Although barbed wire caused small wars in the late nineteenth century, it became a hideous tool of larger wars during the early twentieth century, with

discovered in Greeley County, a reg of the state with few twig trees suit for nest building. Industrious (and brave!) birds built this sturdy hom over the years by picking away at n by fences. "It's the most remarkab thing," says Woods, noting that the also contains a bucket handle and a "devil's claw," a weed with a seed in the form of clinging talons.

The Kansas Barbed Wire Collectors Association, formed in 1967 by a group of long-time collectors, holds its annual "Swap 'N' Sell" session and the World Champion Barbed Wire Splicing contest in La Crosse during the first weekend in May. The contest, which pits competitors against each other in splicing speed and precision, includes a "powder puff splicing" division for women. The "Swap 'n' Sell" session provides a chance for collectors to get together and talk, trade, and admire barbed wire. The museum is often the focal point of these activities.

Clown Prince

Emmett Kelly Museum

202 E. Main St.
Sedan, KS 67361
(316) 725-3470

Hours: Late May-Labor Day, daily 1-5 p.m.; other times by appointment
Admission: Free; donations appreciated
Getting There: Sedan is in southern Kansas on U.S. Hwy. 166, just east of its intersection with Hwy. 99. The museum is on Main St.

Emmett Kelly was quite possibly the world's greatest clown. His "Wearie Willie" character, sweeping a spotlight around a circus, set the stage for the more "serious" clowns who followed Kelly's lead. Sedan was Kelly's birthplace, and his memory lives on in a three-room collection of artifacts from his clown career and that of his son and namesake, Emmett Kelly, Jr. Visitors will find such memorabilia as the two Kellys' makeup, costumes, and props, as well as photographs and accounts of their clowning achievements.

Lasting Impressions

Fick Fossil Museum

700 W. 3rd
Oakley, KS 67748
(913) 672-4839

Hours: Mon.-Sat. 9:30 a.m.-noon; 1-5 p.m. (in summer, 7-9 p.m.); Sun. 2-4 p.m.
Admission: Free
Getting There: Take the Oakley exits from either I-70, U.S. 40, or 83, and head into town. The museum is on 3rd, between Center and Maple.

Fossil museums tend to be as dull and dry as the pieces of rock on display—but not this one. Earnest and Vi Fick, who lived nearby on a fossil-rich section of Kansas farmland, saw these petrified remains of long-gone creatures as the artistry of nature. Vi, especially, imagined the crafty potential in the fossils, and she turned her finds into mosaics and "paintings" of rare and funny beauty.

Vi took common sites and symbols as her subjects, turning the conventional into the unknown by her use of this strange medium. Take the seals of the United States and Kansas on display in this museum—from far away, they look pretty realistic; step closer and you realize they're made from shark teeth and melted wax. This museum has an entire "Wall of Fossils" that is actually a gallery of Vi Fick's fossil art, from snowy landscapes to a Madonna and Child portrait. Vi was also handy with wood and papier mâché, and her creations in these media are on display in the museum as well. But it's her fossil art that is ageless.

This region's rich soil was once the floor of a vast ocean, populated by sharks and mollusks and other water creatures. The Ficks found 11,000 shark teeth in the Monument Rock area alone. But the Ficks weren't the only ones a-fossiling: George F. Sternberg, a renowned paleontologist, found thousands of specimens here, some of which are displayed in the museum. Many of these fossils are quite rare, and frighteningly big, including a 15-foot-long, 5-foot-wide *Portheus molossus*.

The history part of the museum is not as endearing as Vi's fossil art, but intriguing just the same. Exhibits include a sod house, a replica of an early train station, and artifacts from nearby Fort Monument. A battered pioneer's wagon is displayed against wooden planking

emblazoned with the brands of past a present Kansas cattlemen. There is a a delightful display of framed, presse wildflowers from the region, which brings back to mind Vi's fossil art. There must be something in the soul o Kansan that sees beauty, art, and poet in a thing as close to the earth as a fos or a flower.

Odd Eden

Garden of Eden
2nd and Kansas Ave.
Lucas, KS 67648
(913) 525-6395

Hours: March-Nov., daily until dark; Dec.-Feb., by appointment
Admission: Adults, $4; children 12 and under, free with parent
Getting There: Lucas is located on state Hwys. 18 and 232, 16 miles north of I-70. From Hwy. 232, follow the signs to the garden.

It's probably just a coincidence, but L cas is about 22 miles east of a town called Paradise and 11 miles north of

ek called Hell. Whether that explains
y a strange and whimsical man
med S. P. Dinsmoor decided to build
"Garden of Eden" in his front yard is
yone's guess. But build it he did, out
113 tons of concrete and a bit of wire,
estone, steel, and glass.

Dinsmoor was a decidedly eccentric
an—he married his first wife in 1870
ile on horseback and married his
cond wife in 1924 at the age of 81 (she
s 20); he also spent 20 years of his life
ilding the statue-filled Garden of
len and a mausoleum (for himself and
s first wife). A Civil War veteran and
triot, Dinsmoor held a cynical view of
e twentieth century, and his statue
rden reflected his world-weary
sibilities.

If this is what Eden looked like, it's a
onder Adam and Eve didn't joyfully
ip town. The yard of Dinsmoor's
use is occupied by a trapeze-like ren-
tion of good and evil, with statues

mounted on poles and hugging plat-
forms, clambering onto the roof and
balancing on concrete tree limbs. It's a
wonderland of symbolic figures—evil
bankers, lawyers, preachers, and doctors crucify labor in one segment, while
an enormous "All Seeing Eye of Provi-
dence" surveys the entire garden.
Meanwhile, the "Goddes [sic] of Liberty" atop a tree drives a spear through
the heads of the "Trusts." Elsewhere,
biblical characters—including Adam
and Eve, Cain and Abel, the Devil, and
various angels—dangle, cling, and
perch all around, acting out somewhat
altered versions of their dramatic
stories.

Dinsmoor is said to have been a
haughty individualist who built his
"garden" as a personal statement of his
political and religious views. The whole
effect is like walking into a circus from
Hell, but one with a strangely amusing
sense of society. The human statues are

long, lean, skeletal figures with draping limbs and squared-off faces; the animal statues that scamper among the human figures, though more realistic, are still strangely elongated. On the ground below the concrete lattice-work of sculpted trees, branches, and balancing poles, the yard is landscaped with a more Eden-like setting of flowers, walkways, and birdbaths. But all the creatures hanging from the rafters above detract from any tranquility to be found below.

If this weird array of dangling figures makes you curious about the builder, you can see him here, too. During his lifetime, Dinsmoor built his own mausoleum and casket, and left thorough instructions about how his body was to be preserved after his death. When he died in 1934, his young wife followed his wishes. Dinsmoor lies in state in the crypt of his own making, completely visible through the glass-topped coffin.

Dinsmoor had the showing of his corpse all planned, down to the admission fee. In a booklet he wrote about his Garden of Eden, he describes his final resting place thus: "I have a will that none except my widow, my descendants, their husbands and wives, shall go in to see me for less than a $1 . . . and I promise everyone that comes to see me . . . that if I see them dropping a dollar in the hands of the flunky, and I see the dollar, I will give them a smile."

And, if that delightful promise isn't enough to make you visit, the brochure they give out at this strange site clinches the tourist draw. It states that Lucas, Kansas, is "The only place in the world where you can see the 'Garden of Eden' and buy Brant's Bologna."

Leave the Flying to Them

Greyhound Hall of Fame
407 S. Buckeye
Abilene, KS 67410
(913) 263-3000

Hours: April–Oct., daily 9 a.m.–9 p.m.; Nov.–March, daily 9 a.m.–6 p.m.
Admission: Free; donations appreciated
Getting There: Take I-70 to the Abilene exit and drive south for 2 miles to the museum.

The only buses at this hall of fame are the ones in the parking lot—this place is dedicated to the dog's life instead. Opened in 1973, the Greyhound Hall of Fame honors the canines who are certainly a betting man's best friend. The finest of these sleek, fast hounds are inducted into the Hall of Fame and remembered with exhibits on their race records and performance. There are also displays of racing art, greyhound anatomy, antique ticket machines, greyhound genealogy and breeding charts, mechanical lures (an early one was a stuffed rabbit attached to a motorcycle), and racing footage. A miniaturized track brings the action to itsy-bitsy life, and a real live greyhound is usually on hand for petting and playing. In front of the building, a realistic statue of a greyhound acts as a graceful introduction to the exhibits inside. At Christmastime, the statue gets a dose of the holiday spirit when the museum folks dress it up with a shining nose and fake

...tlers; although Rudolph needn't fear ...e competition, the point is well ...ken—greyhounds may be earth-...und, but put them on a track and they ...re can fly.

...ood Shots

...afari Museum

...South Grant Ave.
...anute, KS 66720
...6) 431-2730

...ours: Mon.-Sat. 10 a.m.-5 p.m.; Sun. 1-5 ...m.
...dmission: Adults, $2.50; students, $1; ...ildren under 12 with an adult, free
...etting There: Take U.S. Hwy. 169 and turn ...ht at the exit for Hwy. 39 (Cherry St.), then ...rn right onto Grant St. There are museum ...gns on the highway.

...artin and Osa Johnson were indeed ...unters—but they shot with cameras,

not guns. This museum, dedicated to their honor, has a lively and stunning collection of photographs, films, and ar- tifacts brought back to Kansas by this daring husband-and-wife team. The Johnsons went on their first photo- graphic safari in 1917 and their last in 1935; between those years their docu- mentaries and adventures brought them worldwide fame and a bit of fortune as well. Many of the photos on display here are preserved in albums, lending a somehow more personal feeling to the collection. A short film is also shown, highlighting some of the Johnsons' best footage, and other exhibits display arti- facts brought back from their voyages to the South Seas, Borneo, and Africa. The museum also houses permanent and changing exhibits on tribal cultures. For those who prefer their lions and tigers on celluloid instead of up against the wall, this is a ferociously fine collection.

Kentucky

Coke's On Them

Coca-Cola Museum

Coca-Cola Bottling Company of
Elizabethtown
1201 N. Dixie Ave.
Elizabethtown, KY 42701
(502) 737-4000

Hours: Mon.-Fri. 9 a.m.-4 p.m.
Admission: Adults, $1; students and senior
citizens, 50 cents
Getting There: The museum is in the Coca-
Cola Bottling Company complex on N. Dixie
Ave. in Elizabethtown, which is just west of
the intersection of I-65 and the Bluegrass
Pkwy.

A pause in this museum will certainly
refresh, especially since you'll be offered
a free Coke when you're through. Located in the ultra-modern Elizabethtown bottling plant (complete with a
glittering lobby fish pond), this little
museum is a bubbly tribute to Coca-Cola's history.

The Schmidt Coca-Cola Museum is
the largest privately owned collection
Coca-Cola memorabilia in the world,
with items dating back to the very daw
of the soft drink era in 1886. One of t
most charming of the early Coke artifacts on display is a clock that advertis
the soft drink as "The Ideal Brain Tor
. . . Delightful Beverage Specified For
Headache . . . Relieves Exhaustion."
There are also old-fashioned seltzer bo
tles used to serve the soda, and the ot
reproduced advertising trays with coy
maidens and handsome youths sippin
sweetly away. A center aisle of the mu
seum is taken up with soda fountain
signs and artifacts, and there is a surprising array of remnants from long-
forgotten advertising campaigns, including chewing gum wrappers, playi
cards, candy boxes, and cigar bands
emblazoned with the familiar white a
red lettering.

Lucky Stuff

Colonel Sanders Museum

Kentucky Fried Chicken International
Headquarters
1441 Gardiner Lane
Louisville, KY 40232-2070
(502) 456-8300

Hours: Mon.-Thurs. 8 a.m.-4:45 p.m.; Fri. 8
a.m.-3 p.m.
Admission: Free
Getting There: The museum is housed in
the company's international headquarters,
just off the Watterson Expwy. (I-264) at
Newburg Rd. S.

The secret to the success of Kentucky
Fried Chicken is no secret: Colonel
Harland Sanders was the main ingredient. At the Kentucky Fried Chicken
Headquarters, the Colonel Harland
Sanders Museum pays homage to the
man and his chicken.

It all began in 1930, with a little roadside restaurant in Corbin, Ky., where
Sanders first perfected his fried chicken
recipe using that "secret blend of 11
herbs and spices." Soon thereafter,
Duncan Hines, the premier food critic of
the times, included Sanders' restaurant
in his book *Adventures in Good Eating*,
and by the 1950s, Sanders and his
chickens were winging it across
America.

Among the artifacts of chicken history on display here are an early pressure
cooker, the dress Sanders' wife Claudia
wore while working as a hostess in his
restaurants, and early television com-
mercials featuring the Colonel at his
pokey best. Visitors will learn that
Sanders was made an honorary colonel
in the mid-1930s by Kentucky Governor Ruby Laffoon in recognition of his
culinary contribution to the state. Art

buffs will delight in the Norman Rockwell portrait of this genteel chicken
man. The museum walls and display
cases are also crowded with city keys,
honorary doctorates, proclamations,
plaques, and awards given to the Colonel in thanks for his philanthropy and
pressure-cooker finesse. Among these is
the award that is said to have been
Sanders' personal favorite: the National
Restaurant Association's Restaurateur
of the Year Award, a chicken-wire
sculpture of a hen laying a golden egg.
It's on display in a special glass case
equipped with a button that, when
pushed, activates the sculpture to turn
this way and that.

Although this museum is fairly small,
the tough and tender personality of Colonel Sanders and the empire he built is
evident throughout. It's definitely worth
crossing the road to see.

Still Life

Jim Beam's Outpost

Clermont, KY 40110
(502) 543-9877

Hours: Mon.-Sat. 9 a.m.-4:40 p.m.; Sun. 1-4
p.m.
Admission: Free
Getting There: The complex is about 22
miles south of Louisville. To get there, take
Southbound I-65 (Kentucky Turnpike) to Hwy.
245 (Exit 112, for Bardstown/Bernheim
Forest). Turn left and head 1 1/2 miles to the
Outpost.

In 1964, Congress passed an act that officially named bourbon America's native spirit. But Jacob Beam recognized
the value of a good shot more than a
century and a half earlier when, in

1795, he began making the bourbon whiskey that was to win renown and infamy under the Jim Beam label. Today, at the James B. Beam Distilling Company's Clermont distillery, whiskey is the spiritual inspiration for this tourist spot devoted to acquainting visitors with the story and glory of Kentucky bourbon.

The Jim Beam people have covered all the bases at their American Outpost; attractions range from educational audio-visual presentations to historically significant, if eccentric, exhibits, such as the world's only complete collection of Jim Beam decanters and the "Oldest Still in America."

The best way to drink in all this whiskey history is to start at the beginning, by watching a movie that takes you step-by-step through the manufacturing process of Jim Beam. The film's narrator, Booker Noe (who happens to be Jacob Beam's great-great-great grand son), is the Master Distiller at the Clermont distillery. The film is worth watching if for no other reason than, a the Jim Beam folks so aptly describe, " includes footage of several impossible-to-get-to places, such as the inside of mash cooker."

After you've been enlightened abou the inner workings of mash cookers, it on to the world of whiskey. The Hartman Cooperage Museum features painstakingly reproduced nineteenth-century barrel-making shop. All the accoutrements—from carefully restore cooper's tools and rare machines (the dual-headed horizontal boring machir is considered highly unusual) to the shop's original accounting ledgers—a here for your viewing pleasure.

Next, take a gander at that old still. [On]e of the country's first "moonshine" [stil]ls, it's more aged than any yet to be [fou]nd in the foothills or valleys of Amer[ica]'s whiskey land.

[A]n equally rare find is the display of [Roy]al China Decanters. Featuring more [tha]n 500 beautiful and wittily designed [ves]sels, this is said to be the only com[plet]e collection anywhere. It's a treat to [see] how many symbols of American life [hav]e been transformed into whiskey [con]tainers over the years. There are de[can]ters of covered wagons, antique [gu]ns, and vintage cars. Fish and fowl, [flor]a and fauna, even the Yellow Rose of [Tex]as are represented here, as are such [Ind]ustrial Revolution icons as cable cars [and] early telephones. And if you [tho]ught it was finally safe to go back in [the] Empire State Building, think (or [thin]k) again: King Kong has his own [bott]le. So does Mortimer Snerd, for that [ma]tter. Is nothing sacred?

Funny Lady

Lily Tomlin Gallery

Chez Tomlin
207 Broadway
Paducah, KY 42001
(502) 442-6511

Hours: Mon.-Sat. 10 a.m.-5 p.m.
Admission: Free
Getting There: From I-24, take Exit 4 to U.S. Hwy. 60, which leads directly into Paducah. The gallery is on Broadway, in the heart of town.

Lily Tomlin isn't just one of America's favorite comediennes, she's also the funniest thing that ever happened to Paducah. If you're a Tomlin fan, you'll want to stop by for a visit at Chez Tomlin. Owned and run by Tomlin's family, Chez Tomlin is a tea room and gift/flower shop that's also got a gallery of memorabilia from Lily's career. If you arrive at Chez Tomlin on Thursday through Saturday between noon and 4 p.m., you're in for an even bigger treat: Tomlin's mother, Lilly Mae Tomlin, will be glad to escort you on a personally guided tour of the gallery.

Among the mementos on display are Edith Ann's original oversized rocking chair and a life-size mannequin of Tomlin's famous telephone operator, Ernestine. (A historical note for TV trivia buffs: the Ernestine mannequin was made by Today Show film critic Gene Shalit's daughter). Also included on the three- to four-minute tour (okay, so the gallery is a little small) are several of Lily's costumes, including one from her smash Broadway show, "The Search for Signs of Intelligent Life in the Universe." After seeing the gallery, settle down for a bite to eat in the tea room, where tiny Christmas lights twinkle year-'round—sort of like Tomlin herself.

Drink It Up

Whiskey Museum
Spalding Hall
114 N. Fifth St.
Bardstown, KY 40004
(502) 348-2999

Hours: Nov.-April, Tues.-Sat. 10 a.m.-4 p.m.;
Sun. 1-4 p.m.; May-Oct., Mon.-Sat. 9 a.m.-5
p.m.; Sun. 1-5 p.m.
Admission: Free
Getting There: The museum is in Spalding
Hall on N. Fifth St., just north of U.S. Hwy.
62W as it runs through Kentucky.

Bardstown's Spalding Hall, once the site
of the first Catholic men's college in
Kentucky, is nowadays home to a thoroughly different form of spiritual
devotion—the study and preservation of
whiskey history. The Oscar Getz Museum of Whiskey History opened here in
1984, and displays a collection of whiskey artifacts gathered over a 50-year
period by the late Oscar Getz. A local
businessman who died in 1983, Getz
was so drunk with the joy of collecting
that he gathered items from as far away
as Connecticut (the original permit,
dated 1759, used to sell liquor in that
colony is on display) and as far back as
pre-Colonial times. There are hundreds
of rare bottles and jugs on exhibit, as
well as early pieces of advertising art,
Prohibition posters, a moonshine still
captured by the Internal Revenue Service, and a Carrie Nation display. There's
even an original 1854 bottle of E.C.
Booz whiskey, yielding the word
"booze," and a barroom display with
weird and wacky novelty decanters and
shot glasses.

Also housed in Spalding Hall is the
somewhat more sober Bardstown Historical Museum, which has the same

hours and free admission and displa
such local artifacts as memorabilia fr
the life of Stephen Foster, the will of
John Fitch (inventor of the steamboa
and a velvet cape and antique jewelr
worn by Swedish Nightingale Jenny
Lind, who flew in for a song or two lo
ago. Either museum represents a fin
way to drink in local history and lege

Michigan

Tiny Timber

Iron County Museum
100 Museum Rd.
(P.O. Box 272)
Caspian, MI 49915
(906) 265-2617

Hours: May and Sept., Mon.-Sat. 10 a.m.-
p.m.; Sun. 1-4 p.m.; June-Aug., Mon.-Sat.
a.m.-5 p.m.; Sun. 1-5 p.m.; other times by
appointment
Admission: $1.50; family pass, $3.50
Getting There: Located about 2 miles so
of U.S. 2 (exit for Iron River) on Hwy. 424. A
the exit, turn left up Stambaugh Hill and
follow Washington Ave. through Stambau
to 19th St. At the end of the street (about thr
blocks), turn right onto Lincoln, which merg
into Brady. The museum is on the left in a
large park.

The Iron County Museum is an enormous folk history and art complex fill
with old mining equipment, mill tool
rebuilt log cabins, and pioneer life
displays—but the most famous and
amazing things here are the Monigal
Logging Miniatures. This display, ma
up of 15 major scenes, is considered

e the largest single set of hand-carved
iniature logging equipment in the
orld. While it's a title that few artisans
e carving away to beat, it is an awe-
me spectacle nonetheless.

The miniatures were carved by for-
er lumberman William Monigal, who
as disabled in a 1931 sawmill acci-
nt. Monigal spent the next eight-and-
half years of his life whittling away
ith a jackknife at old utility poles. He
eated more than 2,000 tiny tools, peo-
e, and animals to illustrate the lumber
ocess, all carved at a scale of one inch
one foot. Landscapes filled with real-
ic-looking "snow" and tiny trees help
sh out the story of the lumber indus-
. A little logging camp bustles with
mberjacks and animals, while, in an-
her scene, the logs are carefully float-
downstream to a waiting sawmill.
om the camp cook to the bark peeler,
ery job and aspect of the lumber in-
stry is painstakingly reproduced.

But for all the minute realism of
onigal's Miniatures, he didn't forget
little men's favorite tall tale: a larg-
-than-miniature-life Paul Bunyan
vers above a group of tiny loggers, his
de grin and bristly beard carved with
ectionate care.

agical History Tour

useum of Magic

E. Michigan Ave.
rshall, MI 49068
6) 781-7666

urs: Sat. 10 a.m.-5 p.m.; Sun. and Tues.-
1-5 p.m.; other times by appointment
mission: General, $2 (children under 16
st be accompanied by adult)

AMERICAN MUSEUM of MAGIC

COLOSSAL COLOSSUS OF CONJURING CULTURE

Presents
on the inside for the

Entertainment! Enlightenment!

of come-who-may
Temple of Thaumaturgy
Legerdemain, Hocus-Pocus & Abracadabra
consisting of
MEMENTOES, RELICS,
MEMORABILIA
SOUVENIRS & APPARATUS
of all the
Prominent Professors of
PRESTIDIGITATION
of all time
dating from 1584 to the present.
Arranged to set the senses at defiance!

The whole encompassing both the ground floor and upper
auditorium of the establishment, which a benevolent management, more concerned with the comfort of its clientele
than with paltry profit, has arranged to

Heat in the winter!   Ventilate in the summer!

Free smelling salts to ladies and small children overcome
by the Grandeur of the Notional Whimsies, Cabalistic
Surprises, Phantasmagorical Bewilderments and Unpar-
alleled Splendors displayed within.

Acclaimed by both Press & Pulpit as
Refined & Moral

Collected and assembled by Elaine and Robert Lund from
the most remote corners of civilization's wide domain.

EXHIBITING DAILY, SAVE MONDAY.

No idle bombast at this place.

A Berlinski and Son. Printers by Steam Power

Getting There: The museum is on E. Michigan Ave. in the heart of Marshall, located at the intersection of I-69 and I-94, midway between Detroit and Chicago.

Before you enter the portals of this magical, Victorian building in downtown Marshall, empty your pockets of all your doubts, cynicisms, and worldly cares—bring only your wide eyes and wonder. The American Museum of Magic is like a giant jewelry box filled with hypnotic baubles, endless scarves, trick ropes, cards, and all the other tools of the magician's trade.

The museum was conjured up in 1978 by a collector named Robert Lund, a lifelong magic nut and award-winning journalist whose own home began disappearing under the weight of his collection. Lund and his wife Elaine run the museum as an act of love, taking visitors on 90-minute tours through their maze of amazement. Virtually every conceivable angle of the magic world dating back from 1584 to the present is covered here, from 350 magic kits, 25,000 magician's letters, and almost 3,000 original magic show posters from all over the world, to the Houdini Magical Hall of Fame, which has the giant milk can the great prestidigitator used in one of his most famous escapes. There are also displays of props used in the perenially appealing lady-sawing trick, and a "girl without a middle" disappearing tummy box that remains popular with visitors.

But don't expect to have all your questions answered and your illusions shattered here. Lund is quick to point out that wonder is an essential part of magic, and magic of wonder. "We are all born with a sense of wonder," he says, "but as we grow older, that sense tends to diminish. Magicians give it back."

Minnesota

Just What the Doctor Ordered

Doll Hospital
22 Greenway Ave. N.
Oakdale, MN 55119
(612) 739-1131

Hours: Mon.-Sat. 9 a.m.-5 p.m.
Admission: $2
Getting There: From I-94, take the exit at Century Ave. junction, drive east half a mi on Frontage St./Madison Blvd. to Greenw Ave. N.; the museum is 6 miles east of the State Capitol.

What's a doll to do? For those in need a hair transplant, a hand or two, or ev a complete body makeover, there's n place like "Antie Clare's" doll hospit Clare Erickson, who presides over a d repair business, shop, and museum, h a memorable approach to mannequi she treats them almost like people. Af all, she says that's how children trea them. The repair people in the work shop are known as "doctors," and th exhibits in her 20-scenario museum displayed in "real-life" doll situation like the Saturday night bath or Sund tea party. There are rare and not-so-rare dolls, from Barbies to bisque, an whole section of baby dolls that virtu ly overflows with bald-headed beaut Erickson also offers birthday parties children, who invite their friends an their friends' dolls for an afternoon dress-up, refreshments, even flu shot (for the dolls) administered by the h pital staff.

Million Dollar Babies

rdseye View

olly Green Giant Statue

lly Green Giant Statue Park
ue Earth Area Chamber of Commerce
1 N. Main St.
ue Earth, MN 56013
07) 526-2916

ours: Always visible
dmission: Free
tting There: Blue Earth, in the
uthernmost part of Kansas, can be reached
m I-90 (Exit 119); the statue stands in its
n park and is visible from the interstate.

-Ho-Ho! The valley of the Jolly
een Giant welcomes you, and wants
u to drop in for a visit. The bait? This
nt Giant, who stands 55 feet above
hometown, little Blue Earth. (Motto:

"The earth so rich the city grows.") The
jolly big statue acts as a virtual magnet
to tourists cruising along on nearby I-
90; after all, who could resist a closer
look at the Great Green One?

The Green Giant statue was originally
conceived as a tourism drawing card in
1978. It didn't take long to raise the
money from the eager town folk, and in
the summer of 1979 the statue was dedicated. Jolly cost only $43,000 to build,
a giant bargain as most tourist attractions go. But there was no skimping on
construction: Built from fiberglass, he
weighs in at 8,000 pounds and is painted in two tones of green. He wears size
78 shoes on his 6-foot-long feet, and his
ear-of-creamed-corn-to-ear-of-
creamed-corn grin stretches a dazzling
48 inches.

Minnesota Vikings

Kensington Runestone and Viking Statue

Alexandria Chamber of Commerce
206 North Broadway
Alexandria, MN 56308
(612) 763-3161

Hours: Runestone Museum: May-Sept., Mon-Sat. 8 a.m.-5 p.m.; Sun. 10 a.m.-5 p.m.; Oct.-April, Mon.-Fri. 8 a.m.-5 p.m. (closed weekends); statue always visible
Admission: Free
Getting There: Alexandria is in central Minnesota, on Hwy. 29, just east of I-94 (Exit 103). The statue stands in downtown, and the museum is in the Chamber of Commerce building on N. Broadway.

Is Alexandria really the "birthplace of America?" Alexandrians seem to think so. While this is a pretty vague and lofty claim, the town does have two historical things going for it: the Kensington Runestone and the World's Largest Viking Statue.

America probably wasn't born here but it *was* probably visited during its childhood (in the midfourteenth century) by some big blond Norsemen with battle axes who dropped in for a visit and left their calling stone on the site of a future farm near Alexandria.

In 1898, a pioneer farmer, Olaf Ohmen, pried a large stone from the roots of an Aspen tree on his property. The stone, a piece of Greywack rock, measures 31 inches high, 16 inches wide, and six inches thick. It weighs 202 pounds, and is thought to be one of the common 200-pound ballast stones used in Viking ships. The stone's carved runic lettering was not easily deciphered at first, but eventually the message was identified as having been written in the Norse language, and a translation was made. Dubbed the Kensington Runestone, this Viking postcard to future generations reads:

> "8 Goths and 22 Norwegians on exploration journey from Vinland over the West We had camp by 2 skerries one days journey north from this stone We were and fished one day after we came home [found] 10 red with blood and dead Ave Maria Save from Evil . . . Have 10 of our party by sea to look after our ships 14 days journey from this island Year 1362."

The runestone is Alexandria's pride and joy, and was a big hit at the New York World's Fair of 1964 before coming back for its permanent resting place

wn museum housed in the Chamber
Commerce building. Visitors can
k right up and stare at the big carved
k, which is housed in a special glass
e and flanked by exhibits showing
suspected routes and artifacts of the
ing venturers. Other highlights in
museum include local artifacts such
he fourth Arctic Cat Snowmobile
r made and a 1914 Fordson Tractor.
pite this competition, the Runestone
till the winner in the antique
artment.

lthough there has never been any
olutely conclusive evidence that the
estone isn't an imitation, there have
n plenty of semiendorsements, in-
ding one from a Smithsonian expert
o stated that there was more evidence
avor of the stone than against it. And
s not forget that in 1909, the Minne-
lis Norwegian Society Commission
ed 2 to 1 that the stone was authen-
Records found in Europe back up
long-held Viking explorer theory
h clear evidence that a 1354 expedi-
n, led by a Sir Paul Knutson, was
missioned by King Magnus. Other
dence links eight members of this
ty with a later expedition, dated
66, that was led by the group's navi-
or, Nicholas of Lynn.

listory is dandy, but the stone is ac-
lly pretty undramatic-looking. So, in
ossible fit of Viking vanity, the town
ted "Big Ole," the largest Viking
ue in the world. Ole, who accompa-
d the stone to the World's Fair and
v presides over the town at the north
l of Broadway, stands a mighty 28
tall and weighs a majestic 2,000
nds. He appears cheery enough,
h a yellow and red outfit that brings
the silver in his beard, winged hel-
t, and spear tip. Ole's shield pro-

claims "Alexandria Birthplace of America," which is undoubtedly the very
slogan the original Vikings painted on
their own shields so many centuries ago.

Missouri

Shining Shrine

Black Madonna Shrine
Eureka, MO 63025
(314) 938-5361

Hours: Daily 8 a.m.-8 p.m.
Admission: Free
Getting There: Take I-44 to the Eureka exit,
drive 8 miles south on Hwy. F-F to the shrine,
or take the Pacific exit and drive 8 miles south
on Hwy. F to the shrine.

Creating religious shrines from seashells, stones, and costume jewelry must
have been quite the vogue during the
midtwentieth century, as witnessed by
all the glittering, glistening, twinkling,
entrancing grottoes and shrines built
during that time. None, perhaps, is
more eclectic—or charming—than the
Black Madonna Shrine and Grottoes,
just outside Eureka.

Brother Bronislaus Luscze, founder of
the Franciscan Order of Brothers in this
country, used everything from rhine-
stone brooches to cupcake molds to
make his devout dream come true during the last two years of his life. After
emigrating to America from Poland in
1927, Brother Bronsilaus noticed that
there was no shrine in this country for
his homeland's beloved Black Madonna
portrait. So he built the nation's first

Black Madonna Shrine in a cedar chapel with an outdoor altar in 1938. The original Black Madonna (also known as Our Lady of Czestochowa), cherished as a national and religious treasure in Poland, is said to have been painted during the lifetime of the Virgin Mary by St. Luke, who used as a canvas a wooden tabletop made by St. Joseph. As legend has it, infidels tried to burn the painting in the fifth century, but instead of destroying the work, the flames merely darkened the hands and the face of the Madonna. Similar attacks throughout the centuries have also failed, giving the painting an indestructable reputation.

Unfortunately, the same could not be said of Brother Bronislaus' shrine, which was destroyed by vandals 20 years after it was built. The Brother immediately built a new one, and then set about beautifying the surrounding grounds with unusual grottoes and sculptures. In 1958, his fruitful work began in earnest.

Bronislaus' main materials were concrete, barite rock, seashells, stones, costume jewelry, and other ornamental objects. He cleared the land around the rebuilt shrine, which stands in the foothills of the Ozark Mountains, without the help of mechanical tools. For want of a nearby water supply, Bronislaus hand-carried oil drums filled with water to mix the cement. It was a labor of love, and, during the two short years before his death in 1960, Brother Bronislaus constructed monuments depicting the Stations of the Cross, the Joyful Mysteries of the Rosary, and seven full grottoes, honoring Our Lady of Perpetual Help, St. Joseph, Gethsemani, St. Francis, Nativity, Assumption-Coronation, and Our Lady of Sorrows.

The shapes and ornaments in these sites are a delight—rabbits and other creatures at the Nativity Grotto were made from cake molds, the bases of monuments are implanted with ornate earrings and brooches, and "tulips" shaped from cupcake molds grow from Jello-mold planters—each little cornice, flourish, angle, and shape taking a delightful life of its own from the imaginative use of materials and tools.

Bronislaus had just finished clearing the land for his next grotto, honoring Our Lady of Fatima, when he died. He could not have imagined his work would be finished so suddenly, with only two years of effort expended, but the Franciscan Missionary Brothers who watch over the shrine and grottoes take loving care of them, maintaining the grounds and accepting donations of art and money to keep the place going. The Black Madonna Shrine and Grottoes has grown into a favorite pilgrimage for serious religious travelers to this region. But even those just out for a smile will find a pleasant respite here in the Ozark foothills, where the cupcake flowers grow.

Memories to Spare

Bowling Hall of Fame

111 Stadium Plaza
St. Louis, MO 63102
(314) 231-6340

Hours: Memorial Day-Labor Day, daily 9 a.m.-7 p.m.; fall-spring, Mon.-Sat. 9 a.m.-5 p.m.; Sun. noon-5 p.m.
Admission: Adults, $3; children, $1.50; senior citizens, $2
Getting There: Located in downtown St. Louis, a few blocks from the Gateway Arch, the museum stands at the corner of Walnut and 8th St., next to Busch Stadium. Hwys. 40, 44, 55, and 70 converge within a few blocks of the stadium.

As sports museums go, the National Bowling Hall of Fame and Museum is really quite striking. It's new enough (it opened in 1984) to have been designed with fun in mind, and large enough (three levels, with 50,000 square feet of exhibit space) to cover the history of the game and its great players without mak-ing visitors feel as if they're pinned against the wall.

Aside from the Hall of Fame collec-tions of trophies, champions' portrait and live footage from the Womens In-ternational Bowling Congress and American Bowling Congress, there ar also a number of very interactive exhi

ts. Old and new alleys, side-by-side, allow museum-goers to try out 90-year-
old lignum vitae balls on 1920s lanes
(with real live pinboys setting 'em up),
and then switch to modern lanes showcasing "the latest in bowling technology." And the "Star Talk" exhibit is a
high-tech video board where visitors
can select interviews and clips of their
favorite bowlers. Even the less stellar
stars are represented in an exhibit,
"Hometown Heroics," with a comput-
erized store of information on local and
state Hall of Famers, every known
bowler who has recorded a 300 game,
and unusual bowling facts or events that
have occurred around the country.

The "Tenpin Alley" exhibit takes visitors down a tour of memory's lanes,
with a look back at the earliest forms of
bowling (a child's game from 5,200
B.C. found in an Egyptian tomb),
through the Dutch game of nine-pin
that was introduced into the United
States by immigrants, up to the modern
world of tournament and family bowling. A display of unusual and rare balls
and pins shows the variations the game
has seen over the centuries, and there's
even a tribute to the pinboys of that bygone era before automatic pin setters
revolutionized the game.

Hwy. 54 to the Rte. F exit, turn left onto Rte. F
and proceed to Westminster Ave. Turn left on
Westminster to the memorial, which is on the
campus of Westminster College at the
intersection of 7th St. and Westminster Ave.

inston's Church

hurchill Memorial

estminster College
ton, MO 65251
4) 642-6648

urs: Mon.-Sat. 10 a.m.-4:30 p.m.; Sun.
30-4:30 p.m.

mission: Adults, $2; senior citizens, $1.50;
dren 12 and under, free

tting There: From I-70, go west on U.S.

Missouri seems an odd place to find a
memorial to Winston Churchill, but
here it is. On the campus of Westminster
College, housed in a reconstructed
church building (the Church of St.
Mary, once located in Aldermanbury,
England), the memorial honors the life
of one of England's most famous prime
ministers. The museum exhibits Churchill memorabilia galore, including letters, manuscripts, and photographs, as
well as paintings by Churchill and other
artworks created by his daughter, Sarah, and granddaughter, Edwina. Other

No Bones About It

Osteopathic Museum

311 S. Fourth St.
Kirksville, MO 63501
(816) 626-2359

Hours: Mon. 8-11 a.m.; Tues.-Fri. 8 a.m.-3 p.m.
Admission: Free
Getting There: The museum is on S. Fourth St., on the campus of the Kirksville College of Osteopathic Medicine, which is just west of U.S. Hwy. 63 (City) as it runs through Kirksville

Osteopathy, the art of readjusting the musculoskeletal structure through manipulation of the body frame, is still a controversial form of medical treatment. Nonetheless, Kirskville is proud of its status as the "Birthplace of Osteopathic Medicine," a fact that stems from the town being the birthplace of Dr. A. T. Still, father of osteopathic medicine

The Still National Osteopathic Museum is on the campus of the Kirksville College of Osteopathic Medicine, founded by Still in 1892. It exhibits artifacts from the early days of osteopathy, including textbooks and implements, as well as items from Still's life. Among the more recent and prized additions to the museum is a hand-embroidered linen pillow case, autographed by Still, his two sons, H. M. and Charles, his daughter, Blanche, and the December 1898 and February and April 1899 faculty and classes of the American School of Osteopathy. The museum folks are so proud of it that they have had it framed and "suspended from the ceiling in the Museum Library for the convenience of our visitors for better viewing." With this kind of display, it could well become the most famous case in osteopathic history.

displays include a scale model of Blenheim Palace, a rare map collection, and a look at the life and work of Christopher Wren, architect of this transplanted church that was partially destroyed during World War II. Also located at the college is a comprehensive library with materials on Churchill and his times.

Churchill visited Westminster College in 1946, and it was here that he delivered his now-famous "Iron Curtain" speech about the Soviet domination of Eastern Europe. The memorial was opened in the mid-1960s to commemorate (better late than never) that historic Missouri visitation. Funny thing, though—the building kind of smells like cigar smoke inside.

Nebrasska

ez Who?

Liars' Hall of Fame

3 Mill St.
P.O. Box 172)
Dannebrog, NE 68831
308) 226-2307

Hours: Mon.-Sat. 9 a.m.-1 a.m.; Sun. noon-9
.m.

Admission: Free

Getting There: Dannebrog is on Hwy. 58,
0 miles west of Hwy. 281. The hall of fame is
n the town's main drag, Mill St.

he National Liars' Hall of Fame is
oused in a glistening monolith of Ital-
n marble, with stained-glass windows
d solid-gold stairs. It cost about $2
illion to build, and has won every
nown architectural award in the west-
rn world. And if you believe that, I've
t this great piece of swampland down
Florida for sale, cheap.

Truth be told (and it needn't be here),
e National Liars' Hall of Fame is a
nall but hilarious trip down "I-have-
faulty-memory" lane. It was estab-
hed in Dannebrog in 1986 at the
wn's gourmet dining establishment,
ic's Big Table Tavern, by Roger
elsch and Eric Nielsen. Their purpose,
Welsch puts it: "To recognize and
omote America's second most popular
door sport, lying." In the spirit of this
norable goal, the hall of fame's "Li-
s Gallery" exhibits such mendacious
ementos as a jackalope, fishing li-
nses, and photographs of Presidents
hnson and Nixon. A lie detector facili-
is in the developmental stages and
ould be operational by, say,
norrow.

Membership in the Liars' Hall of

Fame has its privileges—in 1987, for
example, there was a 5,000-millimeter
marathon, and just last month there
were lavish dinner dances on Adnan
Kashoggi's yacht and lectures by Oliver
North and Gary Hart. But the most
prized perk of all is the official "National Liars' Hall of Fame Coupon Book,"
with coupons for a year's free parking in
Dannebrog ("Place this coupon on your
windshield wiper while parking in
Dannebrog for the meter maid's convenience") valued at $100, and $1 off
on Welsch's "famous combination stink
bait and sandwich spread" ("At Home
in Your Tackle Box or Lunch Box").
Nomination packets can be had for a
mere $2.95 by writing to the Liars' Hall
of Fame at the above address. (It's okay
to nominate yourself. Just don't lie on
the application form.)

If you have your doubts about driving
all the way to Dannebrog just to take in
the National Liars' Hall of Fame, never
fear. According to Roger Welsch, there's
another *big* attraction in town as well:
"The nation's only Sasquatch preserve
. . ." Bet it tastes good with peanut but-
ter, eh, Roger?

The Skin Trade

Museum of the Fur Trade

U.S. Hwy. 20
(HC 74, Box 18)
Chadron, NE 69337
(308) 432-3843

Hours: June-Labor Day, daily 8 a.m.-6 p.m.
Admission: Adults, $1; children free if with
parents, 15 cents if alone
Getting There: The museum is on U.S. Hwy.
20, 3 miles east of Chadron.

American fur trading dates back to the early colonial days, when bold trappers disappeared into uncharted wilds, staying for months at a time to trap animals and trade with the Indians. The Museum of the Fur Trade, devoted to preserving the history of this early commerce, has a vibrant and expansive collection showing all facets of the fur trade from colonial times to the present.

Aside from trapping equipment and actual furs (and there are many here, from badger and beaver to wolf and sea otter), there are a number of Indian artifacts, weapons, trade goods (beads, cloths, and trinkets). One particularly rare and compelling exhibit displays a robe of painted buffalo hide tanned by Indians and dates back to 1840. Elsewhere on the museum grounds a restored 1837 trading post is open to the public, and an Indian-style garden grows native American plants.

The museum is a well-lighted, pine-paneled place with exhibits set into glass-fronted alcoves. While the subject matter may not appeal to everyone, there are enough nonfur things to see here to make it a worthwhile and educational excursion in the Nebraska countryside.

On a Roll

Roller Skating Museum
7700 A St.
Lincoln, NE 68501
(402) 489-8811

Hours: Mon.-Fri. 9 a.m.-5 p.m.
Admission: $1
Getting There: The museum is on A St. or the far east side of Lincoln, at the corner of 77th St. The Capital Parkway runs across A S at S. 33rd St.

s is no rinky-dink museum. It
ned in 1980 and has been merrily
ing along to praise and hurrahs ever
ce. For everyone who's ever strapped
a pair of skates and hit (in more ways
n one) the pavement or rink floor for
in or two, this is a museum filled
h universal memories and little-
wn facts.

lthough skates had been around
ce the late eighteenth century, their
hibitive expense and awkward ma-
iverability limited their use at first to
atrical productions and recreation
the rich. But when the year 1863
ed in, an inventor named James
npton introduced the cheap and easy
cking skate," and an international
took off. By the early twentieth cen-
y, official skating organizations in
rope and the United States were
king rules and sponsoring champi-
hips for a whole generation of big
eelers.

he National Museum of Roller Skat-
documents the history of skating
m these early days right up to the
sent with exhibits of advertisements,
ates old and new, profiles of great
aters, and plenty of other items
wned by the skating culture. A col-
tion of personal scrapbooks from
licated skaters provides a sweet and
ing history of this wholesome sport,
h programs, tickets, and favorite
otographs. A display of antique skate
vs will send anyone who grew up with
ttes whizzing right back down memo-
sidewalk.

Plenty of memories are stirred by the
l rink signs and instructors' uniforms,
t the past is just the beginning
re—recent trophies, the perfor-
nces of current champions, and the
ssible future of skating in America are

displayed and explored as well. There's
no better place to learn about the role
skates have played in history—or the
wheels of fortune to come.

Time Warp

Warp's Pioneer Village
Minden, NE 68959
(800)-445-4447 (in NE: 308-832-1181)

Hours: Daily 8 a.m.-sundown
Admission: Adults, $4; children, $2
Getting There: Located 12 miles south of I-
80 at Exit 279. State Hwy. 10, U.S. 6, and U.S.
34 also have exits for the vilage. Signs
abound.

From bathtubs to telephones, swords to
ploughshares, Harold Warp's Pioneer
Village offers visitors a panoramic look
at "The Story of America and How It
Grew." Well—maybe not the early story
of America (this tale starts in 1830) or
even the entire story (the Industrial
Revolution is the main focus here). But
who cares, when an entire village of general stores, schoolhouses, churches, and
Pony Express stations spilling over with
bicyles, washing machines, toys,
snowmobiles, airplanes, carousels, and
steam trains stretches as far as the eye
can see? This is the story of America as

told by its material possessions and motorized obsessions.

Warp opened his Pioneer Village in 1953 as a way of preserving large and usually unwieldy chunks of America's heritage in one enormous complex. His idea began with the sale in 1948 of the little schoolhouse he had attended when he was young. Warp figured if someone could buy and sell schoolhouses, then most of the rest of America's architectural and mechanical inheritance might go on the block as well. He wanted to gather as much of it as he possibly could. Although he may not have gotten everything he wanted, he certainly got enough: Pioneer Village has some 30,000 objects housed in 24 buildings, sprawling over a 20-acre area. A motel, campground, and restaurant are also on hand, for those who can't drag themselves away after a mere day; one admission is good for as many days as you want to stay.

It's an eclectic collection, a gathering of every object imaginable. Among the historic buildings Warp had imported his village and restored are the original Bloomington Land Office, a Fire House a Pony Express station, and a Wild West Fort. And there are 26 "craft shops of the past," including a cooperage, a broommaker's shop, and a blacksmith shop. There are also 21 model kitchens and other rooms dating from 1830 to 1980. Other buildings overflow with collections of speedboats, fishing lures antique china, guns, cars, toys, outboard motors, musical instruments, steam engines, home appliances, farm machinery, the entire "snowmobile evolution: from earliest to modern machines," lighting implements, and motorcyles. One building, known as the "Hobby House," is a complete museum in itself, stuffed with all sorts of collectables from hatpins to trivets.

Perhaps the best explanation of the

ogic behind this vast collection comes
rom Warp himself, as displayed on a
ablet over the main entrance to Pioneer
Village:

"For thousands of years man lived
quite simply. Then, like a sleeping
giant, our world was awakened. In
a mere hundred and twenty years
of eternal time, man progressed
from open hearths, grease lamps,
and ox carts to television, super-
sonic sound, and atomic power.
We have endeavored to show you
the actual development of this astounding progress as it was un-
folded by our forefathers and by
ourselves . . . ."

North Dakota

An Odyssey of Homers

Roger Maris Museum

West Acres Shopping Center
Fargo, ND 58103
(701) 282-2552

Hours: Mon.-Sat. 10 a.m.-9 pm.; Sun. 9:30
am.-7 p.m.
Admission: Free
Getting There: Located in the West Acres
Shopping Center, just off I-29 (Exits 64 or 63),
13th Ave. S.

Everywhere you turn around here,
there's another reminder of Fargo's favorite son of swat, Roger Maris. There's
a Roger Maris Drive, a Roger Maris Memorial, and the Roger Maris
Gardens—but most impressive of all is
the Roger Maris Museum, tucked away
in a sprawling shopping mall.

It's not exactly a walk-in kind of
place—the entire exhibit is housed in a
72-foot-long glass showcase that runs
along a wall in the mall. But this exhibit
has about as much Maris memorabilia
as any fan would ever dare to dream
about. Opened in 1984, one year before
Maris' death, the museum has 150 of his
personal belongings and awards, which
are exhibited on a rotating basis.

Maris' high school football uniform is
here (he also played basketball, but the
diamond was this boy's best friend), as
are his major league baseball uniforms;
other exhibits include medals and
awards, autographed balls and gloves,
and action shots of the great slugger at
bat. Among the trophies on display is
the Page One award given to Maris in
1961 by the Associated Press for generating the most front-page news items.
The 61st home run he hit while playing
for the New York Yankees in 1961 (that
particular crack of the bat shattered
Babe Ruth's 60-home run record) is also
documented here, along with footage of
Maris' last 12 home runs.

Maris was born in Hibbing, Minn., in 1934, but moved to Fargo during his teens. He always thought of Fargo as his hometown, and he is buried in a local cemetery here. His museum has turned West Acres into a baseball mall—not a bad way to honor the state's greatest swinger.

Here's the Beef

World's Largest Holstein
(P.O. Box 393)
New Salem, ND 58563

Hours: Always visible
Admission: Free
Getting There: Salem Sue is visible for miles around, from Hwys. 10 and 31, and I-94. Take Exit 27 from I-94 onto 31 S., or take Hwy. 10 to Hwy. 31 N., and get off at the parking area for the cow.

New Salem has the world's largest Holstein cow, and they're milking it for all it's worth. This fiberglass baby stands a full 38 feet high and 50 feet long, and emptied the town coffers to the tune of $40,000 when she was built in 1974. But that's okay—she was built to call attention to the local dairy industry, and because she practically stops traffic on the nearby highways, it's a safe to assume she is worth every cent.

She's called Salem Sue, and there's even a song, "Ballad of the Holstein," about her. Here's Sue's song, sung to the tune of "I Want a Girl Just Like the Girl that Married Dear Old Dad":

We've got the World's
    Largest Holstein cow,
That looks across our fields.
    Her presence shows
That Salem grows,

With milk—producers yields:
Friends will come and
    View from near and far,
She will tell to all
    Just where we are;
We've got a cow
    World's largest cow
That looks across our fields.

Kind of moooving, no? New Salem has always loved its Holstein business—this area has superb grazing land that made it a prime choice for cattlemen in North Dakota. The town's high school basketball team is even named the Holsteins. But it's old Salem Sue that really put New Salem on the map. Just remember to watch your step

Ohio

Sweeping Success

Hoover Historical Center
2225 Easton St., N.W.
North Canton, OH 44720
(216) 499-0287

Hours: Tues.-Sun. 1-5 p.m.
Admission: Free
Getting There: From State Rte. 43 (Market Ave. N. as it runs through town), go west o Easton St. Follow signs to Walsh College—the Hoover center is across the street.

Housed at the former site of the Hoove family homestead and tannery, the Hoover Historical Center—an extensiv gathering of historical vacuum cleaner and related memorabilia—presents a sweeping panorama of epic scope.
    The machines are displayed in the ol Hoover home, a lovely Victorian farm

...use with tall, shuttered windows and columned front porch. In keeping with the house's charm, the museum pieces are displayed, not in generic glass cases, but standing free and leaning against the walls, or balanced atop delicate side-tables and carpeted stands. The walls are hung with framed prints of early advertisements, and antique curio cabinets display vacuum parts and promotional toys. The effect is both odd and comforting, as though someone actually lived here (albeit someone with a peculiar fixation on vacuum cleaners).

One of the delightful machines on display—for both its historical importance and its amusing design—is the Hoover Company's first model, the 1908 Electric Suction Sweeper. It looks a bit like a dainty walrus, with flowers and tendrilled vines decorating the rounded head and elegant lettering flowing across the surface of the long roller on the front. One can almost imagine the family cleaning lady, her hair tucked under a white cap, her high-waisted dress and apron swishing along the floor behind her as she pushes this pretty monstrosity across the sitting-room rug. Other models evoke similar musings—from the first all-die-cast aluminum cleaner, Hoover's Model 541, introduced in 1923 to a domed 1936 Hoover Cleaner, with a molded hood of the first plastic, Bakelite.

The Hoover Historical Center was opened in 1978, to celebrate the 70th anniversary of the beginning of the company. William H. Hoover, the company's founder, had run a tannery (which has been resurrected in its old building, complete with historic tanning equipment and tools) before starting the company with his family, business associates, and a vacuum cleaner inventor named J. Murray Spangler. William and his son, Herbert W. (no, not the President) ran the fledgling empire, which began as a novelty business and expanded rapidly as more and more homes were wired for electricity. The Hoovers cleaned up.

The Hoover Historical Center is a lively tribute to the development of the vacuum cleaner, a machine that swept the world off its feet and became a household necessity in less than 100 years. "It beats as it sweeps as it cleans" is the old Hoover motto. Add to that, "It ages well, too."

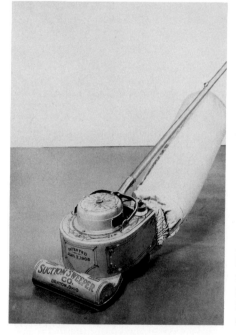

Keeping Zane

National Road/Zane Gre Museum

8850 East Pike
Norwich, OH 43767
(614) 872-3143

Hours: Mar.-April and Oct.-Nov., Wed.-Sa 9:30 a.m.-5 p.m., Sun. noon-5 p.m.; May-Sept., Mon.-Sat. 9:30 a.m.-5 p.m., Sun. noor p.m.
Admission: Adults, $2; children, $1; senio citizens, $1.60
Getting There: Located on U.S. 40, just off I-70 (Exit 164—Norwich). Zanesville is 10 miles to the west.

This ultramodern wooden building wit its slanting roof and angled skylights houses two seemingly disparate but ult mately intertwined historical collections. Half of the museum is given ove to the story of the building and use of the National Road, the first federally funded road built in the United States the other half is dedicated to the life o Zane Grey, author of dozens of popula western novels, who was born in nearb Zanesville.

The National Road (now Rte. 40) stretches from Cumberland, Md., to Vandalia, Ill., and has been the subjec of folklore and nostalgia ever since Con gress appropriated the road's first fund in 1806. The National Road section of the museum houses a 136-foot-long, glass-encased diorama showing the evo lution of the National Road from its ear ly construction, when men with pick-axes and shovels commenced the back-breaking labor of digging the initial roadbeds, through its use as a pioneer route and its eventual disrepair, and finally to its resurgence with the growtl of the automobile. Other exhibits inlude a collection of restored vehicles, from covered wagons to sports cars, and recreations of common roadside services, including a tavern and a wheelwright shop.

At first glance, it would seem odd that Zane Grey would make up the other half of this museum. But there is a deeper connection than the mere proximity of his birthplace: Grey's great-grandfather, Ebenezer Zane, was the man who hacked through the Ohio wilderness to build the area's first public road, known as Zane's Trace. A collection of artifacts, including manuscripts, first editions, and personal mementos, traces the life of Ebenezer's literary descendant. Grey popularized adult western fiction with such novels as *Riders of the Purple Sage*, and his vision of the West was taken up by an entire generation of film directors and cowboy buffs.

It was the National Road that carried settlers out West to build a new America; a half-century later, Zane Grey captured the lives of these pioneers with his pen, guiding his readers to a West that no longer existed except in the frontiers of memory.

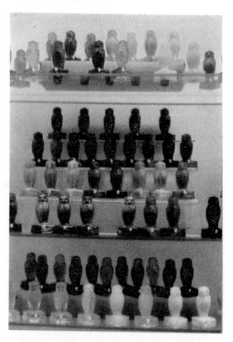

I-77. It's hard to miss, with its tall, woodpaneled, white-lettered sign rising above the parking lot. The museum is also within a few blocks of Rte. 40, Rte. 209, and I-70.

Weights and Treasures

Paperweight Museum

5323 Highland Hills Rd.
(P.O. Box 186)
Cambridge, OH 43725
(614) 432-2626

Hours: Mon.-Sat. 10 a.m-5 p.m.; Sun. 1-5 p.m.; closed in Jan.

Admission: Adults, $1.50; senior citizens, $1; children under 8, free

Getting There: The museum is on Highland Hills Rd., just off Rte. 22, at the intersection of

This Fifties-style rambler of a building houses a stunning tribute to that lowly workhorse desk accessory, the paperweight. On display in this glittering museum are more kinds and shapes of glass paperweights than you could shake a letter opener at, including floral, "window," figural, and name weights. But paperweights are only the beginning: there are multitudes of other glass forms represented here, too. Rows upon rows of clearly wise owls nest on shelves in one room, while fanciful bowls and pitchers, colored goblets, and ornate platters abound throughout the exhibit space.

The museum, established at the bequest of the late Elizabeth Degenhart, is devoted mainly to glassware made from 1850 to the present in western Pennsylvania, northern West Virginia, and Ohio. Much of the collection was created at the Crystal Art Glass Company, a decorative-glass company founded in Cambridge in 1947 and run by Degenhart and her husband John. The factory turned out everything from ashtrays to figurines, but the paperweights, many of which Elizabeth decorated by hand, were the Degenharts' claim to fame.

In 1975, three years before her death, Elizabeth Degenhart was proclaimed "First Lady of Glass" by Ohio's governor. Judging from the size, beauty, and scope of her personal paperweight collection, which includes several thousand pieces, the title is apt indeed. Particularly lovely are the rose weights, with their bright, delicately designed petals frozen in glass. Gazing into these floral crystal balls, one can't help wondering if maybe "Queen of Glass" would have been more appropriate.

Kernel of an Idea

Popcorn Museum
Southland Mall
Rte. 423
Marion, OH 43302
(614) 389-6404

Hours: Mon.-Sat. 10 a.m.-9 p.m.; Sun. noo⟨ p.m.
Admission: Free
Getting There: Southland Mall is on Rte. 423, on the south edge of Marion, just wes⟨ U.S. 23.

The good old days are alive and poppi⟨ at the Wyandotte Popcorn Museum i⟨ Marion. It's got the world's largest co⟨ lection of restored antique popcorn a⟨ roasted-nut vending carts and machines—plus lots of other popcorn⟨ paraphernalia. For visitors with the munchies, there's free popcorn all around, fresh from an antique poppe⟨ But the tastiest things here are the swe⟨ memories evoked by this nostalgic collection.

Although popcorn is a treat that dates ck to the American Indians, it wasn't til a fellow named Charlie Cretors in-ated the first popping machine in 85 that the tasty kernels became a ack-food mainstay. An 1899 No. 1 etors Popcorn Wagon, the third-old-Cretors machine in existence, is on play at the museum. If this early del is representative, it should come no surprise that popcorn vendors re an instant hit with children and the ung at heart—the colorful, nickel-ated cart ornamented with tiny clown ures was an essential stop during any p to the park or fair. There are several er old Cretors at the museum, in-ding a 1927 Model T concession ck that had machines for both pop-n popping and peanut roasting.

For those whose memories don't go ck quite far enough to remember ose halcyon days of state fairs and rk strolls, there are Manley theater ppers. These big popper boxes, with eir bright, rounded tops and the ever-owing mound of popcorn behind the ass, are rarely found in movie houses day, but they're still going strong at e Wyandotte Popcorn Museum. In ct, all the machines here are in pop-ng or nut-roasting order—and the ells that waft throught the museum e utterly delicious.

Other exhibits include a mural of an dian family enjoying popcorn, and ch latter-day artifacts as corn-shell-g machines and testing equipment. yandotte, Inc., which got its start in a tle converted schoolhouse in 1936, is e of the giants in the snack-food in-ustry today. A discount outlet at the useum sells the company's products, ong with some fun-but-tacky popcorn uvenirs, from salt shakers to T-shirts.

Marion is so proud of its homegrown snack that it holds a Popcorn Festival every September, with events ranging from such cultural pursuits as the "Miss Teeny Pop Contest" to a "Tri-Ear-thalon" and "Mixed Kernels Tennis Open" for the more athletically minded. Thousands of people pop in from all over the country to attend the festival. The museum is always a highlight of their visit, but even after the festival tents and stages have been taken down, the museum remains a popular exhibit.

A Major Cancellation

Postmark Collectors Club Museum

Historic Lyme Village
Rte. 113
Bellevue, OH 44811
(419) 483-6052

Hours: Guided village tours, the only "official" way to see the museum: June-Aug., Tues.-Sun. 1-5 p.m.; May and Sept., Sat.-Sun. 1-5 p.m.; other times by appointment
Admission: Guided village tours: Adults, $4; students, $2.50; senior citizens, $3.50. Researchers who contact the curator—(419) 585-7645—10 days in advance can arrange for free admission and special visiting hours.
Getting There: The museum is in Historic Lyme Village on Rte. 113, just east of Bellevue, which is south of the Ohio Turnpike, midway between Toledo and Cleveland.

Unless you've made other arrangements with the museum's curator, you'll have to see the Postmark Collectors Club Mu-seum as part of a package tour of the lovely little Historic Lyme Village—Ohio's version of Williamsburg, with a slightly younger look. The museum is housed in a cute little white clapboard ex-post office that could easily pass for a country church. The post office motif has been preserved, and it's a fitting setting for the world's largest collection of postmarks.

Among the rare and priceless postmarks here are nineteenth-century silk-screened prints, commemorative postmarks, and postmarks from aptly named places on historic days, including one stamped in Old Glory, Texas, on July 4, 1976. There are many kinds of postmarks—aside from the date/place stamps, you'll see everything from the dullest of "Moved, Not Forwardable" statements to the loveliest of commemorative post-office-opening designs. With its vast, letter-perfect collection, this little museum conveys the feel of exotic mundanity that comes from finding a postmark stamped in a far-off place or time.

In for the Kiln

Trapshooting Museum

601 W. National Rd.
Vandalia, OH 45377
(513) 898-1945

Hours: Mon.-Fri. 9 a.m.-4 p.m.
Admission: Free
Getting There: Located on U.S. Hwy. 40 (National Rd.), just east of I-75 (Exit 63).

Trapshooting—shooting at clay targets that have been catapulted into the air—was once a blood sport. Pigeons were the original targets, and even when enthusiasts switched over to nonliving targets, they couldn't quite give up the thrill of the kill at first, so glass balls stuffed with feathers were used to simulate the birds. The Amateur Trapshooting Association's Trapshooting Hall of

Fame and Museum exhibits examples of these glass balls, along with plenty of other fascinating and unusual memorabilia of the sport. Exhibits display everything from early trap machines and targets to such fringe paraphernalia as personalized license plates and gun club patches. The Hall of Fame honors great amateur trapshooters of the past (including one fellow who was even faster with a baton, John Philip Sousa) and records great moments in trapshooting history. It's an interesting collection of those who care for the sport, but anyone with a love for pottery should steer clear.

Warthers' Wonders

Warther Museum

331 Karl Ave.
Dover, OH 44622
(216) 343-7513

Hours: Daily 9 a.m.-5 p.m.
Admission: Adults, $4; children, $2
Getting There: Take I-77/U.S. 250/U.S. 21 Exit 83, and go southeast on Rte. 39. Take a right onto Tuscawaras Ave., another right onto Ninth St., and right again onto Karl Ave.

Ernest Warther was considered one of the world's great carvers, and his wife Frieda one of the world's great button collectors. Their combined talents are displayed in a charmingly offbeat museum planted amid a lush flower garden.

The carvings on display reflect Warther's fascination and skill with miniature trains—among those here are his ivory versions of Casey Jones' engine, the John Bull (the first passenger train), and the Empire State Express (carved from an 81-pound elephant tusk.) Warther had a special notch in his

eart for Abraham Lincoln, and his re-
arkable rendition of Lincoln's funeral
rain is one of the most astounding exibits at the museum: eight feet long,
nd carved from ebony and ivory, the
rain even has a lighted car where curi-
us viewers can peer through the win-
ows and see the President lying in his
offin.

Warther was a master craftsman who
ut a great deal of stock in the intricate
kills needed to master his art (his
econd career, as a knife maker, came
bout because of his own frustration in
inding the right tools for his delicate
arving needs). One of the finest, and
unniest, examples of his skill is the
"Round Tower and Plier Tree" on dis-
lay in the museum. This odd piece of
culpture consists of 511 pairs of pliers,
ll cut from a single piece of wood
"without making a shaving," as one de-
cription states. The main structure of

the tower is carved to look like
brickface, with insets of pliers and family photographs on the bottom, and the
plier "tree" (it actually looks more like a
thornbush from far away) growing out
of the top.

It's a decorative piece indeed, but
even the plier tower can't compete with
Mrs. Warther's button collection on display in the original museum adjacent to
the main exhibit building. The walls
and ceiling are virtually crawling with
stars and diamonds and flowers and
geometric patterns—all created from
buttons. Fully 73,000 buttons, and no
two alike.

If button flowers and plier trees aren't
enough to whet your appetite, the
Warther Museum also has an extensive
collection of Indian arrow heads. All in
all, it's a place where you can indulge in
button-down whimsy and crafty
delight.

Bouncing Back

World of Rubber

Fourth floor, Goodyear Hall
1201 E. Market St.
Akron, OH 44316
(216) 796-2044

Hours: Mon.-Fri. 8:30-4:30 p.m.
Admission: Free
Getting There: From I-76 take Goodyear
Blvd. and turn left onto E. Market St. The
exhibit is on the fourth floor of Goodyear Hall,
part of the corporate headquarters complex
on E. Market St.

Modern life would be pretty hard if it weren't for rubber—no basketball shoes, no rubber bands, no moped tires—so it's a lucky thing that there's the Goodyear World of Rubber to show us just how far we've come since prerubber times. Charles Goodyear, the inventor of the "vulcanization" process (without which this bouncy material would just be so much gooey plant innards), is well represented in the museum. His statue stands prominently in the museum's entrance rotunda, while inside, the Charles Goodyear Memorial Collection displays papers and mementos of his life.

Goodyear was not directly connected with the company that bears his name; he died in 1860, 38 years before the company was founded. But his tireless spirit can be felt throughout the World of Rubber. One of the highlights here is a replica of his workshop, where visitors can see a mannequin recreating the exciting discovery of vulcanization. A simulated rubber plantation is another must-see, and the various couldn't-have-done-it-without-rubber products on display include an artificial heart, two Indy 500 racecars and a bunch of oon tires. There's so much to see at the World of Rubber that you may feel a bit red after your visit—but step outside nd breathe in some of that fresh "Ak-n: Rubber Capital of the World" air nd you'll bounce back in no time.

South Dakota

Maizing Place

orn Palace

)4 N. Main St.
litchell, SD 57301
05) 996-7311

ours: June-Labor Day, daily 8 a.m.-10 p.m.;
bor Day-June, Mon.-Fri. 8 a.m.-5 p.m.
dmission: Free
etting There: From I-90 take the E. 190 exit
to S. Burr St. and follow it into Mitchell.
ke a right onto E. Sixth Ave; the Corn Palace
at the corner of E. Sixth and N. Main St.

here else but in the self-proclaimed rn Capital of the World would you d the Corn Palace? Mitchell is a town

obsessed by its agricultural heritage. The product of this pride is the magnificent Corn Palace. Rising like a corn-fed Kremlin above the flat South Dakota landscape, its bison-painted minarets and twirling towers hold court over the enormous, half-block-long structure decorated from ground to roof with real corn and other grains. No wonder it's also known as "The World's Largest Birdfeeder."

All winter long, hundreds of birds, squirrels, and other cob robbers nibble away at the Corn Palace—but their numbers pale beside the half-million human visitors who travel to Mitchell to gape at this blend of art and agriculture. The biggest crowds come during the Corn Palace Festival, held every September, when Main St. turns into a cotton-candy-infested Midway, and big-name entertainers (Lawrence Welk appeared at five festivals, and Andy Williams has been known to strut his stuff here) come to play the Palace. Indeed, the Corn Palace is multifaceted: behind the exterior of corn cobs and sorghum beats an entertaining heart. The

Corn Palace houses an auditorium where everything from big band concerts to basketball games are held year 'round.

The Corn Palace has deep roots in Mitchell. The original palace was built to showcase Mitchell's first "Corn Belt Exposition" in 1892. This first palace was the grainchild of local citizens seeking to compete with neighboring Plankinton, a town that had recently erected a heralded "grain palace" of its own. With headline entertainment like John Philip Sousa, the Mitchell festival caught on, and a major addition was built onto the original Corn Palace in 1893. Despite the droughts and wars of the following decades, which played havoc with the festival schedule and local crops, three successively larger Corn Palaces were built between 1905 and 1937.

During this time, the exterior geometric corn designs were replaced with annual theme murals depicting South Dakotans at work and play. During the 1940s, the murals depicted the country at war and the corny facades were temporarily replaced with painted wooden panels. From 1948 to 1971, the famed painter Oscar Howe directed the mural designs and execution. Howe also designed five permanent panel paintings depicting South Dakota themes, from pheasant hunting to Mt. Rushmore.

The Corn Palace that stands today is a modern auditorium and exhibit facility of reinforced concrete, complete with fiberglass minarets (the original wooden ones burned in a 1979 fire) and an indoor collection of artwork and South Dakota memorabilia. But the annual changing of the exterior murals still takes place in early September, when workers strip the old facade and apply new corn and other grains to wooden panels covered with roofing paper drawn with exact diagrams for the new design. Local crops of naturally colored corns (including white, yellow, blue, red, and calico), along with oats, sudan grass, sorghum grain, barley, and other grains and grasses are used as the primary decorative material. The resulting designs run along all sides of the Corn Palace, depicting such themes as "South Dakota Fauna," "Relaxin' in South Dakota," and "Modes of Transportation." Murals on the front of the building are usually reserved for portraits of the Festival headliners.

Inside the palace, a series of South Dakota exhibits range from the stuffed trophy animals brought back by local safari hunter F. D. "Doc" Randall, maps and photographs of the state's past and present accomplishments, and adjacent to the stage, the Howe Murals.

The best time to see the Corn Palace is during the festival, when the colorful mural work has just been redone. During the summer months it can look rather scraggly, what with the faded colors and bite marks of marauding squirrels and other creatures. But even during these lackluster months, the Corn Palace, flags flapping in the wind from its plump minarets, is more spectacular than any farmer's fantasy.

Great Wall

Wall Drug
510 Main St.
Wall, SD 57790
(605) 279-2175

Hours: Memorial Day–Labor Day, 7:30 a.m.–10 p.m.; winter, 6:30 a.m.–5 p.m. (Note: closing times throughout the year may

ctuate an hour or more; billboards and
gns in town prominently display the correct
ours for each day)

dmission: Free

etting there: Take I-90 to Exit 110 (you
n't miss it—there's an 80-foot dinosaur
atue at the exit, advertising Wall Drug) and
llow the many signs to the mall, which is on
ain St., a few blocks north of the interstate.

ou'll know you're headed someplace
ecial as soon as you see the 80-foot di-
osaur statue on I-90 that advertises
all Drug. This is one of the few places
here you can buy a bottle of aspirin
d pose for a photograph with a six-
ot rabbit. But it's much more than a
pochondriac's Disneyland: this place
an entire shopping mall filled with cu-
stores and robot-cowboy bands,

doughnut shops and life-sized sculptures of Butch Cassidy.

It all began in 1936 with the simple
gimmick of offering free ice water to
thirsty travelers. Soon, the sleepy little
drug store owned by Ted and Dorothy
Hustead in even sleepier little Wall
("Gateway to the Badlands") was
jumping with parched, teeming masses.
A dynasty was born.

The Wall Drug of today still has a tiny
drugstore, and it still offers free ice water (during the summer, an estimated
5,000 glasses are dispensed daily), but
the robots, statues, stuffed animals,
rides, and souvenir shops in and around
the mall have long since gone from a
sideshow to the main event. During
summers, the "backyard" area is open

for business, and kiddies of all ages flock in to feed quarters to the mechanical hurdy-gurdy man and Indian village—everything, including the Indians, moves around—while posing for souvenir pix with the giant jackalope and stuffed bucking horse. But the backyard is merely the tip of the iceberg at Wall, for the mall itself is even more jam-packed with funny, kitschy displays.

The drug department offers nostrums, of course, plus the life-sized "historical figures" of a one-armed bandit (not the Las Vegas variety) and a gun-toting sheriff. Other historical figures, including Annie Oakley and dirty old "Whiskey Jack," lurk throughout the mall proper, while Calamity Jane reigns over the jewelry store. The Art Gallery Dining Room has the figures of Red Cloud, Crazy Horse, Butch Cassidy, and the Sundance Kid. Mallers are also treated to the Paul Giesel Wildlife Display of stuffed game animals, and the cowboy orchestra, which plays a preprogrammed set every 20 minutes in the Souvenir Shop.

While you'll probably feel the urge to buy, buy, buy at such mall stores as the Big Bull Harness Shop and the Pottery and Iron Shed, you'll be relieved to know that the neatest souvenir of them all is given away free at the Wall mall—a Wall Drug sign or poster, offered to all visitors. It's a touch of public relations genius that has resulted in the dissemination of signs around the world, with such disparate sites as the London Subway and the Taj Mahal harboring Wall Drug ads. On a more local scale, although the once-famous Wall Drug billboards that were erected on highways from sea to shining sea are gone, South Dakota's highways and by-

ways are still dotted liberally with th big, bright signs.

The South Dakota Badlands, now national park, is one of the weirdest na ural environments in America—cent ries of bubbling lava and geologic up roar have turned the earth here into landscape of sharp rock towers and brightly colored, jagged minimountains. It seems fitting that Wall Drug, located a scant eight mile from the entrance to the Badlands, should be found in this odd, desolate part of the country. Wall Drug strikes manically cheerful chord in an otherwise barren zone.

Wisconsin

Yule Love It

Christmas Tree Museum

Friarswood Country Village
3929 80th St.
(P.O. Box 1157)
Kenosha, WI 53142
(414) 697-XMAS

Hours: Oct.-Jan., Tues.-Sun. 10 a.m.-4 p.m (Closed Mon. and holidays)
Admission: Adults, $5; students, $3; childre 6-12, $2; senior citizens, $4
Getting There: Take I-94 to Hwy. 50 East, turn onto 39th St., and drive south to 80th S The museum is at the Friarswood Country Village, at the corner of 39th Ave. and 80th S

The twelve days of Christmas stretch o for four months at the Christmas Tree Story House in Kenosha's Friarswood Country Village. The village, a quaint gathering of craft shops and displays, the perfect backdrop for this unabash edly sentimental collection of Christma trees, ornaments, and other seasonal

aphernalia. The collection is housed
wo buildings—a former barn turned
ter wonderland, complete with a
ffed-animal petting zoo and decorat-
trees representing the four seasons,
d a turn-of-the-century manor house,
h collections filling all of the down-
irs chambers. Displays change year-
but no matter when you visit, you're
und to find room after room of plain
fancy decorated trees. The designs
ige from country charm, complete
h calico ornaments and candles, to
ctorian elegance, with velvet ribbons
d glass and silver baubles. The whole
use seems alive with the holiday spir-
from flickering candelabra to linen-
d-lace window dressings. As the yule-
e approaches, carolers often perform
a gazebo on the grounds—and then,
n Scrooge himself would smile at the
eet tunes rising up all around this
igical museum.

Three-Ring Museum

Circus World Museum

426 Water St.
Baraboo, WI 53913-2597
(608) 356-8341

Hours: May-Sept., daily 9 a.m.-6 p.m. (July
18-August 22, open until 9 p.m.)
Admission: Adults, $7.50; children 8-13, $5;
children 3-7, $2.50; children under 3, free;
senior citizens, $6; family (parents and their
children under 18), $25
Getting There: Baraboo is in south central
Wisconsin. Take I-90/94 to the Hwy. 12 S. or
Rte. 33 W. exits; both lead to Baraboo. Once
in town, follow signs to the museum, which
is on Water St.

Long before Sarasota, Fla. was even a
twinkle in the Ringling Brothers' eyes,
Baraboo was their home-sweet-home.
The Ringling Bros. Circus had its original winter quarters in Baraboo from

1884 to 1918; in fact, a total of six circuses got their start in the Baraboo area.
It's no wonder, then, that Wisconsin
carries the title of "Mother of Circuses."
This nurturing instinct extends itself to
the Circus World Museum, which
claims to be the world's largest, most
comprehensive museum and library facility devoted to the story of the circus.

Circus World was the brainchild of
John M. Kelley, the Ringling Bros. law-
yer and adviser for more than three decades. Kelley hoped to restore the original circus buildings that still stood in
Baraboo and turn the area into a shrine
to this age-old entertainment form. In

59, Circus World became a reality
en two historic circus buildings (once
d for housing and training animals)
re converted into exhibit space and
small collection of circus wagons
l memorabilia was opened to the
blic. Today, the museum site sprawls
er 43 acres of land, encompassing 30
ibit and performance buildings. The
lection includes the world's largest
hering of restored circus wagons
ore than 170), and a vast array of exits ranging from a miniature circus
displays of costumes and examples of
wn makeup and artistry. But these
ibits, although imaginatively ar-
ged and artfully described, can't
tch the live-action emphasis of Cir-
World.

As befits a circus collection (and the
atively high admission price), Circus
rld is a living museum of the most
ring kind: every day, all around,
re are high-wire performances, street
rades, and animal-training exhibi-
ns that combine to turn the whole
ace into a true, all-day circus. Such
ngling Bros. greats as the Flying
allenda family and the controversial
iving Unicorn" have been known to
rform under the museum's original
top, along with a fulltime staff of
wns, ringmasters, acrobats, and oth-
standard circus types. Other high-
hts include the daily Theater of Illu-
n magic shows, steam calliope
ncerts, and demonstrations of wild
imal feeding. There are also elephant
les (additional tickets required; ev-
thing else is included in the general
mission price).

Though Circus World isn't exactly a
placement for a real circus
ow—there aren't as many performers,
as much razzle-dazzle as today's

traveling extravaganzas—it is an exciting way to learn about the history of the
circus. Remember to hold on tightly to
the kids while you're here, or they may
just run off and join the museum.

Hunt and Peck

Crane Foundation

E-11376 Shady Lane Rd.
Baraboo, WI 53913
(608) 356-9462

Hours: Memorial Day-Labor Day, daily 9
a.m.-5 p.m.; May, Sept., and Oct., weekends,
9 a.m.-5 p.m.
Admission: Adults, $3.50; children, $1.75;
senior citizens, $3
Getting There: The center is just outside
Baraboo, which can be reached by taking I-
99/94 to Hwy. 12 (Exit 92) and driving south to
town.

While the Circus World Museum is
Baraboo's biggest attraction, the International Crane Foundation, just outside
of town, is no fly-by-night operation either. For anyone with an interest in con-
servation, nature trails, or just birds
that act funny, this place is a delight.
The foundation is home to the a variety
of crane species, including the nearly
mythical white crane, the rarest and
largest bird in the world, and the sacred
cranes of the Orient, purported to live to
1,000 years old. Visitors can tour the
foundation complex and grounds to see
these gawky-yet-graceful birds perform
during exercise sessions with their "human chick mamas," the name given
their trainers. Another highlight is the
chick-hatching display that shows the
development of crane embryos from
early growth stages through the hatch-
ing process. Walking trails wind

through forests and meadows on the foundation grounds; visitors are encouraged to pack a picnic lunch and venture forth to commune with nature.

Grotto, American Style

Dickeyville Grotto

Holy Ghost Church
(P.O. Box 427)
Dickeyville, WI 53808
(608) 568-7519

Hours: Always visible; guided tours available June-Aug., daily 10 a.m.-6 p.m.; May, Sept., and Oct., weekends, 10 a.m.-6 p.m.
Admission: Free; donations appreciated
Getting There: Dickeyville is near the western border of Wisconsin, 10 miles north of Dubuque, Iowa, on Hwy. 61. Hwys. 11, 151, and 133 also feed into Dickeyville. Follow signs to the grotto, located on the grounds of the Holy Ghost Church.

Father Mathias Wernerus, a Catholic priest, was inspired to create the first his shrines by the World War I deaths three Dickeyville men. Although Ame ca was Wernerus' adopted homeland (he emigrated to America from Gern ny in 1904), his patriotic fervor was a fever pitch when he built the colored stone-and-mosaic soldier's memorial crucifixion group in the cemetery of Church of the Holy Ghost.

Until 1930, the year before his dea Wernerus covered the church ground with grottoes and shrines honoring tl Sacred Heart, the Holy Eucharist, Christ the King, and the Stations of Cross. He worked with bits and pieces stone—fossils, petrified wood, rocks from every state, and colored quartz—as well as archaeological art facts such as broken pottery and Indi arrowheads, and donated materials i cluding old printers' plates, iron doo knockers, and candle holders. Shells were another mainstay of Wernerus'

building materials, appearing most no-
ably at the Grotto of the Holy Eucha-
ist, which has an entire roof lined with
onch and clam shells.

Wernerus' masterpiece, for which the
Dickeyville Grotto is named, is the grot-
o dedicated to the Blessed Mother,
tanding 25 feet high, 30 feet long, and
5 feet deep. Within the recesses of this
littering grotto stands a statue of the
Virgin Mary and the Christ child, sur-
ounded on all sides by a outrageous ar-
ay of jutting rocks, tile mosaics, and or-
amental shells. To the right and left of
he grotto are mosaic interpretations of
he Papal flag above the inscription
Religion," and the American flag
bove the inscription "Patriotism."

A strong sense of patriotism pervades
any of the shrines and grottoes in
ickeyville, but none so much as the
riginal patriotic memorial. A rock and
ass shrine to "Christopher Columbus,
iscoverer of America, 1492," complete
ith an arch and a statue, is flanked by
wall of shells and rocks. A nearby stat-
e of Abraham Lincoln continues the
eme, as does the American eagle foun-
in in the center of this rotunda.

America is home to a number of devo-
nal structures like the Dickeyville
rotto—the Shrine of Redemption in
uth Bend, Iowa, and the Black Ma-
nna Shrine in Eureka, Mo., for exam-
e. All have a distinctly American feel
them. The fact that most were created
immigrants seems as fitting as the
ilding materials used in such
ojects—usually native rock and found
naments. Among the hodgepodge me-
orials built in this potpourri of a na-
n, Father Wernerus' grotto is perhaps
e most unabashedly patriotic. God
d Country meet here, amid a
caphonous symphony of earthly and
avenly delights.

Uplifting Experience

Experimental Aircraft Museum

Wittman Airfield
Oshkosh, WI 54903
(414) 426-4818

Hours: Mon.-Sat. 8:30 a.m.-5 p.m.; Sun. 11 a.m.-5 p.m.
Admission: Adults, $4.50; children and senior citizens, $3.50; children under 8, free
Getting There: The museum is at Wittman Airfield in Oshkosh, off Hwy. 41 at the Hwy. 44 exit.

There are nearly 80 full-sized aircraft on display in this riveting museum at the Experimental Aircraft Association headquarters. Many are famous—in-cluding the Double Eagle V balloon (the first balloon to cross the Pacific

Ocean)—while others are evocative of the most daring exploits of aviation history. There are brightly painted trick planes, light and smooth gliders, and snub-nosed fighter planes. Other exhibits concentrate on such themes as propellers, engines, and aerodynamics. Many of the aircraft in this museum were first-timers—trend-setting vehicles that would spawn new generations of flying machines. Seeing them gathered together under one roof gives a new resonance to the phrase "the sky's the limit."

Sweet Stuff

Honey of a Museum

Honey Acres
Hwy. 67
Ashippun, WI 53003
(414) 474-4412

Hours: May 15-Oct. 31, Mon.-Fri. 9 a.m.-3:30 p.m.; Sat.-Sun. noon-4 p.m.; Nov.-May 15, Mon.-Fri. 9 a.m.-3:30 p.m.
Admission: Free
Getting There: The museum is at Honey Acres on Hwy. 67, just outside Ashippun.

The name of this museum says it all. Located at the Honey Acres honey farm, this collection is a lively introduction to the sweet nature of bees. Exhibits include an active (but safely enclosed) bee tree, displays on the history of beekeeping from its beginnings (honeybees were brought to America by settlers; Indians called the insects the "white man's fly"), and a look at the bee's bitter enemy, the black bear. There are honey tastings, tours of the farm's facilities, and a 20-minute multimedia show called (what else?) "Honey of a Story." Honey Acres is owned by the Diehnelt

family, who have been beekeepers and honey packers here since 1852. Honey products ranging from beeswax candle to honey mustard are for sale in the gif shop on the premises.

Rock Palace

House on the Rock

Hwy. 23
(P.O. Box 555)
Spring Green, WI 53588
(608) 935-3639

Hours: April-Nov. 15, daily 8 a.m.-dusk (ticke sales stop 2½ hours earlier)
Admission: Adults, $10; children 7-12, $6; children 4-6, $1; children under 4, free
Getting There: Located approximately 40 miles west of Madison, on Hwy. 23, halfwa between Spring Green and Dodgeville.

What can you say about a place like th House on the Rock? It is undoubtedly one of America's little-known architec tural wonders, but it is also the site of one of the most extraordinary collections of collections anywhere. Taking tour of this place is like visiting a forei country—there's so much to see, so litt time, and everything is so different fro the world outside.

Technically, the House on the Rock should be called "The House On, In, and Around the Rock, With Addition Sticking Out Here and There." But tha of course, would never fit on a bump sticker. The house probably comes as close to a natural living environment anything has since cave-dwelling day When architect and owner Alex Jorda went looking for an unusual site for h house, he found his dream in this tall jutting outcrop of solid rock. Keeping what Jordan called a strict "covenant

almost feel like scenes out of some private hell—bathed in red light or crammed with frightful wooden carvings of Chinese warriors. But then you enter another room where high windows give a magnificent view of the valley below, or where stained-glass panels cast a dance of colored light rays into the chamber—and the wonder of this castle upon high is apparent again.

Visitors slowly meander up through the house until they reach the pinnacle, which has an observation deck with a view to knock the World Trade Center out of the running. But as panoramas go, the real topper is the "Infinity Room" that juts out 218 feet over the Wyoming Valley and is fitted with 3,244 windows for a floating-in-space feel. The floor even has an inset acrylic window providing a startling view of the forest 156 feet below. Those with a fear of heights should avoid this room.

From the Gate House, it's on to the Mill House, an adjacent rock building where an enormous fireplace and bellows-shaped table are the show stoppers. In addition, there are collections of armor and weapons (including some truly deformed-looking multibarrelled pistols) and a roomful of music machines that "play themselves" thanks to a built-in pneumatic system. There is also a "Ladies Lounge" room filled with an entire wall of glassware and shelves of tiny, dioramic statuary. Other collections in this building include bejeweled eggshells, antique dolls and toys, and an amusing gathering of mechanical banks. But the Mill House is merely the jumping-off point for the enjoyment of Jordan's unique collections. The rest of his odd and delightful hoard is grouped in a series of hangar-type buildings adjacent to the actual House on the Rock.

th nature," he built his house according to the natural lines and strictures of e rock formations.

The resulting home is as lovely as a e-in boulder could be, though it's admittedly uncomfortable with its low lings, dark interiors, and narrow passageways. What the house lacks in comt, it makes up for in ingenuity. The angely shaped rooms of the first sec-n, known as the Gate House, are cked with odd furniture, embellish-nts, and knickknacks Jordan picked at auctions and antique shops und the country. Parts of the house

The "Streets of Yesterday" fills one of these buildings, with a recreated small town complete with a lamp store, toy store, cozy "Grandma's House," firehouse, and all the other hometown accoutrements. While here, don't forget to have a reading by "Esmerelda," a coin-operated fortune teller who can see your future (with about as much accuracy as the Sunday paper horoscopes).

Next, it's on to the "Music of Yesterday" portion, with room after darkly lit room of musical machines, from calliopes to jukeboxes. Many of the pieces here were designed by Jordan, and some are so magnificent that the sound of catching breath is heard all around you—creations like the enormous Mikado machine, a pagoda-like structure with dozens of figures realistically straining as they bang their cymbals or puff away at their tiny clarinets. Other brilliant musical mechanisms designed by Jordan include the "Franz Joseph," an ornate glass-encased machine that rises 27 feet into the air, showcasing an entire orchestra of disembodied brass instruments.

The collections of the House on the Rock go on and on like this for quite some time—building after building of eye-popping machines and lavish objects that leave visitors exhausted from the effort of being constantly amazed. Among the other elaborate offerings here are the "World's Largest Carousel" (a glittering behemoth, 80 feet in diameter and 35 feet high), a collection of giant pipe organs, the "Red Room," with its chandeliered rendition of the Nutcracker Suite, the "Doll Room," with two miniature carousels that slowly twirl the huge collection of dolls, while the "World's Largest Cannon" (its balls alone weigh 7,000 pounds)

stands guard over the itty-bitty carni val. Other sites include a series of min ture circuses, an "Oriental Room," w rare and intriguing carvings and art, and an endless parade of other exoti elaborate treats.

How Now?

Largest Talking Cow
Wisconsin Pavilion
Hwy. 10
Neillsville, WI 54456

Hours: Always visible
Admission: Free
Getting There: *Chatty Belle is at the Wisconsin Pavilion, now the headquarters WCCN FM-AM on Hwy. 10 in Neillsville, which is in central Wisconsin.*

Neillsville has an embarrassment of riches sitting in the yard of the old Wi consin Pavilion, a relic of the 1964 N York World's Fair. The Pavilion, whi looks like a cross between an upside-down umbrella and a UFO, housed a exhibit on the Wisconsin dairy industr and when New Yorkers were set to te it down, Wisconsin brought it back home. Now, the building is home to t Neillsville Chamber of Commerce, lo radio station WCCN, and assorted cheese and gift shops. On the buildin grounds stands a menagerie of genui tourist attractions, the most famous b ing "Chatty Belle, World's Largest Talking Cow."

Chatty will chew the cud with anyo who'll listen, launching into an educa tional lecture on the merits of Wiscons cows and their dairy products. Chatty toddler, the taciturn little "Bullet," is speechless but mighty cute. Chatty Bel

ined by some equally cheesy monu-
nts, including the Cheesemobile, a
,000 tractor-trailer specially built to
sport the World's Largest Cheese
$\frac{1}{4}$ tons) to the World's Fair. There's
a replica of that huge wheel of
ese on display (the original was eat-
nany years ago) and a rock garden
a rock ("exactly this shape when it
dug out of the ground," proclaims
CN) thought by some to resemble
state of Wisconsin.

t Wrenching

edical Progress
useum
S. Beaumont Rd.
ie Du Chien, WI 53821
) 326-2921

urs: May 1-Oct. 31, daily 10 a.m.-5 p.m.
mission: Free
tting There: The museum is at Fort
wford in Prairie Du Chien, which is near
Wisconsin-Iowa border on U.S. Hwy. 18.

st notable about this museum is the
ibit devoted to the pioneer doctor
lliam Beaumont, to whom the muse-
is dedicated. Beaumont's operations
Alexis St. Martin, (a.k.a. the "man
h the hole in his stomach") were the
ndation for modern medicine's basic
owledge of the digestive system. As a
tter of fact, they were also the foun-
tion for Beaumont's credentials as a
ctor; he'd had no real medical experi-
e before St. Martin came along.
ide from Beaumont's instruments,
tes, and other mementos, the muse-
boasts several other collections, in-
ding the infamous transparent twins:

two peekaboo mannequin females exhibiting, respectively, 25 organs and the
skeletal structure. Each body part lights
up as it is discussed, a trick Beaumont
no doubt would have appreciated when
he was rummaging around in Alexis St.
Martin's stomach.

Just for the Halibut

National Freshwater
Fishing Hall of Fame
Hall of Fame Drive
(Box 33)
Hayward, WI 54843
(715) 634-4440

Hours: April 15-Nov. 1, daily 10 a.m.-5 p.m.
(grounds close at 6 p.m.); Nov.-April 15,
Mon.-Fri. 9 a.m.-4:30 p.m.
Admission: Adults, $3; children 10-18, $2;
children under 10, 50 cents
Getting There: Located in northwest
Wisconsin, 2 miles south of Duluth, Minn.
Take Hwy. 53 to Hwy. 63 toward Ashland
and get off at the Hayward exit. Follow signs
to the museum.

For all the fishermen who've ever said,
"You should have seen the one that got
away," never fear: it's been captured
here. It's a huge fiberglass fishie. This
muskie is four and a half stories high,
half a city block long, with a set of jaws
that Steven Spielberg's shark would
give his eye teeth for.
   The mammoth muskie presides majestically over the gardens of the National Freshwater Fishing Hall of Fame and
Museum, but he's more than just a pretty face. He's a walk-through museum,
where visitors can stroll from tip to tail
seeing exhibits on dying fish breeds and
the world's largest nightcrawler (real,
but dead). Then it's on to the observa-

tion deck, perched precipitously inside the muskie's gaping, toothy maw, where visitors can gaze out over the picturesque garden of oversized, frollicking fiberglass fish below. Is this an angler's heaven, or what?

The four-building hall of fame and museum complex houses extensive collections on every conceivable aspect of freshwater fishing. The hall of fame, naturally enough, honors great fishermen and their collossal catches, with records, photographs, and trophies galore. The museum portion has everything from antique outboard motors and hooks that caught fishermen instead of fish to alluring lures and an entire display of tackle boxes. There are exhibits on specific species ("The World of Bass") and displays of rods and reels and tons of other fishy artifacts.

Hayward's own Bob Kutz first came up with the hall of fame idea in 1960 but it was another 10 years before the project really had its head above water. In 1969, the James B. ("Jim") Beam Distillery Company aided the floundering museum with a contract for a series of fishing decanters that would net the much-needed funds. Soon, money poured in from collectors who wanted drink *with* a fish rather than like one and the National Freshwater Fishing Hall of Fame and Museum was under way. The site officially opened in 197 with more buildings and the giant muskie garden being added later on.

Aside from Jim Beam decanters, the Freshwater Fishing Museum has at least one other spectacular money-raising program: the Memorial Wall in the B Fish Angler Shrine. Here, the loved on early departed fishers can have their handwritten remembrance heated onto a glazed ceramic wall tile attached to the memorial wall. The ~~~~ly also receives a walnut plaque, a ~~~~cription to the hall of fame's quar~~ publication, *The Splash*, and a free ~~~~ly pass for the year of purchase. All ~~~ costs a mere $100—no doubt a ~~~~tion of the cost of having a custom-~~ fish-shaped mausoleum built.

~n article published in a museum ~~spaper claims that, at a half-million ~~rs, the big fish was a bargain when ~~ (and shaped by hand, no less) in ~8-79. Today, says the museum, it ~~ld net twice that price. That the Na~~al Freshwater Fishing Hall of Fame ~~ Museum managed to avoid the ~~ue of inflated fish is just one of the ~~y miracles associated with this es~~ ~~ishment. There is a certain lure to ~~ place; it's not just the tackle boxes,

or the outboard motors, or even the giant night crawler—it's something indefinable. It has to do with the big fish. Some visitors come just to stand in the muskie's mouth and stare out at the Wisconsin landscape. Others are hooked for life.

Flour Power

Water-Powered Museum
Hwy. 27
(Rte. 3, Box 129)
Augusta, WI 54722

Hours: May 1-Oct. 31, daily 10 a.m.-5 p.m.
Admission: Adults, $4; students 6-18, $2; children 3-6, $1
Getting There: The museum is on Hwy. 27, 3 miles north of Augusta.

This is an educational little museum, with exhibits showing the history of a

nineteenth-century water-powered flour and grist mill. Owned and operated by the Clark family since 1894, the mill was converted into a museum in 1968, so that tourists could get a first-hand look at the mill's 3,000 feet of belting and 175 pulleys, all water powered. Unfortunately, the best thing about the museum can be seen only if you arrive with a tour group of 30 or more. If you do, you will be treated to the museum's "special show": mill owner Gus Clark and his amazing horse Clementine.

Their claim to fame is the 220-mile ride they took together 1972, with Gus in full Civil War regalia, to commemorate the the 150th birthday of President Ulysses S. Grant. The trip, says a Dells Mill brochure, "received the best wishes of Governor Lucey of Wisconsin, Governor Ogilvy of Illinois, and President Nixon." Now, Gus (still in uniform) and Clementine perform a special show for large groups which starts with a tour of the museum and finishes off with a sing-along of nineteenth-century ballads played on Gus's "gittfiddle," followed by a Kentucky long-rifle muzzle loading and firing demonstration. Just in case word of mouth doesn't bring the tour groups flocking, the folks at Dells Mill are not above generating some grist for their own publicity mill: "We at the museum consider Gus one of the greatest creative talents of our time."

Big Bird

World's Largest Loon
Mercer Chamber of Commerce
Box 368
Mercer, WI 54547
(715) 476-2389

Hours: Always visible
Admission: Free
Getting There: The loon sits on Hwy. 51, just south of Mercer, which is in north-central Wisconsin, near the border with Michigan

So what if Baraboo has the world's largest living bird, the rare white crane? Mercer has the world's largest fiberglass loon, and that's got to count for something. Erected in 1981, the big lug of loon stands 16 feet tall and weighs 2,000 pounds. He rises majestically above a stone-flecked mound, his beak held high with only the slightest hint of a grin. This bird also speaks: push a button at his base and a three-minute tape sends out a plethora of surrealistic sounding loon calls along with tidy bits of information on loon habitat and other fowl facts.

Mercer calls itself the "Loon Capital of the World," and rightfully so: thousands of these graceful water birds call the marshy Mercer area their pond sweet home. The Mercer Chamber of Commerce feathered the nest of the statue project with $10,000 in hopes that the big bird would call attention to the town and also to local conservation efforts aimed at protecting the loon from careless recreationalists and industrialists. A small landscaped park with picnic tables surrounds the statue, so weary travelers can pull over and relax in the shadow of this fabulous fowl.

WEIRD
WONDERFUL
AMERICA

West

Arizona

Over the Hump

Hi-Jolly Monument

Business Rte. I-10
Quartzsite, AZ 85346
Parker Area Chamber of Commerce
Box 627
Parker, AZ 85344
(602) 669-2174

Hours: Always visible
Admission: Free
Getting There: The monument is on I-10's
alternate Business Rte. as it passes through
Quartzsite, about half a block from Ted's
Truck Stop.

The legends of How the West Was Won
with the help of horses, long-horned
steer, etc., are—well—legendary. But
there was a time when folks thought the
West might be won (or at least mort-
gaged for a fixed interest rate) by camels. Lest the West forget this bumpy history lesson, Quartzsite erected a statue
to the camel trainer and driver who
came along for the ride. Haji Ali (Ameri-

cans naturally mangled his name into
"Hi Jolly") left the mild East for the
Wild West in the 1850s when the U.S.
Army imported a bunch of camels to be
used as desert pack animals. Although
Hi Jolly did a fine job of camel-wran-
gling, the Great Hump-backed Experi-
ment never caught on. Gone but not forgotten, Hi Jolly is memorialized in this
stone and concrete pyramid, topped
with a camel.

Yankee Ingenuity

London Bridge

Spanning Lake Havasu
Lake Havasu Area Chamber of Commerce
1930 Mesquite Ave.
Lake Havasu City, AZ 86403
(602) 855-4115

Hours: Always visible
Admission: Free
Getting There: Lake Havasu City is in the
westernmost part of Arizona near the
California border. From I-40, take Exit 9 south
to the city. The bridge spans Lake Havasu in
the heart of the city.

Ever since we won our freedom from the
British, Americans have been trying to
crawl back into the cultural womb of
our revolutionary enemy. From gawk-
ing at royal weddings to gleefully boar-
ing the tops of double-decker buses, we
are a country of starry-eyed Anglo-
philes. In the late 1960s, centuries of
Anglophilia reached an all-time high
with the transfer and reconstruction—
at a cost of $2.46 million—of the genu-
ine, original, one-of-a-kind London
Bridge in little ol' Lake Havasu City.
   In 1962, the British government
learned that London Bridge was liter-
ly falling down due to excessive traffic.
Rather than destroy it, the governme
sold the bridge to Thomas McCulloch,
Yankee entrepreneur, who in turn be
gan the process of importing the brid
to its new home spanning Arizona's
Lake Havasu. The transfer was acco
plished through a complex procedure
that included careful deconstruction,
coding of each individual stone, ship
ping the pieces to California, then
trucking them to Arizona, and finally
reconstructing the bridge with the aid
intricate diagrams and supportive sa
molds. It was a mammoth effort, but

posedly well worth the tourist dol-
that have poured in since Lake
vasu City became America's home-
n England.

here are many ways to enjoy Lake
vasu's London Bridge and environs.
can drive over it in your car, walk
tfully along its historic length, or
n pretend you're yachting down the
imes by taking a "bumper boat" out
he lake for a whiz past those old
hes. Don't forget to stop along the
y to snap a few pictures, and then fin-
off your day strolling through the
er-quaint pseudo-Tudor village,
iplete with candle factories and taffy
es. Hey, who needs Europe anyway?

ting Impression

eteor Museum
E. Birch
gstaff, AZ 86001
2) 774-8350

urs: May 15-Sept. 15, daily 6 a.m.-6 p.m.;
t. 16-Nov. 14, daily 7 a.m.-5 p.m.; Nov. 15-
rch 15, daily 7:30 a.m.-4:30 p.m.; March
May 14, daily 7 a.m.-5 p.m.

Admission: Adults, $5; senior citizens, $4;
juniors 12-17, $2; children, $1
Getting There: Located 40 miles east of
Flagstaff, just off I-40 (Exit 233).

Not many tourist attractions can claim
they were "Founded in 20,000
B.C."—but this place certainly can.
This giant meteor crater is considered to
be the best preserved on the planet.
Measuring 570 feet deep and nearly a
mile wide, the crater was created by a
nickel-iron meteor slamming into the
earth at nearly 45,000 miles per hour. It
naturally made quite an impression—
an impression that closely resembles the
terrain of the moon. That coincidence
did not go unnoticed by NASA, which
trained all of its Apollo astronauts and
tested lunar travel vehicles on the crater's surface.

An observation area has been built
around the crater, where visitors can
stare into the abyss of this alien dent,
then learn about meteors and their
makeup at the adjacent Museum of
Astrogeology. The museum has one of
the world's finest collections of meteor-
ite fragments, with lively and well-ex-

plained exhibits on the physics and geology of meteor formation and travel. At the Astronaut Hall of Fame, also located here, vacationers can view astronaut memorabilia and records, pose for pictures in front of a real space capsule and then have a picnic lunch in the recently established "Astronaut Park," dedicated to crew members of the Apollo and Challenger shuttle missions.

Eek!

Mouse House Museum

3634 Civic Center Plaza
Scottsdale, AZ 85251
(602) 990-2481

Hours: Mon.-Thurs. 10 a.m.-4 p.m. or by appointment
Admission: Free
Getting There: Located on Civic Center Plaza, a half block from Second St., which is at the far southeast corner of the Mall. Enter the museum through the rear parking lot.

Don't bother trying to find a chair to stand on at the Mouse House Museum—every seat and table is taken

up by the residents rodent. But fear n all of the 3,000-plus mice in this ho are replicas, not originals.

The original mouse in this collecti was the collector herself, Olive Atwa Getz, whose childhood nickname "Mouse" stuck throughout her lifetir Little Mouse Getz soon became fasci nated with her namesake rodents, an began a collection that was added to friends and family during their trave around the world. The Mouse House Museum is sponsored by the Getz Fou dation in Olive's memory, as a tribute her single-minded pursuit of mouse memorabilia. Far from being a touris trap, the Mouse House Museum is a squeaky-clean collection of truly nic mice.

Mickey Mouse, certainly the most famous squeaker of modern times, is generously represented with a vast co lection that dates from the 1920s to present, featuring everything from watches amd rocking chairs to pillow gumball machines, and trash cans, a bearing his big-eared likeness. One o the rarest bits of His Mickey-ness on d play is a set of the original celluloids

d to film the 1938 classic "Brave Lit-
Tailor."

mong Mickey's companions are a
use bride and groom, in a music box
sion of the "Three Blind Mice;"
den mice slaving away in a cheese
ory; and mouse firefighters racing
a tiny ladder to save jumping mouse
ims from a mouse-house fire. This
scenario is particularly appropriate:
ve's husband, George, was founder
Phoenix's Hall of Flame firefighting
seum.

he mice here come in all shapes,
s, and media, including mice made
n ivory and clay. In one room, a
r-'round Christmas tree strung with
mouse lights casts a cheerful glow
the surrounding rodents. But per-
s the collection's best exhibit is a
iature nine-room Victorian mouse
se, complete with inhabitants frol-
ng in a backyard hot tub and play-
the scales on a tiny piano.

Man's Home

ystery Castle

E. Mineral Rd.
enix, AZ 85040
2) 268-1581

urs: Oct.-June, Tues.-Sun. 11 a.m.-5 p.m.
mission: Adults, $2.50; children, 50 cents
tting There: The castle is tucked away on
southern edge of Phoenix, just off the far
th end of Seventh St., the major artery
ding to S. Mountain Park.

stery Castle is just that—a wonder-
, sad mystery left by the builder as a
acy of love to the family he had de-
ted 17 years earlier. Boyce Gulley
d Seattle in 1927 without leaving his
fe, Fran, and baby daughter, Mary

Lou, so much as a forwarding address.
Suffering from what he took to be a fatal
case of tuberculosis, Gulley moved to
Phoenix—but within a year he had re-
cuperated. Rather than head home, he
began building a strange, amusing
home out of local materials and found
objects. Gulley was keeping a promise
he had made to his daughter the night
before his disappearance: one day, he
had told the infant, he would build her a
castle.

And build it he did, using local stones
and mortars for the walls, glass refrigerator boxes for windows, and broken
bathtubs for stove hoods. It is an odd
place indeed to wander through—rooms
that jump whole levels, hallways that
suddenly turn into outside walkways.
And in every room there are offbeat design flourishes—beds that roll back and
forth on tracks, mannequins seated at
pipe organs. Most of the eccentricities at
the castle are merely the products of an
odd sense of humor: a tiny, meticulously

built stone tepee is actually a doghouse, while the underground "dugout" bar made from half of a freight wagon was built with an eye toward all the Wild West clichés Gulley could imagine.

For all the Disneyesque leanings within, the castle looks even stranger from the outside—terraces sprawling every which way, cantilevered stair-cases, rickety patios, and cut-out obser-vation areas give the appearance of some half-inhabited ancient Indian ruin, or perhaps a modernist architect's fractured fantasy. There are 18 rooms in the castle, none on the same level or of the same shape, with 13 fireplaces spread throughout the structure. The castle is full of contradictory styles and forms, yet it somehow blends with the rocky, scrubby foothills of the Southern Mountains, from which it seems to grow like a wild stone cactus. The Mystery Castle is such a perfect fit for its fun-house environment that Frank Lloyd Wright is said to have admired the out-rageous, organic nature of the building.

While he was creating this master-piece of odd architecture, Gulley never once communicated with his wife and daughter. Then, 17 years after his dis-appearance, Fran and her teenaged daughter Mary Lou began receiving l[etters] from the lonely, desolate Boyce. Several letters arrived, all addressed from Phoenix, but none explained hi[s] absence. The next correspondence wa[s] telegram announcing Gulley's death

Fran and Mary Lou left for Phoen[ix] immediately, and here, in the enigma[tic] Southern Mountains, they found the Mystery Castle. The mother and dau[gh]-ter moved into the castle, and for yea[rs] to come stumbled on hidden caches [of] artifacts and money. Among these fin[ds,] secured behind a trapdoor and tucke[d] away with a billfold containing $500[,] was a note addressed to "My dear lit[tle] Alice in Westernland" that read, "My love for you and Fran is carved on th[e] foundation of the castle. You see, I haven't forgotten my promise to you when we used to sit in front of the fir[e]place back home reading the beloved fairy books."

It was promise fulfilled too late—a castle foundation built at the price of fatherless childhood. For Mary Lou Gulley, who still lives in the palace h[er] father built for her, that sacrifice will a[l]-ways be the true mystery of this castl[e]

rd Times

etrified Wood Museum

ton & Sons, Inc.
vy. 180 E
O. Box 908)
lbrook, AZ 86025
2) 524-3470

urs: Oct.-April, daily 8 a.m.-5 p.m.; June-
g., daily 6 a.m.-7 p.m.; May and Sept., daily
.m.-6 p.m. Closed Christmas Day and
ring inclement weather

Imission: Free

tting There: The museum is part of a
trified-wood sales outlet and information
nter at the South Entrance to the Petrified
rest National Park on Hwy. 180-E out of
lbrook.

nce the 1930s, Frank DoBell ran a
all but thriving one-man (plus a cou-
e of kids) petrified-wood business,
eating tables and bookends and other

household objects out of this beautiful
wood-turned-to-stone. But sometimes
he came across a chunk of petrified
wood that was just too lovely—or too
weird—to lose, so he'd hold onto it instead of selling it. Friends added to his
collection with gifts made from petrified
wood, and before he knew it, DoBell had
hundreds of rare and remarkable muse-
um-quality pieces. What else was there
to do but open a museum?

This museum is actually just a one-
room showcase of DoBell's collection,
located at the information and sales outlet of Don and Edna Patton's (DoBell's
daughter and son-in-law) petrified-
wood business, Patton and Sons, Inc. It
stands, appropriately, at the entrance to
the Petrified Forest National Park. The
museum may be small, but it certainly
packs some walloping displays of petrified art and artistry. One of the highlights, a priceless clock made in the im-

age of a giant "railroad watch" with a carved chain and fob, took the artist 12 years to complete. Another rarity is a shell-like bowl formed from a 10-inch piece of gem-quality petrified wood.

Petrified wood is the rare product of a centuries-long crystallization process that turns trees submerged in mineralized waters into lustrous agate and jasper gemstone. The DoBell collection is a tribute to the beauty of this rock, which has been much maligned over the years for its gimmicky association with tourist souvenirs. Sure, there are a few tacky souvenirs for sale at the Patton and Sons store, but for free you can gaze at one of the finest gatherings of precious petrified wood in the world.

It's a Blast

Titan Missile Museum

Duval Mine Rd.
Green Valley, AZ 85614
(602) 791-2929

Hours: Nov.-April, daily 9 a.m.-5 p.m.; May-Oct., Wed.-Sun. 9 a.m.-5 p.m. You can see the museum only as part of a regularly scheduled tour; the last tour begins at 4 p.m.
Admission: Adults, $4; children, $2 (under 10 free); senior citizens and military, $3
Getting There: Located about a half-hour's drive from Tucson. Take I-19 S from Tucson to Exit 69 (Duval Mine Rd.), go west 0.10 mile past La Cañada, and turn right at the museum sign.

It's enough to make your blood run cold, stepping out of your car into the desert heat and staring directly across a secured area at the nosecone of a nuclear warhead. Visions of *The Day After* dance in your head as you step cautiously into the entrance building, pay your admission, and settle into an uncom-

fortable theater chair in a small, dilapidated "briefing room." Before long, a tour guide has handed out hardhats to the seated throng. With a congenial smile frozen on her face, the guide relates the size and power of the now-dismantled Titan II missile force—54 in total, with 18 weapons each in the areas surrounding Tucson, Little Rock, and Wichita.

One last request before rolling a grainy, eight-minute Air Force video about deterrence and the "Peace Is Our Business" nuclear weapon theme: as there's still a great deal of electricity being pumped into the missile site, the guide requests that visitors "Please not push any buttons" during their tour. Enough said.

And now, on to the tour. In the yard outside, the emptiness of the surrounding desert and mountain ranges becomes suddenly apparent. The missile site is little more than a cordoned-off military oasis in the middle of nowhere, and this barrenness serves as a discon-

certing backdrop against which to examine the exposed missile re-entry cone that juts out of the earth. It's an innocuous enough piece of metal—no skull and crossbones or rebel flags painted on the facade. It's just a round-nosed cone that could as easily be the front end of an a-

ne or part of a space capsule. But it's
, and the blandness of this mass-pro-
:ed missile head is somehow chilling.
it happens, this is just the beginning.
st of the weapon is still lodged under-
und in its silo.
The few other pieces of equipment
nding in this dusty yard include the
:ket engines (big, beefy-looking
ces of highly mechanical metal), a
:cue helicopter, and a security system
own as "Tipsies" that looks like a
tball goalpost with pinwheels at-
hed, standing guard over the area.
What with peace treaties and all, the
r Force had to prove this is a disman-
d missile base, so the nose cone and
:ket engines were placed above-
ound where the Soviets can take veri-
:ation photographs from space when-
er they want. All other Titan missiles
ve been or are being completely dis-
antled. This particular Titan base was
n alert" (in active service) from 1962
1984, and opened as a museum in
)86 as part of the Pima Air Museum.
The next and final stop on this whirl-
ind tour is the actual missile silo,
hich happens to be the only Interconti-
ental Ballistic Missile (ICBM) silo in
ie world open to the public. A promi-
ent sign over the entrance to the under-
round stairway reads "Watch for Rat-
esnakes." Enough said.
After descending 55 open-backed,
etal mesh steps (high heels and short
cirts are not recommended), you pass
rough a 3½-inch-thick, four-ton con-
rete blast door, walk down a dank cor-
idor and enter the control room. As in
he movies, here are panels of keyholes,
linking lights, and colored buttons
vith ominous labels like "Countdown"
nd "Launch." The guide rattles off a
eries of statistics, including the fact

that the entire launch process takes one
minute and 12 seconds.

At this point, you pause to examine a
big white fuel-protection suit that looks
like the Sta-Puff Man who couldn't
quite stay puffed. "The rocket fuel can
be deadly if it touches the skin," the
guide explains, and points to various
patches on the surface of the well-worn
suit. Then the group is ushered down
long steel hallways that rumble and
echo with every footstep. Now you come
upon the missile itself, all 110 feet of it,
standing upright in its launch silo. Windows have been placed at the observation deck so visitors can get a good, hard
look at missile that has been the nation's
"Peacekeeper" since the early 1960s.

Looking oddly vulnerable, like a pa-
tient in an intensive care unit, the missile has tubes and hoses running into its
body from all directions. Its sheer size
and bulk belie its status as a dinosaur in
this age of swift, silent, and compact nuclear weapons.

"The missile you're looking at," the
guide informs the group, "is basically
just a giant gas tank used for getting the
business end to its destination."

The parts of the silo opened to the
public are only a few rooms and
hallways—the rest of this underground
fortress, with some three levels of living
quarters, operational apparatus, and
military hardware, is still off-limits. But
even a small taste of silo life (manned 24
hours a day by teams who live and work
in these cramped quarters) is enough to
give anyone nuclear nightmares. Back
on the surface again, with the rush of
sunshine and dry desert air, there is a
great sense of relief that this particular
"business end" never saw any business.

To lighten your mood on the way out,
there's a fully stocked gift shop with

such memorable memorabilia as "I Had a Blast at the Titan Missile Museum" baseball caps and bumper stickers, as well as coffee mugs, key chains, postcards, and ashtrays—all emblazoned with the Titan museum logo. Tourists snatch up these pieces left and right, benign souvenirs of a frightening and fascinating trip.

Horse Power

Tom Mix Monument

Pinal County Development Board and Visitors Center
P.O. Box 967
Florence, AZ 85232
(602) 868-4331

Hours: Always visible
Admission: Free
Getting There: Located 18 miles south of Florence, on U.S. Rte. 80-89.

Tom Mix was an American cowboy hero of the first class, but he had a bad habit of driving too fast. On October 12, 1940, at the age of 60, Mix was killed at this spot while pushing his 1937 Cord 812 Super Charge Phantom to 80 mph.

He might have survived the car's loss control had a suitcase precariously perched behind him not come smash down on his head. You can mourn hi passing at his death-site (which has been renamed Tom Mix Wash in his honor). The monument at the spot where Mix passed on to that great du ranch in the sky is a touching tribute i deed: a riderless horse leaps through t air, as if lunging toward the heavens pluck back the missing cowboy.

Thorn of Plenty

World's Largest Rosebus

Rose Tree Inn
Corner of 4th St. and Toughnut
Tombstone, AZ 85688
(602) 457-3326

Hours: Daily 8 a.m.-6 p.m.
Admission: Adults, $1; children under 12, free
Getting There: From I-10, take Hwy. 80 south into Tombstone, turn south onto 4th St and proceed to the museum, which is at th corner of 4th and Toughnut Sts.

mbstone's motto is "The Town That
Museum, a Museum That Is a
wn," and that is true. Add to that its
ssession of the World's Largest Rose-
sh, and you've got one of the must-see
es in Tombstone. The museum houses
ollection of 1880s Tombstone items,
st notably the furnishings of original
s throughout the West, including a
droom set that once belonged to
oss" Tweed of Tammany Hall and a
h Thomas Clock from Wyatt Earp's
iental Saloon. Another highlight is a
nd-carved miniature diorama of the
nous Gun Fight at the O.K. Corral.
Just outside the inn, the World's
rgest Rosebush does indeed grow
ok. The bush, a white Lady Banksia
own from a root brought over from
otland in 1885, now spreads its tan-
d mass of thorny branches over a
000-square-foot arbor. Every spring,
llions of tiny white roses blanket the
bor, which would still smell as sweet
any other name.

of sculpture gardens and parks filled
with industrial-strength statuary. In
fact, the Antone Martin Park's monu-
mental Last Supper façade weighs in at
125 tons. All of the participants in this
enormous tableau are carved in bas-re-
lief, with the exception of Christ, whose
3-D head sticks up into an open window. There are more than 30 statues in
the park, all depicting biblical scenes,
including the "Garden of Gethsemane,"
"Suffer the Little Children," and
"Christ and the Woman of Samaria."
It's an odd setting for such devotional-
ism: the barrenness of the land, with the
hot desert sand and low, scraggly brush,
is anything but inviting. Then again,
concrete is not the world's most delicate
or delightful medium, which may be
why these huge, cold statues fit right in
to this hot, dry landscape. The Antone
Martin Park (once known as the Desert
Christ Park, but recently renamed)
might be moving, if the figures weren't
so heavy.

California

Heavy Scene

Antone Martin Park

7090 Twenty-nine Palms Hwy.
cca Valley, CA 92284
phone

ours: Always open
dmission: Free
etting There: The park is on Hwy. 62
wenty-Nine Palms Hwy.) in southern
alifornia's Yucca Valley.

oncrete seems to be a rather popular
rt medium, judging from the number

Doll of Fame

Barbie Doll Hall of Fame

The Doll Studio
325 Hamilton Ave.
Palo Alto, CA 94301
(415) 326-5841

Hours: Tues.-Sat. 10:30 a.m.-4 p.m.
Admission: Adults, $2; children, $1
Getting There: From Hwy. 101 through Palo
Alto, take a left onto University, another left
onto Waverly, and then go right onto
Hamilton Ave., where the hall of fame is
located in the Doll Studio shop at 325
Hamilton Ave.

Some might call Barbie the ultimate
trendsetter. Born in 1959, she has lived
and dressed through every major (and

many minor) fashion and lifestyle trend in the following decades. She was the first on her block to sport a miniskirt, and she suited up for aerobics faster than Jane Fonda does deep knee bends. Designers like Adolpho and Givenchy have dressed her curvy figure, and men from Ken to GI Joe have thrown themselves at her dainty plastic feet. So it's about time this absolute doll had her own hall of fame to celebrate just how far she's come in less than three decades.

Evelyn Burkhalter is the keeper of the hall of fame, which fills a large part of her Doll Studio shop in Palo Alto. The museum is head-to-toe Barbie, with floor-to-ceiling shelves of the doll wearing many of her chic outfits, her dune buggies and speedboats dangling from the ceiling, and her dream houses and hacienda getaways dotting the room's landscape like so many villas in the Hollywood hills.

Burkhalter, who has been collecting Barbies since the late 1970s, opened the

Barbie Hall of Fame in 1984, the year that marked the 25th anniversary of the doll's introduction. "I decided on Barbie because there were so many things about her that really represent the changes in our country," Burkhalter says.

While Barbie may not reflect all the dramatic changes in American society since the late '50s, she certainly has come a long way, baby, in mirroring the evolution of women's roles during the past three decades. A Barbie in a business suit and sneakers is a common sight now, but when she first showed up on the bedroom floors of America's daughters she was dressed to kill in aprons and hostess gowns. Along the way, and represented in full force on the shelves of the Hall of Fame, Barbie has had careers as a fast food server (she looks smashing in her McDonald's uniform), an astronaut, ballroom dancer, cowgirl, beauty queen (several renditions thereof), stewardess, disco dancer, model, cheerleader, and briefcase toter, to name a

v. An impressive résumé, indeed. The doll herself has changed considably since her youth. Her original inration, a doll named Lilli made in st Germany, was a curvy, quite ult-looking plaything; the very first rbies (measurements: 5¼″-3″-4¾″) micked that look, but were panned toy stores as being too sexy. With ghtly modified proportions, Barbie came a hit. She came with a zebraiped bathing suit (one-piece, natural) and hep-cat sunglasses, and had a ckup line of some 90 outfits and acssories to keep Mom and Dad pulling t the wallet again and again. (At one int in the 1960s, Mattel, Inc., Barbie's anufacturer, became the largest man-acturer of "women's wear" in the orld, with more than 20 million Barbie shions sold annually.) Today's Barbie mes with a catalog of hundreds of acssories, outfits, dream houses, cuzzis, and other wanna-haves. The st Barbies were made of solid plastic, like the hollowed-out models of re-nt vintage, and originally came with ny holes in their feet for the copper ds that helped keep them on their es. And here's the real kicker: Blonde arbie was once a brunette. Although ost of the early Barbies were blonde, a w brunettes were manufactured early n; on today's market, one of these rare onblondes in mint condition can go for 1,500 or more.

But Barbie has not faced the vagaries f style and form alone—and her bud-ies join her in the hall of fame to prove nis point. Displays show a variety of en dolls ranging from prom-date weet to macho man to disco maniac this last dude is pure Travolta), while arbie's female counterparts include id sister "Growing Up Skipper," who

goes from training bra to B-cup with the flick of a wrist. And, as ethnic consciousness swept America in the late '60s, suddenly some of Barbie's "very best friends" were black and Asian (most had Caucasian features; only the skin tone changed). But Barbie herself is still the queen of the quick-change artists, and she looks as drop-dead smashing in her Marilyn Monroe slink dress as she does in her prim Pat Nixon suit.

From America's sweetheart to a boardroom hellcat, Barbie's seen and done it all. Yet she still looks like that innocent, fresh-faced sexpot who was born when America was coming of age so many years ago. The more Barbie changes, the more she stays the same.

Making Up Is Hard to Do

Max Factor Museum
1666 N. Highland Ave.
Los Angeles, CA 90028
(213) 463-6668

Hours: Mon.-Sat. 9 a.m.-5 p.m.
Admission: Free
Getting There: Located in the heart of Hollywood, a half-block south of Hollywood Blvd. and a block from the infamous corner, Hollywood and Vine. (N. Highland is sandwiched between Vine St. and Orange Dr.). Mann's Chinese Theater is a block away on Hollywood Blvd.

Max Factor the man and Max Factor the company are as different as night crème and day moisturizer. With a few brush strokes, Max Factor the man could whisk a set of cheekbones onto a moon-faced starlet or hide a set of jowls on a fleshy leading man. He wielded an almost Frankensteinian power to transform his subjects, creating glamour or of the prosaic. Max Factor the compan has managed to infiltrate every dime-store beauty counter and supermarket sundries aisle with inexpensive, plastic wrapped cosmetics. The Max Factor Museum brings together the man and his company in a partnership of histor and commerce; adjacent to the museur that tells the story of the man and his makeup, a discount outlet hawks the company's wares.

The museum is housed in a three-story art deco building, which Factor began using as a makeup studio in 1928 he eventually had the place completely refurbished and held a gala studio re-opening in 1935. On display is the actu al Max Factor "Scroll of Fame" autographed by many of the 8,000 or so luminaries who attended the gala and by many other stars in following years. The rather ratty-looking scroll, browned and blackened around the edges, is said to bear the world's most complete collection of star's autographs.

Stars of screen and scroll crop up everywhere in this museum. Old advertisements featuring personality endorsements, studio portraits lovingly inscribed to Max, and wig blocks of stars' heads are among the many stellar exhibits. The wig blocks, dating back to a prehair-dryer era—when even macho men like Frank Sinatra and Gene Kelly had to wear hairpieces for that picture-perfect look—were once standard issue for all actors and actresses.

The blocks on exhibit date back to the thirties and forties and resemble the blank Styrofoam heads used to display wigs and hats today—except that each block's "scalp" bears an exacting diagram of the way the wig should be styled. These amusing blueprints for sideburns and pompadours alone make the visit worthwhile.

But the real stars of this show are the legendary makeup and accessories that changed the face—and the faces—of Hollywood forever. Max Factor, in many ways the Thomas Edison of cosmetics, invented everything from tube greasepaint to the first makeup for color television, both of which are displayed here. The Academy Award he received in 1929 for his creation of "Panchromatic Make-Up" is also exhibited, as are circa-1904 machines that made face and body creams, and a set of false eyelashes from 1910.

A visit to the Max Factor Museum presents a disillusioning illusion, because much of the surface glamour that was Hollywood came out of the foundation tubes and rouge pots on display here. Then again, the stars who served as Factor's living canvases were often already the creations of a dream machinery that churned out altered identities, histories, and personalities to suit the tastes of an idolatrous public. Perhaps Max Factor the man and Max Factor the company aren't that different after all: they both gave America what it clamored for—beauty on the big screen and in the corner store.

Myth America

Museum of Modern Mythology

693 Mission, Ninth Fl.
San Francisco, CA 94105
(415) 546-0202

Hours: Thurs.-Sat. noon-5 p.m.
Admission: Adults, $2; children (under 18), 50 cents
Getting There: Located in an office building at the corner of Fourth and Mission Sts., a block north of the Moscone Convention Center. It's accessible by all public transportation.

The premise of this tiny museum is that, as surely as the ancients had their mythical dragon-slayers and harvest goddesses, modern society has its heroes and idols—only ours are Tony the Tiger and the Pillsbury Dough Boy instead of Lancelot and Persephone.

The Museum of Modern Mythology is a nostalgia buff's wonderland and an advertising company's dream come true. The main section is housed in one room on the ninth floor of an aging office building, so there's already a slightly corporate feel to the place. But the full-sized Michelin Man and the eight-

foot-tall Jolly Green Giant that guard the entrance soon allay any fears that the collection within might be—that fate worse than death in mass-media America—boring.

The museum's goal—to be the world's only collection devoted solely to the documentation and preservation of advertising characters—is noble, to be sure. Who, in a world soured by Saturday morning cartoons-turned-sales-pitches, would appreciate the glorification of advertising characters? Yet, when you walk into this exhibit and come face-to-face with the images of Mr. Bubble, Poppin' Fresh, the Campbell Soup Kids, and Charlie the Tuna, there's an almost automatic quickening of the pulse, as though you've stumbled

on an old photo album filled with snapshots of long-gone relatives. Like symbols of a universal language, the very sight of Ronald McDonald or Chiquita Banana sets off associations and memories that often have little to do with the actual product the character was created to promote.

The old buddies to be found in the Museum of Modern Mythology run the gamut from cereal characters like Cap'n Crunch to serialized personalities like the TV stars of "Lost in Space." By inverting the theme of advertising characters to include those who got there the long way around, the museum has justified including the stars of popular TV shows and films who eventually were used to sell anything from lunch boxes

notebooks to candy and fast food.
he collection includes advertising
racters in every conceivable form,
n soft-sculpture dolls and plastic-
lded piggy banks to soft drinks and
wable vitamins. Old favorites, in-
ding Mr. Peanut, as well as new stars,
the soul-singing California Raisins,
featured, as are some of the federal
ernment's very own advertising
rs, including Uncle Sam and the Post
ice Eagle. Advertising "giants," like
bright-eyed hound head that once
sided over a Doggie Diner hot-dog
ve-in, are also represented here.

The current one-room location is
much too small to hold all this
history—most of the museum's collection remains in storage—so the museum
is planning a move to bigger quarters; a
series of traveling exhibits also keep
some of this vast collection on continual
display. The pieces on view at the current museum are a fraction of the collection's holdings, but there's enough here
to spark a few pleasant memories.
Whether these advertising characters
are part of a genuine modern mythology
or are merely fleeting icons of a fast-
paced commercial world is anyone's

guess. For the moment, at least, these words from our sponsors are the stars of this show.

The Reel Thing

On Location
6834 Hollywood Blvd.
Los Angeles, CA 90028
(213) 466-7758

Hours: Sun.-Thurs. 8 a.m.-11 p.m.; Fri.-Sat. 8 a.m.-1 a.m.
Admission: Adults, $2.50; children under 12, free when accompanied by adult
Getting There: On Location is on Hollywood Blvd. on the Walk of Fame, across the street from the famous Chinese Theater.

For anyone who ever thought Hollywood types were small-minded, here's an exhibit that both proves and disproves that theory. Built by master craftsman and cabinetmaker Joe Pelkoffer, On Location Hollywood is a meticulous miniature tribute to the 1940s heydays of this silver-screen city. The collection, located at a neo-neon soda fountain and restaurant, consists of five separate scenarios, including a tiny rendition of Hollywood's 45 main blocks, brought to life with amazing detail (Pelkoffer used photos and maps to get the scale and street directions just right). Meticulous, miniaturized versions of the Malibu film colony, Chinese Theater (the original of which is just across the street), Hollywood Bowl, the Brown Derby, and a typical movie studio were also created by Pelkoffer. Although the Brown Derby model was crushed while traveling and has never been rebuilt, all the others are on display.
The faithfulness is at times astound-

ing, a tribute to Pelkoffer's attention detail. The Malibu colony, for examp measuring 12 feet square, is so accurately reproduced that there are even wooden "waves" rolling into shore at the same speed as the real Malibu waves; Pelkoffer had a friend sit on t beach and time the surf. A fake versi of Hollywood may seem something o redundancy, but this version may be even better in many ways than the original.

Reigning Cats and Dogs

Pet Memorial Park
5068 N. Old Scandia Lane
Calabasas, CA 91302
(818) 347-7037

Hours: Daily 8 a.m.-5 p.m.
Admission: Free
Getting There: The park is west of Los Angeles in Calabasas. From the Ventura Freeway, take the Calabasas Pkwy. exit, tu right on Ventura Blvd., and turn left onto O Scandia Lane to the park.

What do Jimmy Durante, Diana Ross Chief Thundercloud, and Morey Amsterdam have in common? They all ha pets buried at this serene and elabora pet cemetery just outside Los Angeles The L.A. Pet Memorial Park is the fin resting place for hundreds of pampere pooches and coddled cats, not to men tion one rather famous horse: "Topper," Hopalong Cassidy's trusty steed
The list of owners who have pets bu ied or memorialized here reads like a Who's Who of show biz: Lionel Barry more, Rudolph Valentino, Gloria Swanson, Eddie Fisher, Bing Crosby, Linda Darnell, Eva Gabor, Betty Grable, Alfred Hitchcock—the list go

and on. So, too, will this pet ceme-
~~te~~ry: although the park land had been
~~slat~~ted for development, a fast-acting
~~gro~~up of animal-loving activists, Save
~~ou~~r Pets' History In Eternity
~~(S~~OPHIE), managed to buy the park in
~~19~~86. SOPHIE sponsored the first state
~~law~~ ever enacted to protect pet cemeter-
~~ies~~ from development, and the park has
~~no~~w been legally dedicated as a pet cem-
~~ete~~ry in perpetuity.

For Southern California sightseers,
~~the~~ park offers an unusual and touching
~~alt~~ernative to the more conventional
~~and~~ somewhat stale fare of studio and
~~star~~s' homes tours. Finding all the fam-
~~ou~~s animals can become a pet project for
~~the~~ whole family.

~~Rel~~axing Nostalgic

~~R~~ipley's Memorial
~~M~~useum

~~Ju~~lliard Park
~~So~~noma County Convention and Visitors
~~B~~ureau
~~63~~7 First St.
~~Sa~~nta Rosa, CA 95404
~~(70~~7) 545-1420

~~Ho~~urs: March–mid-Dec., Wed.-Sun. 11 a.m.-
~~4 p~~.m.

~~Ad~~mission: Adults, $1; children 9-17, 50
~~ce~~nts; children under 9, free

~~Ge~~tting There: The museum is in Julliard
~~Pa~~rk, at the corner of Sonoma and Santa Rosa
~~Ave~~s. in downtown Santa Rosa.

~~An~~yone who's been to such cultural
~~wo~~nderlands as Las Vegas, Gatlinburg,
~~Ni~~agara Falls, and Ocean City has prob-
~~ab~~ly seen the garish, sideshow-styled
~~Ri~~pley's Believe It or Not Museums, with
~~the~~ir plaster-cast "fattest man in the

world" models and gimcrack displays of
ships made from chicken bones and
two-headed sheep. But this museum in
Santa Rosa is dedicated to Robert L.
Ripley himself, the cartoonist purveyor
of all things weird and amazing.

Santa Rosa was Ripley's hometown,
and the memorial building is, appropriately, the "Church Built From One
Tree!" (a redwood, of course) that
made an appearance in the comics panel
of "Ripley's Believe It or Not." Among
the exhibits in the museum are a life-
sized wax sculpture of Ripley, a bust of
the cartoonist sculptured by a blind
man, and such personal artifacts as his
suitcase, Chinese robe and slippers, and
safari helmet. Original Ripley's cartoon
panels are also displayed, along with
mementos of his friendships with such
luminaries as (believe it or not) Shirley
Temple and Milton Berle.

Trigger Happy

Roy Rogers–Dale Evans Museum

15650 Seneca Rd.
Victorville, CA 92392
(619) 243-4547

Hours: Daily 9 a.m.-5 p.m.
Admission: Adults, $3; children 13-16 and senior citizens, $2; children 6-12, $1; children under 6, free
Getting There: The museum is in downtown Victorville, which is in Southern California, just off I-15. Look for the statue of Trigger that stands in front of the building.

You'll know this museum right off—it's the one with the statue of Trigger out front. The *real* Trigger, stuffed for posterity, greets visitors inside along with his embalmed buddies Trigger Jr., Bullet, and Buttermilk the dog.

Aside from mounted pets, the museum offers a rare glimpse into the lives of

s Wild Western pair, with exhibits of
y's gun collection, Dale's religious
oks and records, and a collection of
cy show costumes. Roy's famed Rose
rade Saddle is displayed here, too, as
scale-model covered wagons and
ge coaches and plenty of trophies,
ards, and honors.

der Your Skin

attoo Art Museum

e Tuttle's Tattoo Studio
Seventh St.
Francisco, CA 94105
5) 864-9798

ours: Fluctuate according to Tuttle's
edule; call to verify times or make viewing
pointment
mission: Free
tting There: The museum, located in a
too studio, is on 7th St., a block east of
rket St. in downtown San Francisco.

e ancient art of tattooing dates back
me 10,000 years, but it still looks
sh in this studio and tiny museum
ned by 25-year tattooer Lyle Tuttle.
u may want to avert your eyes as you
ter, as Tuttle is likely to be perform-
g his craft on some eager biker or star-
as you pass through to get to the dis-
ays. The museum traces the history of
in engraving from the Chinese tattoo-
through the Samoans, Japanese, and
tive Americans, and briefly explores
cultural importance of the tattoo in
ese societies. Another display reveals
me 20 different kinds of tattoo nee-
s and engravers, and there are also
rious artistic representations of tattoo
t, many of which are for sale in the
op.

Out on a Limb

Trees of Mystery

U.S. Hwy. 101
(P.O. Box 96)
Klamath, CA 95548
(707) 482-5613

Hours: Hours vary according to daylight
available. Typical hours: summer, 8 a.m.-8:30
p.m.; winter (after holidays), 10 a.m.-4 p.m.
Admission: Trail fee, adults, $4; children, $2;
museum, free
Getting There: Trees of Mystery is on U.S.
Hwy. 101 in Klamath.

The only real mystery about the Trees of
Mystery is the name— which simply re-
fers to a magnificent redwood forest
through which one must pay to stroll, on
the "Trail of Mysterious Trees." Sure,
there are such anomalies as the "Upside
Down Tree," which grows sideways
over the path, and the "Family Tree,"
with its twelve little Sitka spruces
sprouting from a single trunk that
measures 32 feet around. But even these
are hardly mysterious; they're merely
weird. You can see some that are nearly
as nice simply driving along Hwy. 101,
aptly known as Redwood Highway.

Along with the Trees of Mystery nature trail, there is the "Trail of Tall
Tales," which is spiced up considerably
with a few redwood statues (some
carved with a chainsaw), depicting such
legendary figures as the "Pooped Log-
ger" and "End of the Trail," a replica of
the famous James Fraser sculpture of an
exhausted rider and horse. The most
charming statues here are actually visible from the highway: the giant, colorful
figures of Paul Bunyan and his blue ox,
Babe. Paul stands 49 feet tall, waving
and winking mechanically at the passing cars in hopes of luring tourists to his
home. Babe stands a mere 34 feet tall in

comparison, but his squatty, piñata-like body is endearing. Aside from the nature trail, there is the free "End of the Trail Museum," which exhibits crowded but colorful displays of Native American art and artifacts, including handmade baskets, woven blankets, jewelry, and pottery.

For an attraction with such a promising name, Trees of Mystery is pretty tame stuff. Then again, would a place called "Trees That Are Slighty Weird" attract as many tourists?

Destination: Unknown

Unknown Museum

22243 E. Blithedale Ave.
Mill Valley, CA 94941
(415) 383-2726

Hours: Sun. noon-6 p.m.
Admission: Free
Getting There: *The museum is 10 minutes north of the Golden Gate Bridge. From U.S. Hwy. 101, take the E. Blithedale Ave. off-ramp toward downtown Mill Valley.*

Mickey McGowan is a rare artist with a vision of the past that almost everyone shares—sort of. McGowan's Unknown Museum is filled with hundreds of pop cultural icons, from 250 different television sets to 175 Mr. Potato Heads to life-sized figures of the Michelin Man, Colonel Sanders, and E.T. He's got more than 500 stuffed animals on display, as well as exhibits featuring Batman, Star Trek, Santa Claus, the Beatles, and hamburgers. Think pop, and it's here.

The sheer size of the collection would be statement enough—you know, the medium being the message and all that jazz—but McGowan has gone beyond merely cramming the items together un-

der one roof. He has taken the bubble gum-sweet obsessions of twentieth-century society and turned them upside-down, creating punnish exhibits and pseudo-museum-quality galleries from the images and paraphernalia of every day life. A display titled "TV Dinner" a typical aluminum partitioned frozen food tray filled with choice selections of television tubes and other parts. An elaborately documented gallery of European toilet paper, noting such detail as the location and age of each "find," so funny that you may find yourself wiping away tears of laughter with the exhibit itself. Shoes, atomic reactors, Barbie dolls, astronauts, and war toys get similar send-ups. If the Monty Python gang were let loose in the Smithsonian, the result might well be a museum like this.

All Downhill From Here

Western Ski Museum

Boreal Ski Area
(P.O. Box 38)
Soda Springs, CA 95728
(916) 426-3313

Hours: Winter, Tues.-Fri. noon-4 p.m.; weekends 11 a.m.-5 p.m.; summer, same hours, but closed Tues.
Admission: Free
Getting There: *Northern California's Boreal Ski Area is 40 miles west of Reno and 75 miles east of Sacramento. The museum, located on the Boreal Ski Area property, is about 100 yards from I-80 at the top of Donner Pass as it crosses the Sierra Nevada mountains.*

Like a bear cub tucked away for a long winter's nap, this museum is nestled in the snowy reaches of the Boreal Ski Area on Donner Summit. Opened in 1969, i

owned and operated by the region's ry own Auburn Ski Club, founded in)28 to promote the resurrection of ski- g as a recreational pastime. All but rgotten since the Gold Rush era when ie sport was introduced by Norwegian imigrants out of snowbound necessity, iing started to snowball again at the me the club was founded. The muse- n tells the story of both the golden- iys ski craze (when it was called snow- ioe racing) and the later history of the iuburn Club.

The museum building itself is a toasty ttle solar-heated chalet. Exhibits in- ude displays of early skis, hand-made y cabin-fevered miners and pioneers, ; well as artifacts such as costumes, ophies, and memorabilia of some of estern skiing's great moments and he- >es. And for those who want a more ioving picture of the the slope scope, iere's a videotape theater that plays ick truly great footage.

No Place Like Home

Winchester Mystery House

525 S. Winchester Blvd.
San Jose, CA 95128
(408) 247-2000 (recording: 247-2101)

Hours: Mid-June–Labor Day, daily 9 a.m.-5:30 p.m.; Sept. and early June, Mon.-Fri. 9 a.m.-4:30 p.m., Sat.-Sun. 9 a.m.-5 p.m.; Oct., March-May, Mon.-Fri. 9 a.m.-4 p.m., Sat.-Sun. 9 a.m.-4:30 p.m.; Nov.-Feb., daily 9:30 a.m.-4 p.m. (The house can be seen only as part of a guided tour, which departs from the admission area every 10-15 minutes during the summer and every 30-45 minutes during the winter; the above hours denote the departure times of the the first and last tours.)
Admission: Adults, $8.95; senior citizens, $7.45; children 6-12, $4.95; children under 5, free
Getting There: From I-280 as it runs through San Jose, take S. Winchester St. north to the House of Mystery.

Was Sarah Winchester a madwoman or a psychic? Did the ghosts of people and animals killed with Winchester guns truly haunt her and taunt her into building this terrifyingly strange house, or were those spirits merely the fabrications of a crazy, lonely heiress with more dollars than sense? To this day, there are no definitive answers—spiritualists claim to have had ghostly encounters here, while scientists scoff at the supernatural theories that abound.

Perhaps Winchester herself never knew the truth. And perhaps the truth is only part of the story. Today, it's the legend that counts; the legend of how she built this mansion of staircases that lead nowhere, doors that open onto nothingness, and rooms that have windows but no doors. A sprawling building with dozens of rooftops, chimneys, ad-

ditions, and wings, it was created to hold back the forces of evil she believe might crowd around her at any moment.

After tragically losing both her husband and infant daughter while she wa still a young woman, the rich widow, heiress to the Winchester Rifle fortune sought out a spiritualist in Boston whe told her that the ghosts of the men, women, children, and animals slaughtered by Winchester guns haunted her fortune. The ghosts would hunt her down, the medium told Sarah Winchester, unless she began building a house and never stopped. Only the constant sound of hammers and saws and brick being laid would hold back the vengefu spirits of the dead. In 1884, terrified and vulnerable, Winchester bought an 18-room mansion in San Jose, and be n transforming the house into the suralistic home now trumpeted as "The orld's Strangest Monument to a oman's Fears." It is a well-staked aim indeed.

For 38 years, until the reclusive Sah's death in 1922 at age 82, carpenrs, painters, bricklayers, and other aftspeople worked night and day on r house. They built from strange masr plans that included countless secret llways and hidden rooms, false chamrs, convoluted stairways, and other chitectural anomalies that served no urpose other than as building projects. ne house grew to 160 rooms sprawling er 6 acres, with 47 fireplaces, 52 sky-;hts, and more than 10,000 windows. ne number 13, which Winchester beved had special spiritual meaning, pears again and again throughout the nstruction: 13 blue and amber stones a spider-glass window, 13 lights in e chandeliers, 13 windows and doors the old sewing room. She even divid- her will into 13 parts and signed it 13 nes. Appropriately, the house was signated a California Registered ndmark on Fri. May 13, 1974.

It was not until after Sarah's death at the citizens of San Jose learned of e extent of her obsessive-compulsive ilding project. Authorities were rced to draw maps to help explorers no kept getting lost in the maze of oms and hallways. Among the weirder ids was Sarah's Seance Room (with its coat hooks), where she would con- ict meetings with "friendly" (accord- g to her) spirits. Fearing that enemy iosts would follow her to the room, she vised a complicated route that includ- backtracking through parts of the use, climbing through inside win- ws, and rushing down secret hallways

to get to the room.

Visitors to the house are led through 110 of the mansion's 160 rooms. Popular stops include the staircase that leads up to the ceiling and the regal Palace Ballroom with its rare art-glass windows inlaid with obscure Shakespearean quotes. There are so many astounding Victorian furnishings and flourishes—dozens of Tiffany lamps and windows, elaborate, hand-carved beds and fireplaces, inlaid wood paneling, built-in marble sinks—that the residence would be a worthy museum regardless of its odd architecture.

After the tour, visitors are free to wander through the landscaped gardens and estate grounds. There are also two museums on the premises—the Historic Firearms Museum, exhibiting rare examples of Winchester guns, and the An-

tique Products Museum, featuring other, lesser-known items produced by the Winchester Company, including cutlery, fishing tackle, roller skates, farm tools, and flashlights.

The Winchester Mystery House is one of the strangest pieces of architecture in America. Is it a crazy's castle or a haunted house? The truth was buried with Sarah Winchester.

Colorado

Where the Buffalo Roams

Buffalo Bill Museum

Lookout Mountain
Rte. 5, Box 950
Golden, CO 80204
(303) 526-0747

Hours: Nov.-April, 9 a.m.-4 p.m.; May-Oct., 9 a.m.-5 p.m.
Admission: Adults, $1; children, 25 cents
Getting There: Located on Lookout Mountain, 6½ miles south of Golden. From Hwy. 40 (which runs parallel to I-70 and can be reached from Exits 254, 256, and 259), take Lookout Mountain Rd. 3 miles and follow signs to the museum.

William "Buffalo Bill" Cody was one of the first adventurer-entertainers to realize the commercial potential of the Wild West in all its glory. Cody took the West on the road, with his traveling circus/burlesque/rodeo show, Buffalo Bill's Wild West. But he was more than the P.T. Barnum of the tumbleweed set—he was, at various times during his long and exciting life, a Pony Express rider, a soldier with the Seventh Kansas Cavalry, an Indian scout for the U.S. Cavalry, and an actor. The Buffalo Bill Memorial Museum, located at his gravesite in the Lookout mountains, is a tribute to all facets of Cody's life.

Exhibits in the museum range from artifacts of his life as an Indian scout weapons he used in buffalo hunting—but there's no business like show business, so the memorabilia and memento of Buffalo Bill's Wild West show are t most prevalent and tantalizing on display. The show, which traveled aroun the United States and in Europe unde Cody's management from 1883 until the early 1900s, was originally create as an educational tool to teach audiences about the "real" West; but some how the showmanship always got the upper hand. Performers like Annie Oakley, Buck Taylor, and the bearded Cody himself stole the show with thei sharp wits and sharper shooting. Eve the Indians got into the act, with Sittir Bull drawing standing-room-

y crowds. Worn buckskin costumes
l bright, kitschy show posters are
ong the most compelling artifacts at
: museum, which also displays props
l show guns.

The museum also houses a large col-
tion of western art, much of which
onged to Cody himself, including
rks by Frederick Remington and
arles Schreyvogel. A 12-scene diora-
illustrating major points in Cody's
: and a rare collection of antique
rbed wire are among the other high-
hts in the museum.

Cody died in 1917 at age 70. His
we, near the museum, is marked with
tone-face memorial surrounded by a
ked fence. The view from the moun-
n is a breathtaking monument to
dy's wild, brave spirit. On the Colo-
lo plains below that stretch for miles
d miles, one can almost imagine Buf-
o Bill still riding the range somewhere
h a whoop and a wallop.

Whittle Something

rver's Museum

60 Woodcarver Rd.
nument, CO 80132
3) 481-2656

urs: 9 a.m.-5 p.m.
mission: Adults, $2; children and senior
ens, $1
tting There: From I-25, take Exit 158 and
e west toward the mountains to
odcarver Rd., the first road on the left, to
museum.

lling itself "The Carving Capital of
erica," this museum has chiseled out
lace for itself below Pike's Peak.
ile exhibits change daily at the Na-
al Carver's Museum, the one thing

that remains the same is the artistry that
is inherent in the folk art of wood carving. The collections are uniformly well
lit and nicely displayed, and the gift
shop is fully stocked with all sorts of
carvings, tools, educational videos and
books, and lots of other crafts. Radio
commentator Paul Harvey once called
the National Carver's Museum "a home
base and showcase for the whittlers of
the world," a quote that has been labo-
riously carved in wood by one Al
Schmutz and put on display in the museum. No wasted words (or woods) here.

Larger Than Life

Hall of Life

Denver Museum of Natural History
City Park
Denver, CO 80205
(303) 370-6357

Hours: By scheduled classes only;
information on drop-in classes for tourists can
be obtained from the museum
Admission: Varies; fees usually range from
$1.50-$3 per person.
Getting There: Located in the Denver
Museum of Natural History, on the western
side of Colorado Blvd. (Hwy. 2) between
Business Rte. I-70 (Colfax Ave.) and 32nd Ave.

If Mr. Rogers took you on a guided tour
of your insides, this is where he might
come. The Hall of Life is Denver's answer to health education for kids and
open-minded adults. There are really
big mouths, stomachs, hearts, brains,
and other body parts here that visitors
get a chance to clamber over, walk
through, touch, and tickle. Along with
this oversized anatomy lesson comes a
lecture or two on topics ranging from
"I'm Alive!" (for ages 4-5) to "Teens

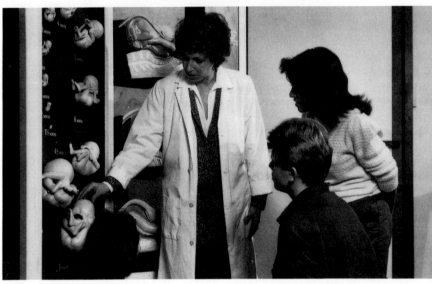

and Tobacco" (for the soon-to-be-smoking set). There's a lot of educational worth here, but all these king-sized body parts are just unnerving enough to make you think you've crawled through Gulliver's belly-button on your way to a soft-sculpted Fantastic Voyage.

Idaho

Unearthly

Craters of the Moon

Hwy. 26
(P.O. Box 29)
Arco, ID 83213
(208) 527-3257

Hours: June 15-Labor Day, daily 8 a.m.-6 p.m.; Labor Day-June 15, 8 a.m.-4:30 p.m.
Admission: $3 per vehicle
Getting There: Located 18 miles southwest of Arco on Hwy. 26.

When early American settlers first sa' this vast, barren lava landscape in the middle of the Idaho wilderness, some thought they had stumbled upon hell earth. This strange 75-square-mile patch of land was avoided for centuri by Indians and other travelers, who pr ferred to take the long way around th desolate environment rather than cut across the tortuous surface. But in 192 the National Park Service designated the area as a national monument, an suddenly this devil's corner of Ameri became a popular vacation destinatio

The park's pockmarked lunar appearance (hence the name "Craters o the Moon") was caused by a rare rup ture in the earth where miles of fissur spewed lava all over the area. The resu is an uneven greyish-brown rock surface that is dotted with jutting lava tubes (the hardened lava crust that forms into monoliths or caves), crater and cinder cones. It is an eerie land, with an unearthly, moon-like surface Yet there is life here, with wildflowers

l gnarly trees growing up between
cks and soft spots in the lava rock,
l tiny mammals, birds, and reptiles
mpering about on the surrealistic
face.

The fastest way to view this park,
ich many believe to be the weirdest
ural environment in the country, is
driving along the well-paved, seven-
le scenic Loop Rd. It passes near some
the most unusual features, including
"Devils Orchard," with its forest of
a fragments protruding from a sea of
ders. Hiking paths and viewing areas
und for the more daring who want to
mber over the jagged landscape to
e into lava tubes or craters.

The last eruptions in the area are be-
ed to have ceased about 2,000 years
, but geologists predict that the land-
pe will erupt again someday. Al-
ugh it's not likely to happen in the
r future, the weak of nerves can al-
ys stay in their cars—just in case.

e Jig Is Up

ddlers Hall of Fame
W. Commercial St.
iser, ID 83672
8) 549-0450

urs: Mon.-Fri., 9 a.m.-noon and 1-5 p.m.
mission: Free
tting There: U.S. Hwy. 95 is called State
as it runs through Weiser; the hall of fame/
seum is in the Chamber of Commerce
lding on E. Idaho at the intersection with
te St.

t's face it, Idaho is not the first place
t comes to mind when you think
ut fiddlin'. The American folk hero
dler, slightly stooped with age, tap-
g his foot as he saws away on his fid-

dle at a summer evening square dance
or a barn-raising picnic just doesn't
seem to fit into the potato-country landscape. Nevertheless, little Weiser is
home of the National Oldtime Fiddlers
Contest, Hall of Fame, and Museum.
The contest, the third week in June,
draws fiddlers from around the world
intent on playing their way into the annals of history and onto the walls of the
hall of fame. The National Oldtime Fiddlers Hall of Fame displays portraits of
the national winners, while the adjacent
museum preserves for posterity the instruments, tunes, and other relics of fid-
dling history and legend.

Montana

The Gravity of the Situation

House of Mystery
7800 Hwy. 2 E.
P.O. Box 500
Hungry Horse, MT 59919
(406) 892-4550

Hours: April-Nov., 8 a.m.-dusk
Admission: Adults, $2.50; children, $1.50
Getting There: The house is on Hwy. 2 E., 3
miles east of Columbia Falls and 3 miles west
of Hungry Horse. Glacier National Park is just
north of the house.

The House of Mystery is at one of those
popular, out-of-the-way places where
gravity stands on its head and squirrels
fear to tread. There are several such
"vortexes" in the United States—
unearthly patches of land where the
forces of nature have gone askew, producing weird magnetic pulls along with
kitschy tourist traps. Although the "Oregon Vortex" is probably the best-

known, the House of Mystery near Hungry Horse claims the unique honor of being located at "Montana's Only Vortex."

"One of the few areas in the world where the natural laws of physics are bent . . . if not broken altogether," states a brochure handed out at the house, with the added warning that "you can actually feel the strange forces as they act on your body." And how, pray tell, do they act on your body? Well, for one thing, visitors here appear to shrink or grow a whole six inches depending on where they stand. Alice would have felt right at home.

The house itself is a tilting, topsy-turvy building that supposedly was a victim of the powers of the vortex. Needless to say, the crooked, disorienting architecture enhances the feeling that the environment is playing hopscotch with your anatomy. And the photos you take here (they encourage camera-toting: "Your pictures will amuse and baffle you for years to come.") are equally enhanced by the house's angular atmosphere. The House of Mystery people are up-front about their efforts to help you "feel" the vortex: "In order to demonstrate how the various senses are affected, we have added a few props . . . but the phenomenon is Real!"

Okay, so maybe it really is a weird place—"A place where birds won't fly," even. But there's got to be a reasonable explanation, right? The House of Mystery folks think so, too. In fact, they propose several logical possibilities, including the theories that the vortex is caused by "geological faults, by sunspots, or crossed gravitational fields." But such farfetched, pseudoscientific notions don't hold much water when it comes to vortexes. So the curators of the House of

Mystery pose another possibility—coul this eerie place and other such "mystery spots" perhaps be "navigational bearing points for extraterrestrial visits centuries ago?" The answer to this question may lie somewhere in the stars, where aliens with 3-D glittery "House of Mystery" window decals on their spaceship flip through a photo album of Montana still amused and baffled after all those years.

Cars and Bars

Old Prison/Towe Ford Museum
1106 Main St.
Deer Lodge, MT 59722
(406) 846-3111

Hours: Memorial Day-Labor Day, daily 8 a.m.-9 p.m.; Labor Day-Nov. 30, weekdays 8:30 a.m.-5:30 p.m.; Sat.-Sun. 10:30 a.m.-5 p.m.; Nov.-Feb., daily 9 a.m.-4 p.m.; March-Memorial Day, daily 8:30 a.m.-5:30 p.m.
Admission: Combined price for both sites: adults, $6; children, $2.50. Separate admissic for each site: adults, $4; children, $1.75
Getting There: Prison and museum are in adjacent buildings on the I-90 Interchange Glacier National Park, a.k.a. Main St. as it rur through Deer Lodge.

Two of America's favorite pastimes, cars and crime, are brought together the tiny town of Deer Lodge. The Old Montana Territorial Prison, in use fro 1871 to 1979, is a heavy, castle-like stone fortress complete with turrets a 20-foot-high walls. Visitors can wand through the prison on self-guided tou or take advantage of planned tours; e ther way, the sights in this dank, cree institution include the "galloping gallows," on which 10 prisoners were

...nged, cell blocks that have been left ...they were when the prison was vacat- ...and the prison yard, where a violent ...59 riot and hostage taking ended af- ...36 hours when the National Guard ...rmed the prison grounds. While some ...ght find this tour depressing, the ...we Ford Museum in an adjacent pris- ...building lightens the mood ...siderably.

...This collection is said to be the ...rld's most complete gathering of an- ...ue Fords on public display. Every ...ar and every model manufactured by ...rd from 1903 to 1953 is here, includ- ...g every roadster and phaeton body ...le from 1928 to 1938. It's an impres- ...e display, with more than 150 cars ...at look as good today as they did when

they first rolled off the assembly line. There are brass and black Model Ts, early V-8s, Model As and AAs, and a vast sampling of Lincolns. A nostalgic look is also paid to postwar Fords, including wood-paneled family touring cars, a few endearing Edsels, and such recent vintage autos as a 1978 Thunderbird; there's also a 1955 Thunderbird. The Towe Ford Museum is the brainchild of Edward Towe, a lifelong car buff and Ford collector.

Within minutes, Deer Lodge tourists can step from behind bars to in front of cars—it's one of the odder museum combinations in the country, but somehow it works. Somewhere between the Old Montana Prison's history of confinement and the Towe Ford Museum's history of the open road, the pleasures and penalties of freedom are illuminated.

Agri Culture

Oscar's Dreamland
S. Frontage Rd.
Rte. 9, Box 4002
Billings, MT 59102
(406) 656-0966

Hours: May 1-first snowfall, daily 9 a.m.-6 p.m.
Admission: $4
Getting There: Located between Billings and Laurel, a mile south of the Market Basket Store on S. Frontage Rd. From I-90 E., take, take King exit to S. Frontage, head west for 3 miles to the Shiloh Underpass, turn left and continue south to the site. From I-90 W., take the exit east of Laurel to South Frontage Rd. to the Market Basket Store; turn right to Oscar's Dreamland.

Oscar Cooke is the agriculture fan and collector/curator of this "dreamland," which at last count included some 5,000 pieces of farming equipment, industrial machinery, and historical buildings. The place bills itself as a tribute "To honor the men and women who pioneered farming in the Northern Great Plains," a goal that, though admirable, makes Oscar's Dreamland Amusement Park and Yesteryear Museum a fairly austere, work-oriented playground. This is no cotton-candy amusement park with college kids dressed as cartoon dogs or mice—instead, it's all hayrides, tractor exhibits, and educational displays. Two acres of the "showground" (as they call it) are "under roof," that is, housed in giant prefab buildings that look like airplane hangars.

Oscar's Dreamland is an odd mix parking lot carnival and country fair hibition, with a ferris wheel, merry-round, and railroad rides competing with such sights as a collection of 1(threshers, "Rare Rd. Building Machines," the church with the second (est steeple in Billings, and a wooden rig. The "Largest Revolving Clock— Diameter" and a display of ancient hand tools are among the other sight be seen.

While Oscar's dreams may not qu add up to your own, the collection d have a meaningful stake in memoria ing the often-neglected history of Am ica's agricultural. There may not be same sugar-coated sheen to be found mainstream parks, but Oscar's Drea land has a certain homespun whole-someness that nearly makes up for it lack of thrills and chills.

Nevada

Rhinestone Showman

Liberace Museum
Liberace Plaza
1775 East Tropicana Ave.
Las Vegas, NV 89109
(702) 798-5595

Hours: Mon.-Sat. 10 a.m.-5 p.m.; Sun. 1-5 p.m.
Admission: Adults, $3.50; children, $2; ser citizens, $3
Getting There: The museum is in the Liberace Plaza shopping center on East Tropicana Ave. in downtown Las Vegas.

Lee Liberace will go down in history one of the most flamboyant, generou schmaltzy, and amusing entertainers the twentieth century. This museum,

ed at his very own shopping center, ‌erace Plaza, does delicious justice to king of glitz.

The Liberace Museum's 5,000 square t of exhibit space is decorated with a , subtle architectural touches includ- mirror-tiled columns, candelabra at ry turn, and heavily draped win- ‌vs, giving the museum that certain s Vegas *je ne sais quoi* that was so . . . ‌erace. The decor is the perfect back- ‌p for the museum's collections, ‌ich include such objets d'art as the ‌rld's largest rhinestone (weighing ‌5,000 karats and worth $50,000), nos studded with rhinestones and ‌ered with disco-ball mirror tile, and ‌tatue of "Mr. Showmanship" himself de from bread dough (a fan's doing). ‌ere are closets and racks filled with ‌erace's extravagant wardrobe— ‌thered capes, sequined tuxedo jack-

ets, gold-embroidered ruffled shirts—said to be worth more than a million dollars. Some of his favorite costumes are modeled by mannequins that could pass for the flamboyant one himself but for their velvet-covered faces and shag-rug wigs. And the cars—oh, those cars—Liberace loved 'em so, and here they are, including a patriotically painted Rolls Royce and a glittery Bradley GT sports car with candelabra detailing.

The Liberace Museum is run by the Liberace Foundation for the Performing and Creative Arts, a charity organization administered by Dora Liberace, the widow of the performer's brother and early musical partner, George. Admission fees go into the foundation's coffers to provide funding for such worthy musical institutions as the American Boychoir School. Liberace's death in

1987 left many of his avid fans shaken and bereaved; his relatives are currently fighting to turn his Las Vegas mansion into a museum/mecca for the faithful. With the sampling of wonderfully gaudy cars, clothes, and kitsch on display at the Liberace Museum, chances are that an entire house full of this stuff would knock Graceland off the top of the Glitzy-Homes-of-Dead-Vegas-Stars charts.

New Mexico

Here's Lookin' at You, Kid

Billy the Kid Museum

1601 E. Sumner Ave.
Fort Sumner, NM 88119
(605) 355-2380

Hours: May 15-Sept. 15, daily 8:30 a.m.-5 p.m.; Sept. 15-May 15 (but closed Jan. and Feb.), Mon.-Sat. 8:30 a.m.-5 p.m.
Admission: Adults, $2; children, $1
Getting There: Located on U.S. Hwy 60/84, 2 miles east of downtown Fort Sumner.

Fort Sumner calls itself the "International Billy the Kid Capital," an amusing claim considering that few foreign cities are likely to try for the title. Pr aside, Billy the Kid (a.k.a. Henry McArty, Kid Antrim, William H. Bo ney, and El Chivo) certainly did terr ize the neighborhood around Fort Su ner and throughout the West, killing least 21 men by the time he was 21 ye old.

Housed in a two-story building th has all the earmarks of an ideal roads attraction—complete with gaudy ba ner signs painted all over the façade, wagon wheels out front, and colorful pees and wagons in the side yard—th museum is more than a collection of K artifacts. In fact, most of the 60,000 plus Wild West artifacts here don't r late to Billy the Kid at all. But, since collection included some Billy the Ki stuff, Fort Sumner's favorite gunsling got his name on the museum.

The collection was first opened as museum in 1953 by Ed and Jewel Sweet. They had been collecting relic and antiques for years; during his care as a traveling salesman and broommaker, Ed often traded his wa for old wagon wheels, coffee pots, an other "junk" sitting around the hom of his customers. The museum is now run by his son and daughter-in-law, Donald and Lula Sweet, and is home

a vast array of objects ranging from old cars to totem poles. While there aren't as many purely Billy the Kid items here as museum-goers might assume from the name, there are enough to give a feel for the Kid's blood-curdling career. His guns, newspaper accounts of his exploits, and a replica of his tombstone are included in the collection.

The Kid shares his real grave with two other "Pals" (as the tombstone puts it), Tom O'Folliard and Charlie Bowdrie, who died in December 1880. They are buried in the Military Cemetery, behind the Old Fort Sumner Museum, four miles south of the Billy the Kid museum on Rte. 272 off of Hwy. 60/84.

Boom Town

Los Alamos Museum

1921 Juniper St.
(P.O. Box 43)
Los Alamos, NM 87544-0043
(505) 662-6272

Hours: Mon.-Sat. 10 a.m.-4 p.m.; Sun. 1-4 p.m.
Admission: Free; a 50-cent donation is suggested for the walking tour booklet
Getting There: Los Alamos is about 45 minutes from Santa Fe and can be reached by taking Hwy. 84 north from Santa Fe and then turning west onto Hwy. 4. The museum is in the center of town on Central Ave., directly across the street from the County Building and Ashley Pond. A walking tour map and guide for the other sites can be obtained at the museum.

This is where all the fuss began: the spot where the first atom bomb was built. The Los Alamos Historical Museum will give you goose bumps when you realize that this little museum isn't any different from other local historical museums in similar small towns—except that this town's local history happens to have played a major role in the history of the world. Here, along with the typical Indian pottery and pioneer history, you'll see memorabilia of the Manhattan Project and its aftermath, including photographs of the scientists at work and crucial archival papers.

Once you've been through the museum itself, set off for a self-guided walking tour of historic sites with an invaluable booklet (developed from an Eagle Scout project by the dutiful John Polzer of Boy Scout Troop 22) provided by the museum. It won't take long to discover that Los Alamosians like to emphasize their "regular" history as much as their "atomic" history, so you'll have to bypass the Indian ruins, and so on, if you are searching specifically for tidbits in the bomb department.

Yet, even as the walking tour glorifies such everyday historical places as old cabins, a rose garden, and a pond, it is clear that the arrival of the Manhattan Project team in this sleepy New Mexico town had vast and lasting effects. Many of the town's buildings and sites were at one time owned or occupied by the Army or the Atomic Energy Commis-

sion, and the tour booklet mentions th Los Alamos' population virtually mus roomed with the influx of Manhattar Project personnel.

One of the few intact Manhattan Project historic sites is the string of r houses where the scientists and milita people settled during their stay. J. Ro ert Oppenheimer lived in the Mae Connell house.

Another chilling bit of atomic lore to be found at the site of the ice hous where the nuclear components of the first A-bomb were assembled. After t project ended, the ice house was destroyed, but in 1965 a monument wa constructed to commemorate the buil ing. Inside the monument there are ph tographs and descriptions of the worl that went on in this seemingly innoce ous shelter.

Did the Los Alamosians resent the virtual takeover of their town? There are enough barbed comments mixed into the tour text that it's hard to belie the scientists and military people wer welcomed with open arms. In describi the Army's temporary Central Schoo for instance, the booklet offers this in sight into military intelligence: "The school was originally conceived as a high school by the Army, who had fo

tten that the average age of the scien-
ts was only 24 years! A nursery school
ould have been more appropriate."
nd why was the school built only as a
mporary structure? Because, the
oklet explains, "General Groves,
ommander of the Manhattan District,
ought that the town would cease to ex-
 after the completion of the bomb
oject."
Did Groves perhaps fear an accident?
 did he just think the Army's leave-
king would spell economic doom for
e town? Long after Groves' departure,
s Alamos has flourished, both blessed
d damned by the infamy of the histor-
project it harbored.

plosive Evidence

ational Atomic Museum

tland Airforce Base
D. Box 5400
buquerque, NM 87115
05) 844-8443

ours: Daily 9 a.m.-5 p.m.
dmission: Free
etting There: From I-66, go south on
yoming Blvd. to the visitors' entrance to
tland Airforce Base. From I-25, take the
bson Blvd. exit east and enter the base at
 visitors' entrance at the intersection of
bson and Louisiana Blvds. Guards at the
trances will direct you to the museum.

is museum was opened in 1969 to
ow Americans their tax dollars at
ork, not at play. And from the 280-
m cannon and giant B-52 parked in
ont of the museum (this one was used
 the last atmospheric tests in the Pacif-
), you instantly know that the Nation-
 Atomic Museum is going to flex some
etty big muscles.

Within these hallowed halls that were
once used as a missile repair facility
there are bomb and missile cases of every age, shape, and description. Exhibits on subjects like "Alternate Delivery
Methods," "Safety and Testing," and
"Building the Bomb" further document
the history and nature of the development of the United States nuclear arse-
nal from inception to present.
Declassified documents and artifacts relating to the Manhattan Project and later research-and-development programs
enhance the displays with factual data.
But as fascinating as these records are,
the more compelling exhibits are the
bomb cases themselves.

Those infamous rogues, the "Fat
Boy" and "Little Man" bombs, are displayed in all their squatty glory. These
weapons, products of the Manhattan
Project, are the only atomic weapons
used to date in warfare, and became the
earliest standard-bearers of the U.S. ar-
senal. Little Man was dropped on Hiro-
shima on August 6, 1945. Its lean,
8,900-pound body, measuring a mere
10 feet long and 28 inches around, delivered a "payload" the equivalent of
13,000 tons of TNT. More than 70,000
people died within seconds. Little Man's
rotund baby brother, Fat Boy, was
dropped three days later over Nagasaki,
Japan, delivering a blast equaling
23,000 tons of TNT and instantly killing more than 45,000 people.

After such a glorious debut, America's grasp on the nuclear age was as firm
as John Wayne's trigger finger; but the
race was on for the rest of the world to
catch up. Other exhibits at the National
Atomic Museum tell the story of the following years, when the development of
nonair drop methods like missiles and
torpedoes was all the rage; "better"

bombs, including the H-bomb, were created; and computer and radar technology raced along at a steady gallop. Displays detailing the safety features of bombs and bomb building, exhibits on above- and below-ground testing, and a look at "Atoms in Space" round out the museum's terrifyingly straightforward collection.

Most of the displays include real examples of the weapons discussed—well, almost real. Only the casings are exhibited, but that's all you need to see what the things look like. The streamlining and perfecting of the atomic bomb is evident in the evolution of the casings shown: the MK-5, for instance, entered the stockpile in 1952 as an improvement on the Fat Man. The insides of both bombs are similar, but the MK-5 has a lighter, aluminum casing instead of Fat Man's steel body, and its tail is an aerodynamic improvement over Fat Man's, which tended to let the bombs wobble as they fell. Other atomic developments on display include the "Davy Crockett," a bazooka-shaped missile that joined the team in 1960 as a "portable" weapon to be taken to the front lines by the infantry, and the "Honest John," a field artillery rocket that is now the oldest missile system still fielded by the United States

Strolling through the museum's 13,650 square feet of exhibit space is almost like taking a walk into the twilight zone. There, right before your very eyes, are the bombs this country has been building for almost 50 years. These are no mythical numbers in a column of arms race statistics—they're real, and they're here. The museum does a fair, if hawkish, job of telling the atomic tale, and it is morbidly fascinating to learn the inside story of the development and

evolution of the bomb. But no amoun nuclear energy could warm the chill produced by a visit to the National Atomic Museum.

On Top of Old Smokey

Smokey Bear Museum and Grave

Smokey Bear Historical State Park
(P.O. Box 64)
Capitan, NM 88316
(505) 354-2612

Hours: Memorial Day-Labor Day, daily 8 a.m.-6 p.m.; Labor Day-Memorial Day, dai a.m.-5 p.m.
Admission: Free (park entrance fee is 25 cents)
Getting There: Located in the center of Capitan, on U.S. Hwy 380, which is about miles east of I-25 (Exit 139).

Smokey Bear has done more, single-paw-edly, for the preservation of Ame ica's forestland from fire destruction than any other mammal, human or ot erwise. Smokey's fuzzy round face topped with a ranger cap is an almos universal symbol of fire safety and ca tious camping. A scorched cub when was saved by rangers from a 1950 inf no on Capitan Mountain, the black be was quickly adopted as the Forest Se ice's mascot, to the delight of childre nationwide. After doing promotional tours, Smokey settled down for a qui life of celebrity at the National Zoo i Washington, D.C., where he lived un his death in 1976. Capitan brought i favorite cub back home at last and bu ied him at the park named in his hon

The museum at his grave site has su memorabilia as a stained-glass wind

picting the bear in an almost
isneyesque fashion, complete with a
uebird on his shoulder, as well as sou-
nir items displaying Smokey's face
id photographs and accounts of his
mous rescue. "Only you can prevent
rest fires," was Smokey's plea to
mericans; only he could tell us how
ith such earnest charm.

he Little Old West

inkertown Museum

rest Rd.
3ox 303)
andia Park, NM 87047
05) 281-5233

lours: April-Nov., Mon.-Fri. 11 a.m.-6 p.m.;
veekends 9 a.m.-6 p.m.
dmission: Adults, $1; children, 50 cents
etting There: Tinkertown is on the
urquoise Trail in Sandia Park, on state Hwy.
55 heading toward Crest. From I-40, take
xit 175 N. to the Trail.

Like some of America's finest folk art
constructions, Tinkertown started as a
hobby that turned into an obsession and
finally into a business. In 1962, Ross
Ward began a wood carving project that
dated back to his childhood love of the
miniature mechanical shows that once
traveled the country with fairs and car-
nivals. Starting with a general store, the
project grew into a small western village, with animated men, women, children, and animals going about their sur-
realistically manic days of dancing,
fishing, shopping, and plain old living.
Ward and his wife Carla built a house
from glass bottles, wagon wheels, and
other cast-off items, and put the growing collection on display as the
Tinkertown Museum.

This is one of those places you just
have to see to believe—tiny, animated
scenes fill every corner of the bottle
building, with elaborately carved and
jerkily mechanical characters heading
west in covered wagons, riding
stagecoaches, and living it up in

saloons—all at the plunk of a coin into the slots that line the glassed-in scenarios. Even without paying up to see Tinkertown come to life, it's a joy to gaze at the intricately carved and crafted pieces. And the bottle building is a glorious piece of junk-art architecture.

Also on the premises are Carla Ward's Pottery Studio and a gallery of Ross Ward's paintings. This is one crafty family, and their Tinkertown museum is as much fun as watching a hurdy-gurdy in full throttle.

Oregon

Ad Infinitum

Advertising Museum

9 N.W. Second St.
Portland, OR 97209
(503) 226-0000

Hours: Wed.-Fri. 11 a.m.-5 p.m.; Sat.-Sun. noon-4 p.m.
Admission: Adults, $1.50; children under 12, free
Getting There: Housed in the Erickson Building, once a famous saloon, located at the gateway to Portland's Old Town Historic District.

Visitors to the museum's 6,000-square-foot exhibit area will see a hushed, wall-to-wall-carpeted display area that, in some areas, has the liveliness of a Manhattan bank lobby; but what the museum sometimes lacks in raw energy, it makes up for with a collection that is genuinely fascinating and informative. Among the rarest items are more than 5,000 original print advertisements dating back to 1683, including commercial works by such modern-day greats as N. C. Wyeth and Norman Rockwell. Roadtrip buffs will delight in the Burma Shave signs gathered here, and video vultures will enjoy the running tapes of classic "words from our sponsors."

Other exhibits include collections of promotional giveaways and "collectibles" such as Coca-Cola trays and neon signs, a look at the advertising process from conception to finished project, and a study of the "Evolution of the Logo," which reveals the economic and graphic considerations that come into play when logos and trademarks are created.

The American Advertising Museum, principally underwritten by the Portland Advertising Federation, stands alone among the small group of advertising and commericial-product muse-

is in America that concentrate as
uch on the business side of advertising
on the often amusing and riveting re-
ts. It's a fascinating look at a world
en relegated to ivory skyscrapers and
rouded in trade secrets.

st Meets West

am Wah Chung Museum

ty Hall
0 South Canyon Blvd.
hn Day, OR 97845
03) 575-0028

ours: May-Oct., Mon.-Thurs. 9 a.m.-noon
d 1-5 p.m.; Sat.-Sun. 1-5 p.m.
dmission: Adults, $1.50; children, 50 cents
etting There: The museum is adjacent to
ty Park

he role of Chinese immigrants in the
inning of the American West is one of
e least-memorialized; but the unusual
d intriguing Kam Wah Chung & Co.
useum goes a long way toward re-
embering the society and lifestyles of
e Chinese who lived and worked in the

Eastern Oregon. The museum is housed
in a restored 1886 building that was, at
varying times, an herbalist's pharmacy,
doctor's office, general store, Chinese
temple, and residence. But despite the
changes, the site remained a gathering
place and cultural center for the Chinese
community until the early 1940s. The
various incarnations of Kam Wah
Chung & Co. are represented with
recreated or restored rooms displaying
original items found in the building,
from shelves of Chinese herbal remedies
to the elaborately ornamented shrines
from the temple. For a taste of Chinese-
American history that has been too little
explored, the Kam Wah Chung & Co.
Museum is a true delight.

Magnetic Attraction

Oregon Vortex
4303 Sardine Creek Rd.
Gold Hill, OR 97525
(503) 855-1543

Hours: March-May and Sept.-Oct. 15, Fri.-
Tues. 9 a.m.-4:45 p.m.; June-Aug., daily 9
a.m.-4:45 p.m.
Admission: Adults, $3.50; children 12-15,
$2.50; children under 12, $1.50
Getting There: Located just north of Gold
Hill, 4 miles east of Hwy. 234 on Sardine Creek
Rd. I-5 runs parallel to this section of Hwy.
234, with interchanges to the Hwy. marked as
turnoffs for Crater Lake. Note: stay on the
short north-south stretch of Hwy. 234 that
crosses through Gold Hill to get to Sardine
Creek Rd; the east-west portion of the Hwy.
that starts in Gold Hill and heads to Crater
Lake (82 miles away) won't get you to the
vortex.

What is it with these vortexes, anyway?
You can't keep a straight posture here,
you shrink or grow depending on where

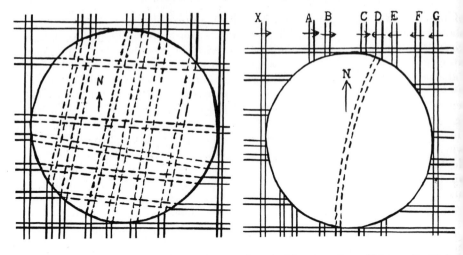

you stand, and small animals avoid these places like the plague—all of which must explain why such sites are popular tourist attractions. The Oregon Vortex, with its requisite "House of Mystery" (all vortexes have to have one of these sideways shacks to prove to tourists that strange things really do happen here), is one of the oldest and most respected weird places in America. It opened as a tourist attraction in 1930, and has been magnetically drawing tourists to its eerie "circular area" ever since.

But as far back as the white settlers, and even earlier, this place was considered a supernatural no-no land. Indians called it the "Forbidden Ground," and in 1864 the first white man to notice the weird pull of the place wrote that he had a "feeling of something wrong" here. In 1914, John Litster, a Scottish physicist, moved to Gold Hill and stayed for the rest of his life, studying the phenomenon and corresponding with the likes of Albert Einstein about it. All of which adds validity to the belief that there really is "something wrong" here.

Due to geological changes in the past decade (the eruption of Mount St. Helens is a favorite scapegoat), the vortex people say it's not as strong as it used to be. That means that visitors can't see such cherished oddities as a broom standing on its bristles, or the wife and kids leaning backwards at unhuman angles anymore. But never fear—there's still enough vortex to go around. That sideways wonder, the House of Mystery, helps out with its wildly tilted floor (you practically have to wear suction cups on your shoes to keep from tipping over), and people still appear to shrink a bit when they stand in certain "mystery" spots. All told, the Oregon Vortex is still a barrel of antigravitational fun and games.

But it's more than that, too—according to the PR machine at the Oregon Vortex, it's also all of the following adjectives: "Natural * Historical * Educational * Scientific * Authentic." Though the science behind this authentic, natural wonder is too educational and historical to get into here, suffice it to say that there's a whole math-filled booklet by Litster, "Notes and Data Relative to the Phenomena at the Area of the House

Mystery" ($2), available at the gift op that purports to explain it all. The st of the data seems to suggest that this tle patch of Oregon is the result of an aberration in the Light Field and other elds" that puts it somewhere in the ague of being "an intermediate vor- x-form between the atom vortex and e galaxy vortex." Got that? In other ords, if you see birds flying upside own or squirrels running backwards the trees around here, don't fret; it's st Mother Nature playing hooky.

oned
━━━━━━━━

etersen Rock Gardens

930 S.W. 77th St.
edmond, OR 97756
(03) 382-5574

ours: Summer, daily 7 a.m.-9 p.m.; rest of e year, daily 7 a.m.-dusk
dmission: Donation requested
etting There: The gardens are on S.W. 77th St., 2 ½ miles west of Hwy. 97, between edmond and Bend.

his compendium of rock gardens, ountains, castles, and monuments was ae work of a Danish immigrant, asmus Petersen, who came to Oregon 1 1906 and began building a fantasy ock land around his home in 1935. 'etersen died in 1950, leaving behind a egacy built in rock. Miniature hurches, the American flag, a replica of he Statue of Liberty, bridges, towers, nd dozens of other architectural and ecorative creations dot the lush, flow- red landscape. Almost all of the rocks 'etersen used to build these wonders rom came within 100 miles, and they nclude such rare and lovely varieties as etrified wood, thundereggs, malachite,

lava, and obsidian. To heighten the al- ready exotic flair of this small, stony wonderland, peacocks roam freely around the grounds—but their brilliant plumage can't compete with the man- made glories of the Petersen Rock Gardens.

Utah

Creature Feature

Dinosaur Gardens

Utah Field House Natural History Museum
235 East Main
Vernal, UT 84078
(801) 789-3799

Hours: Summer, daily 8 a.m.-9 p.m.; rest of the year, daily 8 a.m.-5 p.m.
Admission: Free
Getting There: The gardens are adjacent to the museum, on Vernal's Main St. Vernal is at the intersections of Rte. 191 and Hwy. 40.

The 14 dinosaur statues planted on this little plot of land are no mere papier- mâché and chicken-wire lizards. They are artistic, realistic representations of what these big babies actually looked like. Elbert Porter, a sculptor with a flair for monsters, spent 15 years creat- ing the statues for the million-dollar ex- hibit. Were they worth all that work? You bet! The Triceratops looks just like all the drawings you've seen in history books, and the Stegosauras is so realistic you'd think he lumbered off the set of the "Flintstones."

The dinosaurs are illuminated during summer evenings for those romantic Tyrannosaurus rex–lit strolls. And, to further delight garden-goers, landscap- ers spared no expense in building a love-

ly swamp and a rock outcropping with a bridge and waterfall. The park's trees and shrubbery were also pruned to resemble the kind of greenery dinosaurs were used to way back when.

For an inside view of the big guys, a replica of a Diplodocus skeleton is on view in the gardens. The Utah Field House Natural History Museum next door (same hours as the garden, and free admission) has still more lizard bones to choose from, along with locally culled minerals and Indian artifacts. But the dinosaurs in the garden somehow seem more . . . natural. They look so healthy, you'd think they'd stepped out for a minute instead of being extinct for 150 million years.

Washington

Core Constituency

Apple Industry Museum
North Central Washington Museum
127 S. Mission St.
Wenatchee, WA 98801
(509) 662-4728

Hours: Mon.-Fri. 10 a.m.-4 p.m.; weekends 1-4 p.m.
Admission: Free, donations appreciated
Getting There: From Hwy. 2, take the Wenatchee exit; the museum is on S. Mission St. in the heart of downtown.

Apples are Washington's plum produce, so it's about time there was a museum voted to the history of the state's apple industry. Located in an exhibit annex to the North Central Washington Museum in Wenatchee, the Apple Industry Museum takes a look at the business from its roots on up.

Displays in the museum range from an exhibit of more than 100 apple-box labels (which should make some of today's streamlined corporate logos blush for their plainness) to a workshop where visitors are encouraged to attempt the almost-lost art of building an apple box. No easy task this—getting the nails in just so, the sides up straight—but it was a common job for youngsters and other willing workers who earned a penny per built box. The evolution of apple growing and packaging processes is also explored here, tracing the the industry from its pioneer farm days to modern high-tech methods.

The most amusing item displayed in the museum is a 1923 Price sizer that weighed apples by flinging them across room. Lighter apples flew farther, landing in the appropriate, far off bins;

heavier apples would soar only a few feet before plunking into the nearer bins. The result of this far-flung sizing concept: apples so badly battered and bruised that even the museum has resorted to using tougher, lead-weighted plastic fruits in place of tender, real apples. It just goes to show that one bad sizer can ruin a whole bunch of apples.

Tall Tail

Whale Museum

62 First St. N.
(P.O. Box 945)
Friday Harbor, WA 98250
(206) 378-4710

Hours: June-Sept., daily 10 a.m.-5 p.m.; Oct.-May, daily 11 a.m.-4 p.m.
Admission: Adults, $2; students and senior citizens, $1.50; children, 75 cents
Getting There: Friday Harbor is on San Juan Island in upper Washington State's Puget Sound. The only way there is by ferry, and the museum is two blocks (mainly upward) from the ferry landing, at the top of First St. Hill.

Taking the ferry to Friday Harbor, chances are you'll see a few real whales before you ever get to their museum. The big, swimming mammals consider Puget Sound their own personal fishbowl, much to the delight of whale watchers and researchers, who would otherwise have to take to the vast ocean to see these normally deep-sea-going creatures. After catching sight of a tail or two (if you're lucky), you'll dock on San Juan Island and trudge up a rather steep hill to the museum, where everything you ever wanted to know about whales is explained with exhibits and audiovisual presentations.

As you enter the museum, you will be greeted by recordings of "whale songs," which are so haunting that you may want to just stand still for a minute and drink in the lilting, somber whistles and moans. Then it's on to the exhibits,

where you'll learn that orcas are actually dolphins rather than whales and that there are more than 75 species of cetaceans (whales and their swimming mammalian cousins), ranging in size from the 15-ton, 100-foot-long blue whale to the 100-pound, 5-foot-long harbor porpoise. If you need more information, there's a phone you can use to chat with the whales directly.

Other exhibits include skeletons (those flippers actually have tiny, "hand-like" bones in them), scale models illustrating the different sizes and styles of whales, and a collection of·stomach-turning whale parasites. The museum also has a video viewing room that shows whale documentaries, and a children's room with hands-on games and puzzles about whales and their preservation. A "hotline map" in the museum shows the locations of the lat-

whale sightings in the area as called
to the museum's 24-hour whale-
tch hotline.

The Whale Museum was opened in
79 by the Moclips Cetological Socie-
a nonprofit research group that has
en studying the whale population in
d around Friday Harbor since 1976.
le group is dedicated not only to sav-
y the whales, but also to understand-
y them and disseminating whale
owledge to other people. Hence, the
hale Museum itself and related
ojects, like the "Orca Adoption Pro-
am" ($35 to "adopt" any one of more
an 70 local orcas) and "Whale
hool" (university-accredited field
urses in whale biology). A museum
ft shop sells cetacean sundries, from
lphin-shaped cookie-cutters to whale
welry and whale-shaped soap.

This is one of the most well-thought-
t natural science museums in the
untry, with a flair for teaching with-
t preaching.

Wyoming

Mail Bonding

First-Day Cover Museum
702 Randall Blvd.
Cheyenne, WY 82001
(307) 634-5911

Hours: Mon.-Fri. 9 a.m.-5 p.m. (closed noon-
12:30 p.m.)
Admission: Free
Getting There: Cheyenne, Wyoming's
capital, is at the crossroads of I-25 and I-80.
On I-25 N. from the intersection with I-80,
take Exit 6E and follow signs to Randall Blvd.
Drive east on Randall (toward the State
Capitol and away from Warren Air Force
Base). The museum is on the north side of the
street.

Many stamp collectors would give their
eye teeth, not to mention their week's
pay, to own some of the first-day covers
on display here. The collection of this
museum, valued at close to $1 million,

includes one of the world's single most valuable first-day covers, along with dozens of other rare, much-prized examples.

First-day covers are envelopes bearing a postmark dated the first day of a stamp's issue, usually from the one post office officially designated to issue the stamp. Because these postmarks are only stamped during a single day and by a single post office, first-day covers are sought after by stamp collectors with the same vigor as book collectors tracking down first-edition volumes. Nowadays, the issuing of stamps themselves produces revenue, so the process of getting a first-day cover in today's market is usually as simple as mailing an order to the issuing government's postal service well in advance of the stamp's issuance date. But before stamp collecting became an international hobby and trade business, stamps were created merely as symbols of postage paid.

Which is why the collections of the National First-Day Cover Museum are so highly touted: many of the first-day covers on display come from times when little hoopla was made over a stamp's issuance, and thus, no more than the average day's postal business of first-day covers were issued. The very first first-day cover is owned by the museum—the first postmarked issue of Great Britain's famed "Penny Black" stamp, dated May 6, 1850. Worth a pretty penny, it is housed in a specially designed case, set off from other displays with appropriate respect for age and stature.

Other displays include first-day covers from around the world and pieces of original art from which cachets (the drawing or painting reproduced on an official first-day cover envelope to commemorate the stamp's issue) are produced. Many of the first-day covers and their stories are displayed against glossy black backgrounds with neon-colored text, an exhibition design that creates an excitingly modern feel for a museum subject usually victimized by stodginess of display.

The museum also houses an "Old Time Post Office and General Store," complete with antique coffee bean grinders and other old-fashioned store displays, along with a replica of a turn-of-the-century Wyoming post office. It's a charming reminder that many of the first-day covers in the museum date back to a time when folks strolled in both to pick up a pound of sugar and to drop off a letter to Aunt Mable in Memphis—and what a nice treat to send it off with that brand new stamp that just came in, too.

Index

Credits

East

Page 9: Courtesy, Edward Clark Streeter Collection of Weights and Measures, Medical Historical Library, Yale University. Page 10: Courtesy Johnson Memorial. Page 12-13: Courtesy The Potato Museum. Page 14-15: Courtesy Bryant Stove Museum. Page 17: Courtesy The Peary-MacMillan Arctic Museum. Page 17: Courtesy Babe Ruth Museum. Page 23: Courtesy Cranberry World Visitors Center, Ocean Spray Cranberries, Inc. Page 25-26: Courtesy Paper House. Page 27: Courtesy Salem Witch Museum. Page 32: Courtesy New England Ski Museum. Page 33: Courtesy Lawrence L. Lee Scouting Museum. Page 35: Courtesy Miniature Kingdom, Inc. Page 36: Courtesy Discovery Seashell Museum. Page 38: Courtesy Alling Coverlet Museum. Page 39: Photo by Carla Shaprio, courtesy of Museum of Holography. Page 40: Courtesy National Bottle Museum. Page 42: Courtesy Onondaga County Department of Parks and Recreation, Office of Museums and Historical Sites. Page 44-46: Courtesy The Strong Museum. Page 47: Courtesy The Trotting Horse Museum. Page 50: Courtesy Little League Baseball, Inc. Page 51: Courtesy Mr. Ed's Elephant Museum. Page 50: Courtesy Julius Sturgis Pretzel House. Page 57: Photo by Laura A. Bergheim. Page 59: Courtesy Bob Hoffman Weightlifting Hall of Fame. Page 62: Photo by Mark Sadan, courtesy of Bread and Puppet Museum and Theater. Page 63: Courtesy Vermont Marble Co. Page 65: Courtesy Palace of Gold.

South

Page 70: Courtesy Boll Weevil Monument. Page 71: Courtesy Key Underwood Coon Dog Graveyard. Page 73: Courtesy Elna M. Smith Foundation. Page 74: Courtesy Daisy Manufacturing Company. Page 76-77: Courtesy Lum 'N' Abner Museum. Page 79: Courtesy Mitchell Wolfson Jr. Collection of Decorative and Propaganda Arts. Page 80: Courtesy Coral Castle. Page 81-84: Courtesy Cypress Knee Museum. Page 85: Courtesy Don Garlits Museum. Page 86: Courtesy John Gorrie State Museum. Page 87: Courtesy Xanadu, Home of the Future. Page 88: Courtesy Oldest Store Museum. Page 90: Courtesy International Swimming Hall of Fame. Page 91: Courtesy Tiki Gardens, Inc. Page 92: Courtesy Tragedy in U.S. History Museum. Page 96: Courtesy Elberton Granite Association. Page 97: Courtesy Juliette Gordon Low Girl Scout National Center, Girl Scouts of the U.S.A. Page 103: Courtesy New Orleans Historic Voodoo Museum. Page 104: Courtesy International Checker Hall of Fame. Page 107: Courtesy Marvin and Mary Johnson Gourd Museum. Page 109-110: Courtesy Enterprise Square, USA Page 111: Courtesy Broadcasting Museum. Page 117: Courtesy General Shale Products Corp. Page 119: Courtesy Memphis Pink Palace Museum and Planetarium. Page 121: Courtesy Museum of Tobacco Art and History. Page 123: Courtesy Buckhorn Hall of Horns Page 125: Courtesy Del Camino Motor Hotel. Page 127: Courtesy Orange Show. Page 129: Courtesy Texas Ranger Hall of Fame and Museum. Page 130

rtesy Bedrooms of America Muse-
Page 131-132: Courtesy Enders
eral Home, Inc. Page 133: Courtesy
rge Washington Masonic National
norial. Page 137: Courtesy National
acco-Textile Museum.

lwest
e 140: Courtesy Billy Graham Mu-
m. Page 142-143: Courtesy Illinois
's Oliver P. Parks Telephone Muse-
, Page 144: Courtesy Rockome Gar-
s. Page 146: Courtesy of The Time
seum. Page 147: Courtesy Tinker
ss Cottage. Page 148: Courtesy Na-
al Shrine of Our Lady of the Snows.
ge 150: Courtesy Bird's Eye View
seum. Page 154: Courtesy Van Horn
ck Museum. Page 156: Courtesy
tto of the Redemption. Page 157:
rtesy The American Film Institute.
ge 158: Courtesy Jasper County His-
cal Society. Page 162-163: Courtesy
den of Eden. Page 165: Courtesy
tin and Osa Johnson Safari Muse-
. Page 168-169: Courtesy James B.
m Distilling Company. Page 171:
rtesy American Museum of Magic.
ge 173: Courtesy Antie Clare's Doll
spital. Page 174: Courtesy Alexan-
a Chamber of Commerce. Page 176:
rtesy Black Madonna Shrine and
ttos. Page 178-179: Courtesy Na-
al Bowling Hall of Fame and Muse-
. Page 180: Courtesy Winston Chur-
ll Memorial Library. Page 182:
rtesy Museum of the Fur Trade.
ge 184: Courtesy Harold Warp's Pio-
r Vilage. Page 185-186: Courtesy
st Acres Shopping Center. Page 187:
rtesy Hoover Historical Center.
ge 187: Courtesy Degenhart Muse-
. Page 193: Courtesy Warther Carv-

ings. Page 194: Courtesy Goodyear
World of Rubber. Page 195: Courtesy
Corn Palace Concessions/Mitchell
Chamber of Commerce. Page 197: Pho-
to by Ken Dorgard, courtesy Wall Drug,
Inc. Page 199-200: Circus World Muse-
um. Page 202-203: Courtesy
Dickeyville Grotto. Page 205: Courtesy
The House on the Rock. Page 208:
Courtesy National Freshwater Fishing
Hall of Fame.

West
Page 213: Courtesy Meteor Crater En-
terprises, Inc. Page 215-216: Courtesy
the Mystery Castle. Page 217: Courtesy
Patton & Sons, Inc. Page 218: Courtesy
Pima Air Museum. Page 220: Courtesy
Rose Tree Inn Museum. Page 222-223:
Courtesy Mattel Inc. Page 224: Courte-
sy Max Factor. Page 227: Courtesy On
Location. Page 230: Courtesy Broad-
casting Magazine. Page 233: Courtesy
Western America SkiSport Museum.
Page 234-235: Courtesy Winchester
Mystery House. Page 236: Courtesy
Buffalo Bill Memorial Museum. Page
238: Courtesy Hall of Life. Page 241:
Courtesy Powell County Museum and
Arts Foundation. Page 243-244: Cour-
tesy Liberace Museum. Page 239: Cour-
tesy Billy the Kid Museum. Page 246:
Courtesy Los Alamos Historical Muse-
um. Page 249: Courtesy Tinkertown
Museum. Page 250: Courtesy U.S. De-
partment of Energy. Page 251: Courte-
sy Kam Wah Chung & Co. Museum.
Page 252: Courtesy House of Mystery at
the Oregon Vortex. Page 254: Courtesy
Utah Field House Natural History Museum. Page 255-256: Courtesy The
Whale Museum. Page 257: Courtesy
Unicover Corporation.